The Politics of Juvenile Crime

Sage Contemporary Criminology

Series editors

John Lea ● Roger Matthews ● Geoffrey Pearson ● Jock Young
Centre for Criminology, Middlesex Polytechnic

Sage Contemporary Criminology draws on the best of current work in criminology and socio-legal studies, both in Britain and internationally, to provide lecturers, students and policy-makers with the latest research on the functioning of the criminal justice and legal systems. Individual titles will cover a wide span of issues such as new developments in informal justice; changing forms of policing and crime prevention; the impact of crime in the inner city; and the role of the legal system in relation to social divisions by gender and race. Throughout, the series will relate theoretical problems in the social analysis of deviancy and social control to the practical and policy-related issues in criminology and law.

Already published
Jeanne Gregory, *Sex, Race and the Law: Legislating for Equality*

The Politics of Juvenile Crime

John Pitts

SAGE Publications
London ● Newbury Park ● Beverly Hills ● New Delhi

SAGE Publications Ltd
28 Banner Street
London EC1Y 8QE

SAGE Publications India Pvt
Ltd
C-236 Defence Colony
New Delhi 110 024

SAGE Publications Inc
2111 West Hillcrest Street
Newbury Park, California 91320

SAGE Publications Inc
275 South Beverly Drive
Beverly Hills, California 90212

British Library Cataloguing in Publication Data

Pitts, John
    The politics of juvenile crime. — (Sage
    contemporary criminology).
    1. Juvenile corrections — Great Britain
    I. Title
    364.6   HV9145.A5

    ISBN 0-8039-8132-5
    ISBN 0-8039-8133-3 Pbk

Library of Congress catalog card number 87-051529

Printed in Great Britain by J.W. Arrowsmith, Bristol

Contents

For Deborah

It is impossible to see modern life steadily and see it whole, and she had chosen to see it whole.

E.M. Forster, *Howards End*

Preface

I have spent years talking about the ideas in this book. I have talked to so many people over such a long time that I can no longer remember where any particular idea came from. I do know that it usually was not from me.

John Miller first interested me in working with young people, and because he made it so interesting and such good fun, I became intrigued and have stayed intrigued for over twenty years. I have been talking to Dave Garnett about these ideas for almost as long — he's a very good listener. At Blackfriars Settlement the late Aida Tennant influenced the ways I thought about working with disturbed and deprived children and young people. Harold Marchant persuaded me of the importance of permissiveness in work with estranged young people in 1971, and I remain persuaded. The section in Chapter 4 about the Wincroft Youth Project owes a great deal to recent discussions with Harold. At the Polytechnic of North London, Randal Metzger made me think about power, poverty and crime and the shift from agonising to organising. At Middlesex Polytechnic Mike McKenna, John Lea and Jock Young continue to make me rethink my ideas. Any traces of intellectual rigour in this book are largely attributable to them and John Bousfield at the University of Kent.

Roger Matthews has, as usual, offered help, support and friendship, and Geoff Pearson has always been willing to talk and listen. The time I spent with Lesley Day, Dennis Dobson, John Dennington, Geoff Gildersleeve, Graham (Clarke Kent) Robinson, Charlie Burr and Eddie Joyce in the *Eureka* editorial collective was a very happy one. They taught me about practical politics, collective working, and how to lose gracefully at darts, and for that I am very grateful.

Many of the ideas in the final three chapters were developed as a result of the anti-racist training sessions I did with Theo Sowa, Lorna Whyte and Alan Taylor. At the West London Institute of Higher Education I have discussed parts of this book with Marie McNay, Marilyn Lawrence, June Roberts, Angela Foster, Cathy Aymer, Robin Roychowdry, Rachael Hetherington, Lesley Day, Andrew Cooper, and particularly, Philip Smith. They have always been encouraging, generous and indeed, indulgent, towards me, and that is one of the many reasons I enjoy working with them. Jane Schauerman typed a beautiful manuscript and was very nice about my bad handwriting and peculiar politics. Jane Linklater knows more about the practice of IT than most and always offers me new ways of looking at old problems. Helen Edwards from the NACRO Juvenile Offenders' Team, and Judy Lester from the Rainer IT Fund both spent time telling me about current developments in IT.

For various reasons I am indebted to the Bermuda Department of Tourism, VW Audi UK, the Military Police Archives Section at Chichester Barracks, the Daily Telegraph Information Service, the NACRO Information Service, The Conservative Central Office library, The Labour Party headquarters library and Cynthia Winifred's brother-in-law.

Milan Kundera says that the compulsion to write, 'graphomania', develops because those we love the most get fed up with listening to what we have to say and so we are forced to search for a larger, albeit anonymous, audience. This may not be true in my case. For example, my children, Matthew, Adrian and Lisa, often asked me how the book was going, they crept away when I suddenly started to scribble on pieces of paper, and once they even asked me to read them a bit of it aloud. They have been tolerant and generous when I have given to the book time and attention which was rightfully theirs: Deborah has listened patiently to most of this book in its various forms and has always seemed interested when I have looked up. They have made me feel that what I was doing was important. What more could I have asked for?

John Pitts
Streatham Hill

1 The rise and fall of welfare and treatment

We are refining and we are restating our socialism in terms of the scientific revolution . . . The Britain that is going to be forged in the white heat of the technological revolution will be no place for restrictive practices or outmoded methods.

Harold Wilson to the Labour Party
Conference, October 1963

There aren't any good brave causes left.

Jimmy Porter in John Osborne,
Look Back in Anger

The rediscovery of the class connection

Above the main entrance of the Central Criminal Court at the Old Bailey are carved the words: *Defend the children of the poor and punish the wrongdoer.* This apparently straightforward injunction has proved extraordinarily difficult to carry out because in the juvenile courts of England and Wales it appears that the wrongdoers are also the children of the poor. This has led many people to speculate about the relationship between crime, justice and social class.

The issue of social class is always bubbling just beneath the surface of any serious discussion of juvenile crime. The Ingleby Committee on the working of the juvenile court in England and Wales, established in 1956, rediscovered this class connection (HMSO, 1960). Their report argued that delinquency might be an indicator of social deprivation and that this deprivation might be prevented by the infusion of welfare resources into neighbourhoods which produced high juvenile crime rates. To this end, the report advocated the establishment of family advice centres. It also alerted us to another problem: an over-emphasis on the social compensation of deprived offenders delivered, via the justice system through the medium of welfare or treatment, might shade into a denial of the legal rights of the young offender. This important consideration was largely ignored in the subsequent debate within the Labour Party about the role and function of the juvenile court but it emerged again, with much greater force, from a variety of political quarters, in the mid-1970s.

Longford and psychoanalytic socialism

Ingleby had raised the question of social class, social deprivation, and its connection with crime. What was clear to most observers, however, was that the majority of members of the most deprived segment of society were not identifiably criminal. If then the juveniles who appeared before the juvenile court were drawn from the most deprived segments of society then either they were peculiar or they were responding to their deprivation in a peculiar way. The Labour Party reformers opted for the latter view. The hapless subjects of the juvenile court were no different, it seemed, from their law-abiding neighbours; they merely responded to this shared deprivation in a different way.

If then this criminality was in fact no more than a particular reaction to deprivation, then to respond to the crime rather than the causes of the crime was absurd. The Longford report stated the matter thus:

> No understanding parent can contemplate without repugnance the branding of a child in early adolescence as a criminal, whatever offence he may have committed. If it is a trivial case, such a procedure is indefensible, if a more serious charge is involved this is, in itself, evidence of the child's need for skilled help and guidance. The parent who can get such help for his child on his own initiative can almost invariably keep the child from court. It is only the children of those not so fortunate who appear in the criminal statistics. (Labour Party Study Group, 1964)

Longford's plea is for a set of therapeutic facilities which can be made available to the deprived in order to restore their children to social and mental health. This plea echoes earlier Labour Party responses to Ingleby.

The Labour Party rejoinder to Ingleby (Donnison and Stewart, 1958; Donnison et al., 1962) is essentially concerned with the organisation of a new family service. This family service was to be aimed at the small residue of families which had slipped through the net of welfare state provision and did not slot neatly into the range of needs which existing social work agencies were established to meet, and those others who were 'too ignorant or apathetic to make use of the services offered to them' (Donnison and Stewart, 1958: 3).

Donnison and Stewart (1958) write: 'One study after another has shown that the personal social services devote most of their resources to a small proportion of their clientele, and many of these people need help from several different services.' (This concentration of helping resources becomes important in terms of delinquency because: ' . . . it is now generally agreed that unhappy and broken homes play an important part in producing the delinquents who enter the approved school } (Donnison et al., 1962)

The approach to the problem of juvenile crime presented here is that of a mopping-up operation. The new family service is to identify, penetrate and clear out the last residues of unwarranted social maladjustment. Its potential clientele is presented as a kind of proletarian hangover from an earlier primitive era whose problems are compounded by official responses to their behaviour.

The problem of juvenile crime as formulated by Donnison et al. (1962) and the Longford Study Group is a psychological one. Juvenile crime may flow from inadequate parenting but it is essentially a problem of lack of access to skilled help. What appears to distinguish the deprived from the privileged in this account is that while the privileged have information about where to find skilled help and the economic wherewithal to pay for it, the deprived do not. The deprivation experienced by the deprived is a deprivation of information, a deprivation of motivation, and an economic deprivation, the major consequence of which appears to be to prevent deprived families from paying for psychoanalysis for their errant offspring. This deprivation, it is argued, is compounded by the stigmatisation which is the inevitable consequence of a court appearance. Such stigmatisation would, it seemed, only serve to propel the juvenile deeper into a deviant career.

In the hands of the Fabian reformers the ideas of class and poverty are transformed. To understand this transformation it is necessary to know something of the 'new-look' labour politics of the early 1960s.

A high-tech decade

Harold Wilson divined correctly that if Labour was to stand a chance of winning the 1964 election it had to modernise itself. The world he presented in the early 1960s was a world in which the 'white heat of the technological revolution' would eradicate poverty and iron out social inequality. Through the expansion of educational opportunity, full employment and an enlarged welfare state, opportunity, prosperity and security would be created for all. Here was a new-style Labour Party with its appeal to the new and the old 'working class'. It was going to proceed on the basis of consensus. By distributing the rewards of a technologically sophisticated society more fairly, social discontent would be quelled and the legitimacy of the new order secured.

In the murky depths beneath this wave of optimism, however, poverty was in the process of being rediscovered. Brian Abel-Smith and Peter Townsend (1965) showed us that discrepancies of wealth and opportunity remained as stark in the early 1960s as they had been in the immediate post-war period, suggesting that the welfare state had not done what it was supposed to do and that the new society which Wilson and the Labour Party were marketing so successfully was not quite what it appeared to be. This rediscovered poverty had to be tackled if the Wilsonian dream was to be realised — but how could class inequality exist in a classless 'meritocratic' society? There was, then, a problem of explanation and a problem of strategy.

Whereas the traditional orthodoxy of the Labour Party and the labour movement had emphasised the antagonistic relationship between capital and labour, this new ideology stressed the idea of a stratified, open society in which distinct class differences had dissolved into a continuum of statuses. Traditional class differences were supplanted by a notion of a world of opportunities to be grasped by those with sufficient skill and merit. An expanded educational system would exploit the abilities of the less fortunate and enable those with the talent to participate successfully in the new society. The diminishing need for unskilled and semi-skilled labour would be paralleled by a spectacular increase in the financial rewards for such labour. The British car industry was cited as the example par excellence of this tendency. The unskilled worker would be subject to an embourgeoisement which would shake him free of his traditional working-class lifestyle and loyalties (Goldthorpe and Lockwood, 1968; Westergaard, 1968).

If then, in this new world, there remained those who lived in poverty, then clearly they did this because they had failed to get the message. They were in some way unaware of the new educational and occupational opportunities and persisted in an essentially pathetic reproduction of lower working-class lifestyles and behaviour — a sort of 'culture of poverty'. Thus, being 'working-class' became synonymous with being a victim of an ensemble of problems, deficits and defects which a benign state would have to address and eradicate. In the new classless society people who continued to act in working-class ways were to be educated, helped and cajoled into the new meritocratic classless consensus.

So class was not central to the new politics. Class struggle was no longer the motor of social change. Being a member of the working class emerged as a reprehensible anachronism. People who remained so were seemingly labouring under a misapprehension. They were, it was argued, located in small pockets, in localised areas which the new doctrine had failed to penetrate. A mopping-up operation was necessary and in the spirit of the times this operation had to be scientifically informed and technologically sophisticated.

Enter the eggheads — the appliance of science

With the election of the Wilson administration we witnessed a rare, and perhaps never-to-be-repeated, phenomenon because Wilson had gathered around him a group of academic social scientists which included Donnison, Jay and Stewart, and asked them first to define, and then to devise solutions for, Britain's social problems. This was not, of course, original. John F. Kennedy had done precisely this at the inception of the American poverty programme in 1960 and the British 'poverty programme' bore a resemblance to the Kennedy initiative. The idea of a new Camelot in which the king surrounded himself with the most esteemed righters of social wrongs was a mark of the humanistic idealism which was the necessary complement to an enlightened 'high-tech' administration.

The endeavour was essentially to de-politicise social issues. It was an attempt to remove questions of poverty, educational opportunity and crime from the place they had occupied in the old class politics, namely as a manifestation of social inequality, and put them on to the agenda of social anomalies to be eradicated by an apolitical process of social engineering. This alliance with social science had a profound impact on Labour Party juvenile justice policy in the 1960s.

The reformers attempted to reshape our perception of the problem of juvenile crime and our ideas about the most appropriate responses to it. This attempted transformation had five central features — depoliticisation, decentralisation, preventive intervention, decriminalisation, and treatment.

Depoliticisation Juvenile crime is transformed from a social evil or a manifestation of class inequality into a residual problem which arises as a result of rapid social change and resides in families and neighbourhoods which have been unable to avail themselves of the opportunities proffered by a prosperous technologically sophisticated society. The problem of juvenile crime is subsumed within the larger problem of deprivation. This deprivation is defined not as a consequence of objective class inequality but rather as a self-perpetuating subjective culture of poverty which is out of tune with political reality. Thus juvenile crime emerges as a temporary pathological phenomenon amenable to social engineering.

Decentralisation The power to place a child or young person in a confined space against his or her will is taken from the courts. The administration of this confinement is taken from the Home Office and placed in the hands of the employees of democratically elected local authorities. Young offenders are restored to their local community and are subject only to those constraints which will be determined locally with due regard to their needs. In effecting this change the possibility is opened up of the construction of a localised democratically answerable system of youth control beyond the influence of central government crime control policies or strategies.

Preventive intervention The role of welfare is transformed from a reactive to a pre-emptive one. Welfare resources are to be targetted-in on crime-prone neighbourhoods and families in order to offer them corrective and compensatory experiences which will put them in touch with (a) *information* about resources, (b) *advice* about opportunities and (c) *help* in the child-rearing task. Welfare is to be used as an educative device and its objective is to equip the small residue of deviant families with what is needed to participate successfully in the mainstream of society.

Decriminalisation The Fabian transformation of crime into a socially determined pathology renders the category of crime, with its connotations of culpability and choice, irrelevant. If then the major mechanism established to deal with illegal youthful misbehaviour is still geared to questions of guilt, innocence, culpability and mitigation, it is clearly not only anachronistic but a pernicious stigmatising mechanism wherein the problem of juvenile crime is actually worsened. It therefore becomes necessary to transform the juvenile court into an agency which addresses the real problem of deprivation and pathology rather than the false problem of criminality. It follows that the juvenile criminal justice system must be decriminalised (Bottoms, 1974; Clark, 1980).

Treatment If crime is transformed into individual or family pathology the juvenile court must be transformed into a diagnostic clinic. If the privileged can buy the services of child curers then the state is obliged to provide them free for the less well off. Thus it follows that a family service, employing psychologically or psychoanalytically trained professionals who can enter the homes and minds of pathological families and children, must become a central feature of any official response to juvenile crime.

What is being proposed here is a substantial shift in power, away from central government and towards local authorities; away from the courts and the legal profession, and towards welfare professionals and experts. It is an assault on the dominance of a system of justice which the Labour Party had traditionally viewed as being in the pay, and working in the interests of, the privileged. Beyond the apparent 'scientific' 'rationality' of the reformers' proposals lay a deeper political antagonism towards a system of justice which was seen to perpetuate social injustice. It was a struggle between a new generation of red-brick high flyers and the Oxbridge old guard, a struggle between the traditional ancien regime and the new scientific order.

Welfare versus justice?

By 1965 the stage was set for the struggle to transform the juvenile criminal justice system into a mechanism which dispensed welfare and treatment. The vehicle for the first assault was the White Paper, *The Child, the Family and the Young Offender* (HMSO, 1965) and the vehicle for the second was the *Children in Trouble* White Paper (HMSO, 1968).

It is important to remember that questions of age and social deprivation had already been a consideration in court proceedings for juveniles for more than a century. The creation in 1908 of a separate juvenile court had been an acknowledgement of this and the establishment in 1933 of approved schools was further testimony to this acceptance that children and young people in trouble had special needs.

The argument in juvenile justice in the post-war period prior to the 1960s had been about the relationship between the concern for justice and the concern for the welfare of the child and the ways in which these concerns might complement each other. This political polarisation of 'welfare' and 'justice' was peculiar to the 1960s and 1970s.

Did he jump or was he pushed?

The 'justice model' is derived from the utilitarian philosophy of the enlightenment and, more specifically, from the social contract theories of Hobbes, Montesquieu and Rousseau. Together this body of theory is known as classicism:

> The central tenet of classicism was that the rights of men had to be protected against the corruption and excesses of existing institutions; and these vagaries were nowhere more evident than in the legal systems of eighteenth century Europe. Punishment was arbitrary and barbarous, 'due processes' of law being absent or ignored and crime itself being ill-defined and extensive. (Taylor et al., 1973: 1)

Classicism poses a model of an ideal society. In this society a social contract has been struck between the government and the governed. This contract says that if each citizen relinquishes a small proportion of his or her personal freedom to the government, the government will, in its turn, operate a system of justice consistent with the principles of equality before the law and the minimisation of interference with individual freedom. It will, moreover, operate a system of punishment in which penalties are no harsher than is necessary to recompense the victim and to deter other potential offenders. Governments act rationally on behalf of the people, and the people, being rational, effect a rational choice which permits governments to do this. In this ideal and rational society crime becomes an irrational act.

What was quite clear, however, was that a lot of people in the real world, the very poor in particular, seemed reluctant to honour their end of the social contract. The implicit psychological theory which underpinned classicism is familiar enough; it also underpins behaviourism. It asserts that human beings are motivated by the pursuit of pleasure and the avoidance of pain. Thus a system established to discourage crime by increasing its pains and decreasing its pleasures, but simultaneously offering all citizens, irrespective of wealth and social position, the same level of pain could not cope with those who lived in such abject misery that crime, the possibility of the pain of judicial punishment notwithstanding, seemed a preferable option to the pain of living in poverty.

Classicism as a system of abstract thought could not accommodate the reality of social inequality. Just as classical economic theory posed a model of an ideal, or perfect, economic market, classical criminology posed an ideal, or perfect, moral market. Classical economic theory was therefore unable to account for instances of 'market imperfection', 'market failure', and 'market collapse'. Similarly, classical criminology had no way of accounting for imperfections, failures, and collapses occasioned by social inequality in the moral market place.

There were two ways out of this challenge to classicism. One, which had extremely radical implications, was that the impoverished could not be bound by the social contract because they were severely handicapped in the moral market place by dint of their poverty. The other, favoured, account was that poverty should be seen as a condition which, under certain circumstances, constrained the rationality of the poor, and as such limited their culpability for their crimes. Indeed, Locke distinguished between 'those members of the poor who had chosen depravity and those who, because of their unfortunate circumstances were unable to live a rational life' (Macpherson, 1962). Neo-classicism was born.

Neo-classicism emerged as a way of accommodating these unpalatable social realities while preserving classicism more or less intact. In this new formulation the world was divided up slightly differently: 'In the neo-classical schema man is still held to be accountable for his actions but certain minor reservations are made, the past history and the present situation of the actor are held to affect his likelihood to reform' (Taylor et al., 1973: 8).

Because the rationality of criminals might be constrained by poverty, enfeeblement, madness or immaturity, the range of penalties is expanded and a movement away from penalties which fit the crime towards a range of penalties which fit the criminal is set in train. For neo-classicism the social world still retains its rational centre but on the margins there exist small ghettos of irrationality which the legal system increasingly attempts to accommodate by the administrative manipulation of penalties. Thus we see the introduction of discharges, probation and suspended sentences, on the one hand, and the adjustment of existing penalties like fines, on the other, in order to accommodate the principles of impaired rationality or diminished responsibility.

The neo-classical revision of the classical schema had a more profound impact than this, however. Neo-classicism provided an entree for the sciences of behavioural determination, and the techniques of behavioural change into the sphere of crime and justice.

Neo-classicism had saved classicist theory from collapse by accommodating the problem that inequality might limit freedom of choice. In doing so, it acknowledged that certain behaviours were not freely chosen but shaped by invisible or barely visible social or psychological forces. What it had not done was to explain the nature of this determination of behaviour. As an administrative correctionalist criminology neo-classicism needed (a) an explanation of behavioural determinants — a *criminology* — and (b) a set of techniques whereby the determined criminal actor could be transformed into a freely willing undetermined actor — a *social treatment* — if the world described in classicist theory was to be transformed into a social reality. Thus it was neo-classicism, a philosophy and a theory which dominated the sphere of crime and justice, which gave the impetus, set the paradigm, and specified the problem which the emergent sciences of behavioural determination and techniques of behavioural change in the field of crime and justice were to solve. Indeed, it even lent criminology classicism's somewhat simplistic and pessimistic psychological theory.

If this scientific or scientifically informed endeavour was successful then the world of classicism would be realised. If the determinants of criminal behaviour were identified, explained, and then cured, then irrational criminals could be restored to the rational consensus.

It was this essential complementarity of welfare and justice which was ignored or misunderstood by the protagonists in the welfare versus justice debate of the 1960s and 1970s. The project of criminology and social treatment was the restoration of the legal subject to rationality. By the early 1960s, Harold Wilson's social scientists had adopted both a theoretical cause and a theoretical cure for criminal irrationality.

Durkheim, Freud and Harold Wilson

By the 1950s and early 1960s the dominant intellectual influences on criminology, social welfare and the practice of child care were those which originated in Durkheim's sociology and Freud's psychoanalysis.

Durkheim's argument with classicism was that it was a political ideology and not a description of social reality. He castigated classicism because it was unscientific and gave a false account of the relationship between individuals and the state in capitalist societies. He argued that industrialised societies were characterised by a forced division of labour in which individual freedom was curtailed by an industrial system which denied opportunity to all but the privileged. Instead of a consensus, or in Durkheim's phrase a 'conscience collective' society was characterised by a multiplicity of mutually antagonistic groups who were not bound together by an over- arching morality or ethic. In these circumstances, as Taylor et al. (1973) have argued, three types of deviant will emerge:

1. *The biological deviant*, who deviates because of situational factors or genetic inheritance irrespective of social opportunity. These people would deviate under any social system.
2. *The functional rebel*, who is in revolt against existing social inequality and lack of access to opportunity. These people would not deviate in a society in which there was a spontaneous division of labour and individual ability, individual utility and not privilege, determined one's social position.
3. *The skewed deviant*, who is a victim of the 'anomie' or normlessness which arises when the forced division of labour negates the possibility of a conscience collective and an institutionalised social egoism which arises out of this anomie and allows free reign to the appetites of the individual.

Taylor et al. (1973: 83) contend that: 'for Durkheim, biological positivism would be the prime explanation of deviant motivation only in a perfectly regulated organic society. In such a situation, anomie, egoism and the need for functional rebellion would not obtain.'

The skewed deviant is, in Freud's terms, a victim of an undeveloped superego and an inadequate ego which is unable successfully to sublimate the primitive drives of the id into socially useful activity. As for the functional rebel, Freud (1928: 15−16) would argue: 'It goes without saying that a civilisation which leaves so large a number of its participants unsatisfied and drives them into revolt neither has nor deserves the prospect of a lasting existence.'

In arguing thus Freud finds strong resonances with Durkheim. Both Durkheim and Freud were critical bourgeois thinkers who laid bare the social contradictions of industrial society and found within them the social determinants of deviant behaviour which lay beneath the classicist facade. Importantly, however, both were intent not only to reveal these contradictions but also to specify the conditions under which the contradictions and the determinants might be transcended and a rational world, analogous to the world, posited by classicism, realised.

Durkheim's concern is that if actors are to participate in the classicist game on equal terms then we must, through social and economic intervention, make sure that the board is flat. Freud is concerned that when the board is flattened, the pieces will be facing the right way. The ideas of Freud and Durkheim had profoundly influenced Harold Wilson's academic social scientific policy advisers. Their popularity was due in no small part to the fact that they were theories which could be read as being optimistic about, and offering a blueprint for, substantial social change without radical political change.

Harold Wilson's administration claimed to be completing the work of the welfare state. By expanding the personal social services it was adding an educational and therapeutic layer to the welfare state and in doing this it was bringing into being a society which offered universal material security and social support. Through economic intervention anomalies of wealth would be ironed out. Through an agreement with the trade unions which Wilson himself styled 'the social contract' industrial strife was to be supplanted by industrial harmony. Through the expansion of higher education, the new universities, the polytechnics and the open university, citizens who had previously been denied opportunity were to be given a fair chance. Through the Educational Priority Areas programme and the Community Development Projects residual pockets of poverty were to be attacked.

Wilson offered a new enlightenment, a new 'social contract', in which human rationality need no longer be constrained by poverty and inequality. He seemed to be attempting to bring the ideal classical world of Rousseau into being. This was also Durkheim's world of 'organic solidarity' — an open, meritocratic society with a spontaneous division of labour based on ability and social utility rather than rank.

It was a world in which the functional rebel and the skewed deviant had no reason to deviate. Thus an initiative in the sphere of juvenile justice must be geared to the functional rebel and the skewed deviant who were temporarily out of step with the new enlightenment. The functional rebel would be diverted from crime by education and the provision of legitimate opportunity. The skewed deviant would receive therapy, education and opportunity. The biological deviant would be contained by a humane state.

What is ultimately so astounding about welfarism in the Wilson era is that the logical outcome of the 'welfare' endeavour, had it been successful, was not simply that the redundant juvenile court would be replaced by the diagnostic clinic which, having done its work, would itself become redundant. It would become redundant because, in restoring its patients to the rational consensus in which crime became an impossible option for the rational actor, it would have ushered in the crime-free society. The only people who would break laws would be biological deviants who, by definition, could not be described as criminal. That was the idea anyway.

It is strange that governments which claim to be appropriating the future on behalf of the people are usually engaged in appropriating the past, albeit a mythical past, on behalf of an abstract idea of how the world ought to be. It was the fictional individualistic bourgeois world of classicism which the Wilson government strove to bring into being. Collectivism and socialism had been abandoned along the way. It was a yearning for this fictional world which inspired much sociological and criminological theory. These political, theoretical, and social endeavours were measured against the mythical achievements of a non-existent golden age.

Reform, resistance and pragmatism
The 'justice versus welfare' debate was ultimately a debate about means rather than ends. The radicalism of Longford and the Fabians consisted in the novelty of the means they wished to employ to engender social conformity among the young in a rapidly changing advanced industrial society. The dispute was between those who believed that social harmony and conformity could be engineered and those who believed it would evolve as a result of the operation of the hidden hand of social and economic forces and the imposition of penalties.

Stripped of their philosophical and theoretical trappings the parliamentary politics of the 1960s concerned productivity and conformity. The problem presented was to engage education, management and the trade unions in a co-operative venture to maximise personal and national productivity. In a similar vein communities and social welfare agencies were to engage in a co-operative endeavour to create social harmony and conformity. The personal social services was one of the means whereby available, but non-conforming, human resources might be utilised more effectively in the service of an expanding economy.

If one aspect of the welfare state emphasised care, the other emphasised duty, responsibility, conformity, and the avoidance of waste. The protestant ethic, with its emphasis on duty, responsibility and conformity was alive and well in the strong strand of grass-roots Methodism in the Labour Party of the 1960s. This was an ethic with a double edge, for in as much as it advocated a responsible caring society it wanted that society to be populated by responsible careful individuals.

Many Labour MPs remained unimpressed by what they saw as the Fabian intellectuals' attempt to excuse the bad behaviour of the young and thus promote the very irresponsibility they claimed to be curing. In a similar vein conventional criminology, whose project had been to identify that which was peculiar about criminals, complained that the proposals of *The Child, the Family and the Young Offender* (HMSO, 1965) involved an unjustifiable lumping together of the deprived with the depraved, which would stigmatise and corrupt the poor but virtuous by thrusting them into close association with the feckless and the delinquent. Magistrates who would lose their jobs were appalled by the White Paper. The police, who would lose power, were antagonistic. The probation service, which would lose clients, was scathing. Lawyers, who would lose work, were hostile. The bulk of Conservative MPs did not understand the White Paper and did not like it either.

The Child, the Family and the Young Offender proposed the abolition of the juvenile court and its replacement by a family panel composed of social and psychological experts and social workers. The panel was to act as a referring agent to a range of specialised treatment facilities. The White Paper proposed an expansion in the numbers and types of people who could report children and young people to the panel either because of what the youngsters were doing or what was being done to them by others. Teachers, youth workers, police officers, social workers, and parents would all have access to the panel, its expertise and its resources. The White Paper proposed that the age of criminal responsibility be raised from 10 to 16 years, but that nobody under 18 should enter a prison department establishment.

In parliament, the White Paper was seen to be going too far too fast and foundered as a result of political resistance, but importantly also as a result of lack of parliamentary time to navigate a contentious bill towards the statute book. Thus in 1965 the government made a strategic withdrawal and returned to the drawing board. Interestingly the Kilbrandon report (HMSO, 1964) which proposed similar changes for Scotland was successful, and its proposals were incorporated into the Social Work (Scotland) Act 1968. This suggests how finely balanced the political forces of the time were on the issue of juvenile justice, and how the 1965 White Paper was perhaps as much a victim of bad timetabling or a lack of a sense of political priority on the part of the government, as of political resistance.

The major thrust of *The Child, the Family and the Young Offender* was its attempt to transform the structure of the juvenile criminal justice system of England and Wales. The subsequent *Children in Trouble* White Paper left the structure intact but attempted instead to transform its functioning.

In its attempt to ensure a smoother passage for its projected reforms at the second attempt, the government leant very heavily on the expertise of the Home Office child-care inspectorate and in particular its Chief Inspector Joan Cooper and Derek Morrell, the Assistant Under-secretary. These two people, committed as they were to a treatment orientation, to a belief that social deprivation produced juvenile crime, and to deinstitutionalisation, were the major architects of the *Children in Trouble* White Paper (1968) and the Children and Young Persons bill 1969. Cooper and Morrell produced a piece of legislation which, while acceptable to political, administrative, and professional constituencies, retained the more radical features of the earlier attempts at reform.

Within these more modest confines the 1969 Children and Young Persons Act (CYPA) attempted to achieve its radical objectives in three ways. First, it created a *buffer* between the juvenile court magistrate and the young offender. While the act empowered the magistrate to impose care orders and supervision orders on juvenile offenders, the social worker was given complete autonomy in the execution of these orders. Thus if the court imposed a care order, the social worker would decide whether the child should be removed from his or her home to a Community Home and if so, for how long. Prior to the Act the magistrate would simply have imposed an Approved School Order and the child would have been escorted from the court to an approved school. Similarly, after the act a magistrate could impose a supervision order but the social worker would decide what, if anything, the young person had to do in order to comply with that order. Prior to the Act the magistrate would have imposed a Probation Order and if the child or young person had failed to comply with the conditions of that order, which had been specified by the court, then the probation officer, an officer of the court, was required to initiate breach proceedings in which the offender would be returned to the court and could be sentenced both for the breach of the order and for the original offence. This change meant that magistrates could have been placed in a position where they served as mere rubber stamps for social workers and their therapeutic intentions.

Second, the Act attempted to *curtail the magistrate's power to imprison*. Prior to the Act the magistrate had been able to remit juveniles of 15 and over to Crown Court for borstal sentencing. This was done because magistrates were not empowered to sentence juveniles to substantial periods of custody. Had the 1969 CYPA been fully implemented nobody under 18 could have been remitted to Crown Court for borstal sentencing and the juvenile would therefore have had to be dealt with by the penalties available within the juvenile court.

Meanwhile, of course, the Act set the scene for the abolition of the other custodial sentencing option available to the juvenile court, the detention centre. It did this by stating that as forms of 'Intermediate Treatment' (IT) were developed, so the attendance centre (AC) and the detention centre (DC) would be phased out. This 'phasing in' of IT and 'phasing out' of the AC and the DC was both politically and practically necessary. If the 1965 bill foundered because it went too far too fast, the 1969 Act was offering to go quite far but more slowly. Given that IT existed in name only, it was also impractical to substitute a non-existent IT for the existing ACs and DCs. What is clear, however, is that if the Act had been fully implemented then this pincer movement would have completely removed the juvenile magistrates' power to imprison.

Third, the Act attempted to *minimise criminalisation* by raising the age of criminal responsibility from 10 to 14. This would have brought Britain into line with many other European countries; Italy for example raised the age of criminal responsibility from 9 in 1867, and its effect would have been to reduce substantially the numbers of children passing through the juvenile court. The children diverted from the court by this change were to be dealt with within the social welfare apparatus instead.

The 1969 CYPA represented the high-water mark of more than a decade of attempts at reform in the juvenile criminal justice system in England and Wales. It was an uneasy compromise between the reformers and their opponents. For the proponents of a 'welfare' position it constituted a gain, for the 'justice' lobby a loss. Seen in retrospect it appears that, like the Treaty of Versailles, the attempt to patch up one struggle sowed the seeds for the next. This struggle took place in 1981/2 and resulted in the 1982 Criminal Justice Act.

The 1969 Act may have been a compromise but it attempted to buy time and to create the terrain upon which the struggle for reform could continue. It offered a large foot in the door for reformers and it probably did as much as it could have done, given the political climate in which it was born. The pragmatism of, and the confused and disparate motivations behind, this legislative endeavour should not however obscure what was truly radical about it. Taken together the provisions of the 1969 Act added up to the abolition of imprisonment for children and young people and herein lies its claim to radicalism rather than mere novelty.

The most important thing about the Act, as it emerged, was not the change in the balance between 'welfare' and 'justice' within the juvenile criminal justice system, but the change in the balance of central and local government control over young offenders and the challenge this posed to the prison. This is evidenced by the invention of IT. It was not the case that something called Intermediate Treatment had been shown to be more effective in terms of reconviction, rehabilitation, or resocialisation. The call to replace imprisonment with IT was not based on the technical superiority of this untried response. Indeed, well into the 1970s large and expensive conferences continued to founder on the question 'What is Intermediate Treatment?'. The most significant thing about IT was not what it was but what it was not. What it was not was imprisonment. The other significant thing about IT was that it was to be operated by local authorities. The importance of the *Children in Trouble* White Paper (HMSO, 1968) and the CYPA 1969 lies as much in what they do not say as in what they do say. What they do not say, but what gives them unity and coherence as a legislative endeavour, is that in our dealings with children and young people in trouble we do not need prisons. Indeed, we need them so little that we do not even need to talk about them. The only points at which the bill and the Act come anywhere near a discussion of the prison is where they discuss its alternative. In this they avoid the trap of justifying the alternative in terms of the aims and objectives of the prison.

The 1969 Act was an attempt to keep the abolition of imprisonment for children and young people in England and Wales on the political agenda. It came at a time when faith in the capacities of governments to effect positive and constructive social betterment was waning and it came too late.

2 The rise and fall of delinquency management

The 'Twentieth-century Dream' has had three central interwoven strands:

1. The belief that, through science and technology, we should be able to unlock all the secrets of the universe. We should be able to 'master' nature, and thus create a materially secure and comfortable life for the majority of mankind;

2. The Utopian belief that, through drastic social and political reorganisation, aided by the greater use of State planning, we should be able to create an entirely new kind of just, fair and equal society;

3. The belief that through the dismantling of all the old repressive 'taboos' and conventions of the past — whether in social attitudes or the arts — individuals would be able to enjoy a much greater degree of freedom and self-realisation.

The importance of the seventies was that, in each of these great avenues of human exploration, they had marked a 'moment of truth', a point at which, more obviously and inescapably than ever before, the dream ran out.

Christopher Booker, *The Seventies*

Internal rather than external conflict could be the concern of the decade.

Edward Heath to the UN General Assembly, 1970

An expanded system
The Labour government through its policies and legislation had laid the ground for a new apparatus of juvenile justice, and in the creation of the Local Authority Social Services Departments, the Family Service, had brought into being a group of professionals who would operate it. In consequence, the Heath government inherited a substantially expanded set of resources with which to pursue its law and order policies and to manage its deviant populations. It is interesting that while many Conservatives in parliament and beyond bemoaned the passing of the 1969 Act the only parts which the Heath government

failed to implement were those which would have placed limits on the resources available to deal with young offenders. It did not raise the age of criminal responsibility to 14, ensuring that the supply of young deviants to be dealt with was not diminished; it did not phase out the Attendance Centre and the Detention Centre in favour of the new Intermediate Treatment as the Act had intended; but it placed no impediment in the way of the development of IT. It did not prevent young people under 18 being sentenced to borstal training by the courts, but it gave social workers the discretion to place these young people in the revamped approved school — the Community Home (with Education) (CHE). In so doing, it substantially increased the numbers of people who could decide whether or not a child should be removed from home.

In the early 1970s we saw the emergence of a juvenile criminal justice system which was not, as the Fabian reformers had hoped, transformed, but substantially expanded instead. Those elements of the system which had been brought into being by the Act were absorbed into a system of juvenile justice which retained its traditional commitment to imprisonment as the ultimate disciplinary backstop. It was a system in which more things could be done to more young criminals more often than at any time since 1908 when a separate system of juvenile justice had been formally created in England and Wales. The cruellest irony for the reformers was that these new system components had been devised in an attempt to stop young people being defined as criminal and thus projected into a criminal career. By default or design the reforming endeavours of the Fabians had been incorporated into a more pervasive and more punitive system of juvenile justice. Social welfare and social work had been annexed and put into the service of the law and order state.

The restructuring of welfare
Heath offered a new, harder version of Conservatism to match the starker economic realities which followed the short-lived economic boom of the 1960s. He had promised to control inflation, the unions, public expenditure, and crime and, as we now know, he failed spectacularly in each of these endeavours. The election of Heath in 1970 signalled a shift from government by consent to government by constraint. There is of course a profound irony in these Conservative crusades since, despite the fact that they advance behind the banner of 'less government', they are almost invariably accompanied by increased state interference in the lives of citizens and increased state expenditure on criminal justice activities.

Gough (1979) has noted that despite changing governments and changing ideologies, the proportion of the Gross National Product

(GNP) expended by the state on welfare, crime control, and industry continued to grow during the period in question (see Table 2.1).

The significance of this increased expenditure in the sphere of juvenile justice lies in the ways in which these increased human and material resources were deployed within the revamped juvenile criminal justice system. The non-implementation of key sections of the 1969 Children and Young Persons Act and the implementation of the 1970 Social Services (Reorganisation) Act created new relationships between system components. Thus we must speak of a restructuring of state welfare expenditure and not merely of its expansion. This restructuring of welfare brought the practice of social work into a relationship of uneasy interdependence with the junior penal system.

The struggle for the delinquent body
Social work and the junior penal system constituted the two aspects of the expanded juvenile criminal justice system. While the former offered to cure offenders in order to restore them to conformity, the latter strove to effect a similar change through punishment. If what followed was a struggle for the delinquent body, then it was a struggle which the junior penal system won hands down.

What we now know is that the 1970s witnessed a massive expansion in the numbers of children and young people who were imprisoned. Between 1965 and 1977 the numbers of young people aged 14 to 17 entering detention centres rose from 1404 to 5757. In the same period the borstal population remained fairly static but the proportion of 15-to 17-year-olds in that population rose from approximately 12.3 per cent to over 30 per cent. In 1965 21 per cent of convicted young offenders aged 14 to 17 were dealt with by police-administered attendance centres and prison department administered detention centres and borstals. By 1977 this proportion had risen to 38 per cent indicating that during a period which saw the unparalleled expansion of social work, its significance as a response to juvenile crime declined rapidly. This view is

Table 2.1   *The growth of social expenditure in the UK*

| | Percentage of GNP at factor cost | | | | | | | |
	1910	1921	1931	1937	1951	1961	1971	1975
Welfare	—	1.1	1.8	1.8	4.5	0.3	0.1	1.1
Health	—	—	—	—	—	4.1	5.1	6.0
Justice and law	0.6	0.8	0.8	0.7	0.6	0.8	1.3	1.5
Industry	1.8	4.5	3.2	2.8	6.9	4.9	6.5	8.3

Source: Gough, 1979: 77

further reinforced when we note that the proportion of young offenders being supervised in the community by probation officers and, in the wake of the implementation of the 1969 Act, social workers, dropped from 18.5 per cent of those convicted in the 10–17 age group in 1965 to 13.5 per cent in 1977 (Pitts, 1982).

Table 2.2   *Convictions of 14- to 17-year-olds, 1973 and 1977*

Offence	1973	1977
Violence against the person	5283	5184
Sexual offences	804	679
Robbery	1312	883
Burglary	23,459	29,357
Criminal damage	9661	9546

Source: Pitts, 1979

When called on to explain this rapid and spectacular rise in youth imprisonment, governments through the 1970s were content to make vague references to the 'crime wave'. The crime wave has been a consistent part of the British political landscape in the post-war period. Crime waves are however elusive things. They are epidemics which always seem to have shifted just at the moment when governments are about to cure them, yet remarkably they never seem to infect a very large number of people.

The crime wave which was allegedly afflicting Britain in the early to mid-1970s was similarly elusive. At a commonsense level one would expect an increase in the incarceration of the young to be related to an increase in the numbers of young people perpetrating serious offences. When we look at the incidence of serious offences for which 14- to 17-year-olds were convicted in the years 1973 and 1977, the period of the crime wave, we find little evidence for this (Table 2.2).

Table 2.3   *Receipts into custody under sentence as a*
          percentage of those found guilty

	Male	Female
1967	4.8	0.7
1970	6.2	0.8
1973	8.2	0.9
1976	10.9	1.3

Source: Prison Statistics, 1977

It is certainly the case that the period witnessed a remarkable increase in the proportion of convicted 14- to 17-year-olds entering custody under sentence (Table 2.3).

That this was an indication of hardening reactions rather than worsening crime is evidenced by the fact that young people aged 15 to 17 entering borstal in 1976 tended to have substantially fewer previous convictions than their older contemporaries or their counterparts of a decade before (Table 2.4).

Table 2.4   *Borstal admissions*

| Number of previous convictions | All age groups | | | | | | 15–17 years 1976 | |
| | 1966 | | 1972 | | 1976 | | | |
	No.	%	No.	%	No.	%	No.	%
0	166	4	200	4	255	4	255	10
1–2	854	20	1121	20	1299	20	841	32
3–5	1989	46	1961	36	2730	41	969	37
6–10	1178	27	1880	35	2018	30	473	18.4
11 +	94	2	165	3	215	3	30	1.0
Total	4281	99	5327	98	6580	98	2568	98

Sources: Prison Statistics, 1977; Spiers, 1977

Spencer Millham stated the matter thus:

In 1975 . . . some 6,000 boys aged between 14 and 16 underwent a spell in Detention Centre. During the same year 1,200 boys aged 15 and 16 were received into Borstal Institutions. This means that during this period more children experienced a spell in security than at any time since 1908, a fact emphasised more when we link these figures with the 5,400 juveniles remanded to adult prisons or remand centres. (Millham, 1977: 22)

The facts are fairly clear, but the reasons for this renaissance of juvenile incarceration in the 1970s became a source of considerable controversy.

The 'justice backlash' thesis
David Farrington (1984) maintains that when considering the statistical evidence:

A plausible interpretation of these figures is that after the 1969 Act was introduced in 1971 the magistrates were avoiding sentences for which social workers were responsible. This led to an increase in the more lenient sentences (discharges and fines), and also in the more severe institutional sentences.

Here Farrington implies that the increased use of custody for juveniles is due to the continuing struggle between 'welfare' and 'justice', with justice, in the form of the juvenile court magistrates, using all the means at its disposal to impose its solutions on the problem of juvenile crime.

In this account greater severity in sentencing or growing authoritarianism on the part of the bench is attributable to the struggle for power and control between social work and the juvenile bench. The increase in custodial sentencing is seen as a consequence of attempts by the bench to minimise the potential role and function of social workers in the court. Social workers are left, it seems, to deal with less problematic offenders and to explore 'prevention' with 'pre-delinquents' or youngsters with only a minimal involvement in crime rather than take control of, and impose 'welfare' solutions on, 'hard-core' young offenders. This leads to a 'spreading of the net' in which new delinquent, or potentially delinquent, populations are subjected to state intervention, albeit the intervention of the relatively benign social worker.

Farrington suggests that the juvenile bench initiated a division of labour in which it dealt with the bulk of offenders who had traditionally inhabited the juvenile court while social work was bequeathed a newly identified, less problematic, population.

Social work is offered its own sub-system as a consolation prize for not gaining control of the whole system. The statistics indicate that the sub-system social work was bequeathed, the system of preventive intervention, supervision, care orders and the CHE was a contracting one.

The Approved School Order, which could only be imposed by a magistrate, was replaced, on the implementation of the 1969 CYPA, by the section 7.7 Care Order which gave social workers the power to place juveniles in a CHE. Between 1965 and 1971 the numbers of young people placed in these institutions rose from 5821 to 7543. Following the implementation of the Act on 1 January 1971 and the transfer of this power from magistrates to social workers the figure dropped gradually to 6033 in 1977 (Pitts, 1979). As we have already noted the use of Supervision Orders underwent a far more dramatic decline in the period following the implementation of the CYPA 1969.

The 'professional entrepreneurism' thesis

The 'justice backlash' thesis locates the cause of the explosion in juvenile imprisonment in the 1970s in the behaviour of juvenile court magistrates. The 'professional entrepreneurism' thesis, by contrast, locates the causes of these unprecedented incarcerations in the behaviour of local authority social workers who are, it seems, bent on an attempt to annexe delinquency as their own exclusive professional domain.

Giller and Morris have argued:

Increasingly, as the mechanisms of these processes are researched and investigated, the traditional ascription of responsibility for these results to an unsympathetic magistracy or judiciary cannot be substantiated . . . A fuller picture suggests that the benign and helping agencies can, and do (often unwittingly), contribute to the production of punitive juvenile justice. (Giller and Morris, 1983: 151–2)

The research referred to is research into 7.7 Care Orders and the frequency with which social workers place juveniles in CHEs (Thorpe et al., 1980), and research into social workers' recommendations to magistrates in cases where custodial sentences are imposed (Lupton and Roberts, 1982). The former research contends that a substantial section of the CHE population should not be so confined since according to a strict reading of the conditions of a 7.7 Care Order the order should not have been imposed in the first place. The latter research indicates a fairly close correspondence, up to 70 per cent, between social workers' recommendations and magistrates' eventual disposals. The implication of this research is that social workers' recommendations may have a significant impact on magistrates' decisions. What is obvious, but sometimes overlooked, is that in all cases in which a care order or a custodial sentence is imposed, it is the magistrate who either imposes the order or sentence, or remits juveniles to a higher court for sentencing.

Morgan (1981) in pursuing the 'professional entrepreneurism' thesis, runs the risk of confusing the respective roles of magistrates and social workers in precisely this way. In her attempt to implicate social workers as the major force behind the growth in incarceration, Morgan's distaste for 'pinko liberals' and her mistaken belief that secure residential and penal establishments are primarily populated by 'dangerous, repeated, or serious delinquents' add fire to her prose; even if they do make for a somewhat misleading argument:

It is part of the progressive folklore typified in the *Guardian* and *New Society* that responsibility for the expansion of secure places or 'intensive care' is to be laid at the door of the public's and the magistrates' intolerance of dangerous, repeated or serious delinquents. Both are accused of converting the care order into an instrument of punishment and public protection. However, this ignores the fact that transferral within the care system is completely dependent upon the evaluations and decisions of its own staff. (Morgan, 1981: 57)

Here again the argument is actually about care and not imprisonment, and it is actually about what happens after a magistrate has imposed a 7.7 Care Order. To argue that the imposition of a Care Order by magistrates may make possible, or set in train, certain actions or processes which lead to greater levels of control is not the same as arguing that social workers carry the major responsibility for the initial imposition of controlling orders or sentences.

A central problem for the professional entrepreneurism thesis is that it fails to account for the diminishing significance of social work and social workers in the British juvenile criminal justice system in the 1970s. This again is fairly obvious and yet these arguments are used by the proponents of the 'professional entrepreneurism' thesis as a rationale for a reversion to a strictly judicial system of juvenile justice from which social workers would be effectively banned.

If one attempts to achieve a synthesis of these two positions in order to get closer to the truth, a third thesis suggests itself.

The 'collusion and cock-up' thesis

This thesis is most clearly stated by Thorpe et al. who argue that:

> It was the decision-makers — policemen, social workers, probation officers, magistrates and social services administrators — who effectively abandoned whatever potential for reform the 1969 Children and Young Persons Act contained. Quite simply, cumulatively these disparate bodies of professionals made the wrong decisions about the wrong children at the wrong time. (Thorpe et al., 1980: 3)

This is an attractive thesis in its commonsense simplicity but sadly, like the other two theses, it ignores government and the role of the state in elaborating both an ideology and an apparatus of youth control. It was not social workers or magistrates who planned and built the new secure units in community homes in the 1970s, it was the government. It was not social workers or magistrates who expanded the numbers of places in borstals and detention centres, it was the government. It was not social workers or magistrates who from 1972 instituted cutbacks in social welfare expenditure which resulted in thousands of young people who were the subjects of supervision orders remaining unsupervised, it was the government. Most importantly, it was not social workers or magistrates who failed to implement those sections of the 1969 CYPA which would have effectively prevented the imprisonment of children and young people, it was the Heath, Wilson, Callaghan and Thatcher governments. Parker identifies the increased power given by governments to magistrates as a key factor in the move towards greater authoritarianism in the juvenile criminal justice system in Britain in the 1970s:

> The potential social work influence in criminal proceedings ... is not crucial however and the probation role in court merely aggravated and failed to check the court's punitiveness rather than caused it ... The scapegoating of social work has been propagandist, diverting attention away from the fact that power is vested in the police and magistrates who have been using it in a similar way to produce the punitive disposal patterns of the past decade. The critique of the social welfare component of juvenile

justice by radical criminologists ... and liberal reformers like Morris and Giller has perhaps colluded with this misrepresentation of social work influence in criminal proceedings. Indeed, as the powers of lay magistrates and their armoury of disposals via more attendance centres and even harsher detention centres are extended, the marginal influence of social workers and probation officers will become even more apparent ... In part this is made possible by the erosion of due process and its restructuring by court workers to allow pseudo legitimacy to extraneous social and moral judgements. Furthermore the passive performance of many solicitors and probation officers allows this production to continue unchecked. (Parker, 1980: 259)

Criminologists looking for explanations of the 1970s juvenile imprisonment bonanza seem to search endlessly among the actors within the system for the culprits. It is almost as if government stands like a concerned, anxious but powerless parent on the sidelines of the juvenile justice system. The target of criticism is always these low-level agents of control, the mistakes they made, and the unintended consequences of their actions. Similarly the target for intervention and change is always the behaviour of these 'zoo-keepers' of deviance. The fact that they are employed by somebody to do something and that the something which they do fits into a much broader set of political and bureaucratic arrangements is ignored. Commenting on a previous generation of criminologists, Matza observed that:

Their contributions were to be absorbed into a tradition of enquiry whose first premise was the separation of crime and the state; thus the absorption was not without a certain measure of distortion or misfit. Left unassaulted, the historic misconception of the positive school — the separation of crime and state — could remain the cornerstone of a sociological study of deviation that heeded the possibility that the correctional system's effects sometimes boomeranged. But as long as the misconception was maintained, such a possibility could be regarded as easily rectified, instead of a profound irony lodged in the very nature of the intimate relation between crime and the state. (Matza, 1969: 144)

Meanwhile, back at number 10

Back at number 10 in 1970 the Heath administration was attempting to work out what 'getting tough on law and order' meant. It seemed clear that the moral fibre of the country had to be refurbished and that things, particularly economic things, were getting out of control, but to identify a problem is not to find its solution. Unsurprisingly the Heath administration began to rework neo-classicism in order to come up with a criminal justice strategy.

Whereas the Wilson administration was concerned to identify and eradicate the social causes of crime, the criminal justice strategy which emerged from the Heath administration emphasised the more efficient, effective and economic use of the apparatus of detection, deterrence and rehabilitation. This changed strategy reflected not only radical change in political ideology but also a change in the kinds of people who were influencing policy. Harold Wilson had surrounded himself with academic experts in psychology, sociology, and social policy. Edward Heath tended to turn to barristers, policemen and accountants for his advice.

As James Q. Wilson has observed, the problem with seeking advice from academic sociologists or criminologists is that their stock-in-trade is the pursuit of ultimate causes. He writes:

> But ultimate causes cannot be the object of policy efforts precisely because, being ultimate, they cannot be changed. For example, criminologists have shown beyond doubt that men commit more crimes than women, and younger men more (of certain kinds) than older ones. It is a theoretically important and scientifically correct observation. Yet it means little for policy-makers concerned with crime prevention, since men cannot be changed into women or made to skip over the adolescent years. (Wilson, 1978: 50)

While Wilson fails to observe that an understanding of ultimate causes is in fact extremely useful to governments which want to effect radical social change, he expresses very succinctly the spirit of scepticism which affected governmental crime control strategies through the 1970s. It stands in stark contrast with the Wilsonian spirit of optimism of the 1960s. It is pragmatic, policy-orientated and concerned with what can be done now rather than what should be done eventually. It is part of a broader philosophical and ideological change which affected reformers and their reactionary adversaries alike and seemed at times as if it would bring the political programmes of the right and the left to a point of convergence.

The Heath criminal justice strategy was concerned with the causes of crime only to the extent that an understanding of causes would suggest policy initiatives which would lead to the more effective containment of crime and criminals. While accepting the need for 'treatment' for some people, the strategy retained its commitment to the due process of law and the necessity of punishment as a means whereby the rational citizen might be encouraged to conform. Young offenders were not seen simply as the victims of deprivation as they had been by the Fabians. Some were, but a majority were rational choice-making individuals for whom the penalty was part of the calculation of the advisability of the deviant enterprise. There were therefore two types of creature to whom the system must respond. One, whose behaviour was determined by factors beyond his or her control, and another whose actions were freely chosen in the knowledge of their likely consequences. Classical actors in a classical social drama.

Any criminal justice strategy therefore needed to contain both that which could respond to the actor whose rationality was impaired by social, emotional or material deprivation, and that which could respond to the rational, calculating actor. In the hands of the Heath administration neo-classicism cast off the radical imbalance placed on it by the Fabians and reverted to its more traditional form. It was humane where humanity was warranted and severe where severity was necessary. It was also potentially very expensive because it would require the expansion of both the welfare services and the junior penal system, and this posed a serious problem for a government committed to reducing government expenditure. This expansion was necessitated because Heath had made an election pledge to do what previous post-war governments had failed to do. He had pledged that he would do something about the 'crime wave'.

'Community corrections' for a crumbling prison system
Heath's major initiative in the sphere of justice was embodied in the 1972 Criminal Justice Act, and the Younger report (HMSO, 1974). The 1972 Act increased the minimum penalty for the possession of firearms to endanger life or to resist arrest from 14 years to life imprisonment while it allowed police officers to take people who might otherwise be charged as drunk and disorderly to detoxification centres.

The Act introduced Community Service Orders and Day Training Centres as alternatives to custody for adults, and these alternatives were to be supervised by the probation service. Power was given to Probation Committees to create Bail Hostels, Probation Hostels, and Probation Homes. Simultaneously Mark Carlisle, a Home Office minister of state, announced a 30 per cent increase in probation officers' salaries and increased the number of trainee places from 200 for 1972 to 600 for 1975. At a NACRO AGM in 1972 Carlisle spoke of the probation service as the central pillar of government crime control strategies for the next 20 years.

In 1974 the Younger report, *Young Adult Offenders*, was published. Younger proposed a mode of 'reinforced supervision' in which probation officers were to be given the power to return clients to 'secure houses' in the community for brief spells of custody if they violated the very tight conditions of their order.

The 1972 CJA and the Younger recommendations were to be the mechanisms whereby the Heath government would develop its community correctional system, a system aimed at the efficient, cost-effective management of law-breakers. This initiative signalled the beginning of a new era in government responses to crime. It marked the advent of 'delinquency management' which was to reach its fullest flower in the juvenile criminal justice system a little later in the decade.

The development of a community correctional system was in no small part a response to the problem of the prison. British prisons from the early 1960s, at least, had been in a state of crisis. They were chronically overcrowded, staggeringly expensive, and on the face of it they systematically worsened the problem to which they were allegedly a solution. With the 1972 Act, Heath's administration attempted to deal with this crisis by instituting a system of delinquency management. This development had five essential features: repoliticisation, bifurcation, the restoration of the prisoner to the community, the imposition of the prison on the community, and annexation.

Repoliticisation

Whereas Harold Wilson's administration attempted to remove crime from the political arena and re-describe it as social pathology, Heath restored crime to the realm of morality. Wilson's criminals were a residual population of social casualties, victims of an inequitable social order which the new socialism had all but vanquished. Heath's criminals were, by contrast, frequently parasites and subversives, only a minority of whom were not responsible for their behaviour. They were testimony to what happened when an overdeveloped welfare state took away personal responsibility, dignity, and motivation.

Heath's assault on crime was an assault on one crucial aspect of a much broader problem which was seen to create not only crime, but industrial strife and inflation as well. The broader problem was that too much state intervention in the lives of citizens in the post-war period had made us soft and had therefore produced the conditions for economic decline. We were living in the 'something for nothing' society. This was why industry was not competitive. This was why our growth rate was so low and our inflation rate so high. We needed to 'slim down'. 'Dead wood' had to be 'cut away'.

Conservative governments in the 1970s and 1980s, however sophisticated they might be in other respects, are ensnared by 'Conservative theory's' explanation of economic decline. This is an explanation which is an article of faith for the party's rank and file. It is an explanation which transforms economic into moral problems. Within this theory there is always the mob which is not prepared to do a fair day's work for a fair day's pay and constantly threatens to wrest the legitimately acquired wealth of the responsible and prosperous away from them either by excessive pay claims or by robbery.

Conservative assaults on crime are a powerful political symbol of governmental determination to attack the pervasive social malaise of decadence which is seen to have afflicted the mob. 'Law and order' means more than law and order for Conservative governments, it means 'defending civilisation as we know it from anarchic mob rule'. For Conservatives, crime is the symbolic key to the problem of economic decline, and crime control must always be a central political plank for a Conservative government in periods of economic crisis. For Edward Heath the repoliticisation of crime was unavoidable.

Bifurcation
Bifurcation is a mechanism whereby governments can have their law and order cake while they eat their public expenditure one too. The 1972 Criminal Justice Act demonstrated its commitment to tough punitive responses by extending the penalty for a small number of armed robbers to life imprisonment. Meanwhile it strove to effectively decriminalise public drunkenness and in so doing divert from jail a large part of the vast army of homeless alcoholic recidivists, who are the stock-in-trade of the magistrates court and the prison. A bifurcated policy allows governments to get tough and soft simultaneously. It requires a redescription of the deviant population in which a few offenders will be described as more dangerous and threatening and will therefore be subject to higher levels of attention and intervention, while a larger group will be redescribed as less threatening and as such not meriting the harsh punishments to which they were previously subjected. This clears the way for either taking this larger, newly-defined group out of the prison altogether or, at least, reducing the sentences that they will receive, thus effectively reducing the prison population.

Bifurcated policies are often part of a strategy to develop non-custodial alternatives since if the previously imprisoned group can be redescribed as relatively innocuous, judges will, it is argued, be more inclined to return them to the community and the community will be more inclined to accept them. Part of the purpose of bifurcation then is to move certain categories of offender back towards a relative 'normalisation'. These policies are a way in which the pressures on the prison and the costs of imprisonment are reduced while governments may still claim to be getting tough on law and order.

It goes without saying that those offenders who are selected to undertake the harsher punishments feel more than a little aggrieved by bifurcated policies. Since, however, these policies are primarily informed by political pragmatism and an attempt to minimise state expenditure, little heed is paid to the gross injustices which they require.

The restoration of the prisoner to the community

One of the saddest features of the British penal system is that a substantial minority of prisoners are in prison because they have nowhere else to live. A few actually commit offences in order to take advantage of the comfort and security offered by the prison. Thus the introduction in the 1972 Criminal Justice Act of Bail Hostels, Probation Hostels and Probation Homes, must be seen as a progressive measure whereby the need for accommodation could be met without the necessity of imprisonment. This was an important attempt to restore the prisoner to the community.

The case of the Community Service Order, and Day Training, is slightly different. If it could be demonstrated that everybody who was sentenced to community service or day training would otherwise have been imprisoned, then one might sustain the argument that here was a further example of the restoration of the prisoner to the community. If however community service and day training emerged as sentences which subjected offenders who would previously have received a lesser penalty to greater levels of surveillance, intervention, and control then we would have to conclude that we were witnessing the imposition of the prison on the community.

The imposition of the prison on the community

The reality is that community service and day training were very ambiguous additions to the sentencing repertoire. Research suggests that in as much as community service has diverted about half of its clients from prison the other half would not have received a custodial sentence anyway. As a decarcerating strategy community service must thus far be viewed as a 'goalless draw'.

If community service and day training inadvertently imposed the prison on the community in the form of higher levels of surveillance, intervention and control, the Younger recommendations strove to introduce a prison regime into the community in very explicit ways. One of these ways was to transform the probation officer into a peripatetic prison warder and it was this proposal, to annexe the probation service to undertake these new surveillance and control functions, which gave rise to the 'screws on wheels' controversy.

Annexation

Annexation involves the attempt to annexe agencies, practices and practitioners who have a degree of autonomy from central government in order to use them to implement the intentions of central government in very specific ways. Had the Younger recommendations been implemented the role of the probation officer would have been transformed to resemble that of the American parole officer. Younger received support from the upper echelons of the probation service because the proposals offered a further vehicle for expansion of the service. The rank and file were almost universally opposed, arguing the case for professional autonomy and a commitment to the best interest of the client. They refused to have their social work-based activity annexed and their professional autonomy constrained in the service of such intense levels of control and surveillance.

The National Association of Probation Officers' rejoinder to Younger (1975) states: 'An examination of recent developments in the service suggests that a corollary of increasing control over the client is increasing control over the Probation Officer by management'. The Younger report marked the point beyond which probation officers were not prepared to go in helping the government impose the prison on the community. They resisted annexation and so the Younger proposals foundered (National Association of Probation Officers, 1975).

'Community corrections' for crumbling borstals

While the 1972 Criminal Justice Act and the Younger report were not concerned specifically with juvenile justice, they were designed as a response to a crisis in the prison occasioned in no small part by an influx of young prisoners under 25 years of age. We have already noted that the borstal changed in the period 1965 to 1977 from an institution which catered primarily for the 17 to 21 age group to one which, in 1977, had a 15- and 16-year-old population of at least 30 per cent. This effective annexation of one-third of all borstal places by the juvenile criminal justice system meant that an increasing proportion of young people of 17 and over were being forced up into the adult system.

The response of Younger and the 1972 Act was to create a system in which the prison was surrounded by a set of ancillary institutions and practices which offered differential levels of surveillance and control. This was precisely the model which the imposition of the remnants of the 1969 CYPA upon the existing juvenile criminal justice system had created. By the mid- to late 1970s, the adult and juvenile justice systems were attempting to develop virtually identical strategies in order to manage an expanding population of identified young offenders more effectively. While the juvenile system placed greater emphasis on the deprivation of its subjects, the mechanisms through which these subjects were processed were strikingly similar.

In the adult system the integration of community corrections and the prison was made easier because all the system components came under the control of the Home Office. The juvenile justice system by contrast was comprised of: (a) prisons controlled by the Home Office, (b) attendance centres controlled by local education authorities, (c) CHEs, remand and assessment centres and field social workers controlled by local authorities and (d) community correctional facilities controlled by local authorities and voluntary organisations. Thus the attempt to produce analogous adult and juvenile justice systems required central government intervention in the functioning of local authorities and the voluntary sector. As the 1970s progressed we witnessed the Heath, Wilson, Callaghan and Thatcher governments attempting to exert more and more control over those elements of the juvenile criminal justice system which were the responsibility of local authorities and the voluntary sector. Although there was a change of government in 1974 the policies and initiatives of the Heath administration were not seriously modified by the Labour administrations of Wilson and Callaghan in the period 1974 to 1979. They showed no enthusiasm for attempting to resuscitate the badly mauled 1969 Act. The political tide had turned and the spirit of the times was against such idealistic social engineering. Seemingly we were all hard-headed delinquency managers now, and besides, being a Labour government and a law and order government seemed less contradictory in 1974 than it had done in 1969.

We can observe the processes of repoliticisation, bifurcation, the restoration of the prisoner to the community, the imposition of the prison on the community, and annexation, at work in the juvenile criminal justice system of the mid-1970s.

Repoliticisation

In 1975 the Expenditure Committee on the working of the 1969 Children and Young Persons Act reported (Home Office, 1976). The preoccupation of the report was political rather than financial. It stated that the Act had not been wholly effective in 'differentiating between children who need care, welfare, better education, and more support and the small minority who do need control and an element of punishment'. David Farrington notes:

> Less than three years after the Act was brought into effect (in December 1973) the House of Commons Expenditure Committee began an inquiry into its working ... the inquiry was based on the assumption that the Act was not working although no evidence was quoted in favour of this. The membership of the Committee (set up under a Conservative government) included at least two former magistrates and one former manager of an approved school, but nobody with close working or personal connections with the social work profession or social service departments. (Farrington, 1984: 85)

This spectre of a band of sophisticated committed young criminals whom no amount of kindness will touch has loomed in the reports of all law and order governments, all the manifestos of authoritarian moral crusaders, all the speeches of those who wish to make this 'once great country of ours great once more', and all the writings of right-wing conspiracy theorists.

They are never named, they are never counted, they are never located in time and place, and they are always on the increase. They are the 'hard core', they are that 'certain element', they are the 'trouble makers', they are the 'ringleaders', they are the ones without whom the others would not do it. They have been with us for hundreds of years but they are always a contemporary phenomenon. They are the example par excellence of what is going wrong in our society. They are the ones that the hard edge of bifurcated crime control policies are going to fix.

Bifurcation

This bifurcation of children and young people in trouble provides evidence of governmental toughness while the way is cleared for reshaping child-care and custodial provision in response to economic reality. The 1976 White Paper which followed the Expenditure Committee Report is a useful illustration of these processes at work. There are three significant government decisions in the White Paper.

The first is that magistrates should be able, in certain cases, to recommend to a local authority what it should do with a child, including a recommendation for secure accommodation (para 27) and that the government would use its powers under the 1975 Children Act to make direct grants to local authorities to build more secure accommodation in community homes (para 42). This is an attempt to resolve the financial problems of local authorities by offering enhanced resources for extending prison-like provision and marks an important central government intervention into the sphere of local government.

The second decision is that the educational welfare service should be empowered to take responsibility for children under supervision whose main difficulty is their refusal to go to school (para 65). The White Paper questions the assumption that persistent truants are in need of care and control (para 71). It is interesting to note that a high proportion of children and young people in CHEs at that time had committed relatively few offences but were detained primarily on the grounds that they were persistent non-school attenders. Had this attempted normalisation and redistribution of truants been successful it would have resulted in a substantial reduction in the demand for CHE places, thus hastening their eventual demise. This discussion of truancy took place against the backdrop of a burgeoning 'out of school' industry in which off-site units and alternatives to formal schooling were mushrooming.

The third decision requires that non-residential treatment, such as intermediate treatment schemes, day care, supervision, and fostering, should be given priority by local authorities (para 61). It is also suggested that local authorities should consider using CHEs for day as well as residential care.

Thus the decarcerating thrust of the second and third decisions should theoretically at least more than compensate in financial terms for the increased costs necessitated by the first decision. David Ennals, speaking in 1977 at a NACRO AGM, contrasted the £34,000 spent on 100 children engaged in intermediate treatment with the £2,000,000 spent on 700 children in residential care. Bifurcation holds out the possibility of substantial economies which hard-pressed local authorities recoiling from wave after wave of government spending cuts were very keen to make. Thus there was a calculating edge to the humanitarian endeavour to restore the prisoner to the community.

> What does this mean in terms of money and other resources? Islington councillors and officers were forced last year (1976) into some fresh thinking as we were faced with the horrifying cost of residential provisions of all sorts. We concluded by agreeing to close two children's homes, change the character of two others and to transfer part of the revenue savings into increased votes for the community-based provision of fostering and Intermediate Treatment ... Our Intermediate Treatment projects vote is increased to £10,000 which we hope will be our 25 per cent contribution to an Urban Aid grant. (HMSO, 1977)

Bifurcation may have offered a solution to some financial problems for some interest groups in the juvenile criminal justice system in Britain in the mid-1970s but it did not solve the problem at which the policy was aimed, namely the problem of a collapsing penal system. There is a recurring problem with bifurcated policies of crime control which each government adopting them seems to have to discover afresh. Box and Hale (1986) point out the ways in which magistrates and judges have routinely subverted government attempts to limit incarceration. This was the dilemma that Heath and the subsequent Labour administration faced. They developed bifurcated policies to allow them to manage larger populations of delinquents more economically and more effectively but were either unwilling or unable to control the major power-holders in the system, the bench and the judiciary.

The problem seems to be that governments have given magistrates and judges two messages. Home Secretaries as politicians have said we must get tough, while Home Secretaries as penal administrators have said we must limit custodial confinement. The bench and the judiciary have always responded to the first message and ignored the second. The fate of 'delinquency managers' large and small, in the post-1969 period, has been sealed by the legal establishment.

The restoration of the prisoner to the community

At first sight, the fact that in 1976/7 8000 children and young people participated in schemes of intermediate treatment, the measure which was to replace the attendance centre and the detention centre, might lead us to believe that we were witnessing decarceration on a large scale. In fact, of this 8000 a substantial majority were aged 8 to 15 years and only a small minority were subject to a court order. As such they were not a population in any serious danger of entering the care or custody systems. By the mid-1970s, IT was being used as a catch-all for social compensation, compensatory education, personal growth, therapy, outdoor activity holidays for children with no money, and here and there and from time to time as an alternative to custody. It is not therefore possible to argue that in the mid-1970s IT represented a decarcerating endeavour. It resembled instead a patchwork of often quite interesting explorations in work with deprived, neglected and mildly delinquent children and young people. The children who were being decarcerated or diverted were mainly those placed in residential care for reasons other than delinquency. What frustrated many practitioners in the field of Intermediate Treatment was that IT was making no effective impact on the imprisonment of juveniles. This concern was echoed in government and resulted in the establishment of a working party at the Personal Social Services Council which published *A Future for Intermediate Treatment* (Personal Social Services Council, 1977).

The future envisaged by the report coincided at certain points with the ethos and methods of the ill-fated Younger report (1974). The most significant contributions made by the report are the suggested reintroduction of legal controls and sanctions into the conditions of an Intermediate Treatment requirement imposed on a juvenile by the court, and the redefinition of IT's potential client population. Section 8 of the report is entitled 'Intensive Intermediate Treatment: A Provision for the Persistently Delinquent'.

The report suggests that Intensive IT (IIT) might well pose an alternative for some young people who were at the time languishing in CHEs, borstals, and detention centres, and correctly notes that many were there as the result of a tariff system in which a string of minor offences resulted in custodial disposals, irrespective of the needs or problems of the child or the suitability of his or her home circumstances. Intensive IT, to paraphrase the report, would have two components. The child would go from the court to the IT centre where he or she would reside for two weeks. During this time the 'programme' for the second component, day care, will be devised and 'the parameters of acceptable behaviour and control both during the residential placement and the daily programme of intermediate treatment' will be agreed 'by all concerned'. There will, the report suggests, probably be a need for some 'preparation of attitude' during this residential period. Should this preparation not be wholly successful and the subject experience 'problems in his personal, family, or school life' or if difficulties are being encountered in meeting the requirements of his 'programme', he or she can be taken back into residence for 'a more total form of care and supervision' to 'provide the support needed'. The subject's progress would be supervised by one team member, who would ensure the subject's attendance and exert day-to-day control.

A Future for Intermediate Treatment was produced by a group of people noted for their progressive, and indeed, in certain cases, radical, views about children and young people in trouble and their needs. The report was first and foremost however a tactical attempt to get IT off the sidelines and back into the law and order game. Intensive IT was to be the Trojan horse which would get radical liberals inside the walls of the law and order state.

The model of IIT developed in the report resembles very closely the California Youth Authority Probation Subsidy Project. This was the model which had inspired the Younger report (HMSO, 1974) and found favour with the Heath government, since, on the face of it, it appeared to be the perfect mechanism whereby one might appear tough while simultaneously curbing the rush of young offenders into the prison. One of the central aims of the Probation Subsidy Project had been to encourage the courts to divert offenders away from the prison to a community project and, in so doing, to divert some of the money saved, away from the prison in the form of a subsidy to fund the project. The project was concerned with changing behaviour. It strove first to change the behaviour of judges by offering inducements and second to change the behaviour of offenders by threatening penalties.

IIT was not going to be sold to children, their families, or their social workers on the basis of a voluntary agreement as earlier government pronouncements on IT had envisaged. It was going to be sold to juvenile court magistrates, and judges. It was to be sold on the basis that if it were to work then magistrates must have the power to enforce the conditions of the offenders' supervision order and that this would involve legal sanctions. The PSSC report recommended that the law be changed so that, where a supervision order arose from criminal proceedings, the subject could be taken back to court for breaches of the conditions of the order. The 1977 Criminal Law Act gave the courts the power to fine a young person for a breach of an intermediate treatment requirement or, in the case of a boy, to send him to an attendance centre.

The onus of intervention switches from the needs of the child or young person to his or her social obligations. As part and parcel of this the report distances itself from questions of need and therapy and moves instead to a paramount concern with behaviour. Nobody is going to be psychoanalysed in IIT, they will be too busy pulling up their socks. This marks an important shift away from interventions which had implicitly or explicitly identified the mind as the site of change. Now it was the body or the actions of the body which came increasingly under professional scrutiny. Cohen has observed that:

> Here is where the new behaviourism appears: it offers the modest prospect of changing behaviours rather than people, of altering situations and physical environments rather than the social order. To be sure, the pure Skinnerian model was a highly ambitious one: a totally synchronised and predictable environment. But the realists of crime control will settle for a derivative pragmatic version, sharing with the original a refusal to accept consciousness as a variable. As long as people behave themselves, something will be achieved. The vision is quite happy to settle for sullen citizens performing their duties and not having insights. (Cohen, 1983: 124)

The objects of intervention are no longer Longford's psychologically impaired working-class children. The new offender is the young citizen motivated by the pursuit of pleasure and the avoidance of pain who has reneged on his end of the social contract. The response is to elaborate around the offender an apparatus of rewards and punishments which will offer a direct lesson in the value of conformity. The object of the reformers' endeavours in the juvenile criminal justice system in Great Britain in the mid-1970s comes once again to resemble the object of the justice system of Great Britain in the late 1790s — classical man. Reformers no longer seek the social or psychological causes of offending, for in this model there is no mystery surrounding deviant motivation. The offender effects choices, possibly on the basis of imperfect information, but choices nonetheless. Young offenders make a rational calculation and then act. The task of the delinquency manager is to inject a sufficient measure of pain into the equation to dissuade the would-be deviant. The task of radical liberal reformers it to annex what they might of the apparatus and minimise the harm done by official intervention in the lives of young offenders. The site of reform moves from intervention in the social factors which predispose young people to crime, to intervention in the system and its apparatus in order to restore the prisoner to the community.

The imposition of the prison on the community

We have already noted the ambiguous nature of community correctional endeavours, and IIT was, and is, not immune from this ambiguity. The problem with Trojan horses, to mix a metaphor, is that they have a nasty habit of turning around and biting the hand which carved them.

The problem once again is that if we wish to take the offender from the prison then we have to appear to be taking something of the prison with us into the community. As would-be reformers we find ourselves always justifying the alternative in terms of the aims and objectives of the prison. We find ourselves constructing an alternative which apes the prison in its attempts to gain credibility with the bench and the judiciary. We build a bridge over which we hope the prisoners will rush from the prison to the community but we do this with no guarantees and no promises from the magistrates, the judges and the politicians who have the power to make our ambitions a reality. We undertake our endeavours in the shadow of the prison which stands at the end-point of social discipline, doors open, anticipating our failure.

As IIT developed through the late 1970s the population of juveniles in prisons continued to grow. As this population became demonstrably less delinquent so the alternative was of necessity applied to even less delinquent offenders in an attempt to keep them in the community. In so doing the prison was imposed more effectively on the community.

Annexation

From its inception IT was an instrument whereby central government attempted to annex bits of social welfare and educational provision, which had previously had nothing to do with crime and offending, for its own law and order purposes. The Department of Health and Social Security booklet (1972: 13–14) identified the object of treatment as bringing 'the child into contact with a different environment' to help him or her form 'new personal relationships', participate in 'constructive activities of a social, educational or therapeutic nature', in fact anything which would be 'beneficial to his development as an individual and as a member of society'. These aims were to be achieved by allowing 'delinquents' to participate in activities available to 'normal' children and young people. The intention was that participants should be projected into the 'non-deviant' world. It was hoped that a broad range of youth service organisations, uniformed and otherwise, further education, outdoor pursuits and sporting facilities would be pressed into service. The attempt to annex these previously autonomous social, recreational and educational resources did not go unresisted however and the Community and Youth Service Association rejected IT on the grounds that young people might be directed to its members, projects or centres by the courts.

As we have already noted, by 1976 an entire phase of urban aid money, money made available as part of the British poverty programme, was re-designated to be spent on IT. Here we see a trend which developed throughout the 1970s in which central government intervenes to implicate local authorities and the voluntary sector in the furtherance of central government policies. The funding of secure units in local authority community homes is, of course, the example par excellence of this tendency towards centralised control. In a similar way established voluntary organisations like Dr Barnardo's and the Save the Children Fund are offered substantial central government money to develop IIT. Meanwhile government funding for voluntary social welfare agencies engaged in work which does not involve the management of delinquents is steadily reduced.

The introduction of sanctions for a breach of a supervision order with an IT requirement, and the development of secure units, implicates professional social workers in a far more controlling role and thus effectively annexes them into central government law and order strategies. Bernard Davies (1982) has observed that:

> Deliberately and progressively state policy for youth throughout the '70s and '80s has become more coherent, more firmly the direct responsibility of state agencies exercising state power and implementing state intentions, and increasingly concerned with satisfying the needs of the nation rather than the needs of young people.

By the end of the 1970s the capacity of the juvenile criminal justice system to control children and young people in trouble had been enormously expanded, but it was still not big enough for Margaret Thatcher.

3 The rise of vindictiveness

No one would remember the Good Samaritan if he only had good intentions. He had money as well.

Margaret Thatcher, 1980

I call it Sado-Monetarism.

Denis Healey, 1983

Just before the 1979 general election a journalist asked Margaret Thatcher what the most important task to be undertaken by a future Conservative government would be. Without hesitation she answered that it would be 'the restoration of the rule of law'. 'What laws might they be?' the disingenuous reporter enquired. 'The laws we are going to introduce', she replied. This was not the last time that the national interest and the pragmatic concerns of Mrs Thatcher and her cabinet colleagues were to be presented as one and the same.

Margaret Thatcher, the iron lady, as she came to be known, inevitably chose law and order as the central motif with which to adorn the rich ideological tapestry of her right-wing populism. Within this rhetoric 'lawlessness' was presented as both a cause and a consequence of the contemporary social malaise. Stuart Hall (1979) has noted how Thatcherian rhetoric traded on a widespread social anxiety in weaving together the disparate horrors of IRA terrorism, unemployment, mugging, skyjacking, profligate public spending, the red menace, football hooliganism and trade unions which held the country to ransom. Her appeal was simple but direct: 'Do you want a home of your own?', 'Do you want the medical treatment you need when you need it?', 'Do you want safe streets?', she asked, and because she had traded on real anxieties and real desires a majority of the electorate replied that they did.

The juvenile justice policies developed by Wilson and Heath may have had their problems and limitations but nobody could argue that they were not interesting, innovative, and indeed fairly thoughtful. Wilson showed us what a fully-fledged, radical, welfare-oriented policy would look like, while Heath pioneered an original delinquency management approach which was accepted and perpetuated by the subsequent Labour administration. Whatever one may have thought about these initiatives one had to acknowledge that they were quite well done. We don't have to approve of the direction in which the ship is sailing to appreciate that there is a professional hand on the tiller. If we pursue this nautical analogy though, it has to be said that the crew of the Thatcherian law and order lugger had apparently dropped all its oars into the water before the boat was out of the harbour.

The election of Margaret Thatcher in 1979 marked the renaissance of amateurism in the sphere of British juvenile justice policy formation. It was not so much that William Whitelaw, the Home Secretary, and Patrick Jenkin, the Minister of State for Health and Social Security, were amateurish but rather that the traditional Tory tendency towards a 'commonsense' amateurism in matters of crime and poverty was accentuated by the Thatcherian landslide which had filled the Tory back-benches with right-wing MPs who held radical views on law and order issues. One such was Warren Hawksley, elected to represent the Wrekin in 1979, employed by Lloyds Bank since leaving school, who at the committee stage of the 1982 Criminal Justice Act attempted to reintroduce flogging for the 10-plus age group for an offence which he styled 'provocative language'. To suggest that Hawksley, whose name was brought up in accusations of right-wing entryism to the Tory party, was typical is to overstate the case, but it is important to remember that the curfew introduced by the 1982 Act was inserted in the bill at committee stage as part of a compromise with Hawksley and his supporters, who had brought proceedings to a standstill on the provocative language/flogging amendment. The juvenile justice policies which emanated from Margaret Thatcher's government were constructed with more than half an eye to the right wing which constituted the rump of the Thatcher government's parliamentary majority.

William Whitelaw confronted similar problems to those encountered by Heath and the subsequent Labour administrations. The difference was that by now, as a result of the failure of the bench and the judiciary to co-operate with governmental attempts to limit the prison population, the problem was much larger. The political problem for the Home Secretary was equally pressing. This government had adopted a harder, more radical profile on law and order than the Heath government. It was moreover a government which was destined for historical reasons to measure its success against Heath's failure. The personal struggle between Heath and Thatcher manifested itself in many ways and ensured that Thatcher would never knowingly be seen to compromise with criminals, miners, or scroungers.

It became necessary to demonstrate that the government 'was going in hard on law and order'. But as usual in the Home Office the Home Secretary was sitting among election manifestos, demands from sympathetic pressure groups like the Police Federation and the Magistrates' Association, Saatchi and Saatchi's latest poll results, projections of anticipated parliamentary majorities on a variety of issues, pay claims from the Prison Officers' Association and surveyors' reports of crumbling walls in top security prisons. Amid this sea of potential troubles William Whitelaw was hurriedly developing a criminal justice strategy. He had at least seven problems which he had to solve before he could publish his *Young Offenders* White Paper (HMSO, 1980) and pilot the Criminal Justice Act (HMSO, 1982) on to the statute book. They were:

1. How could he deal with a chronically overcrowded prison system which had been subject to a series of violent disturbances and in which a race riot was anticipated? This problem was made no easier by the fact that the Conservative commitment to the 'rule of law' led inevitably to a 'hands off' policy in relation to any attempt to limit the sentencing powers of the bench and the judiciary.

2. How could he placate and control the substantial majority of right-wing authoritarian back-benchers and a prime minister who supported hanging, flogging and life sentences as rational responses to norm violation in the final quarter of the twentieth century?

3. How could he accommodate the demands of the Magistrates' Association which from 1972 onwards had been promised by successive Conservative Home Secretaries a restoration of the powers taken from them by the 1969 CYPA? This was particularly problematic since all the evidence suggested that a restoration of these powers would lead to substantially increased pressure on residential and penal establishments.

4. How could he accommodate the demands from the police for the changed legislation and stiffer penalties which, they argued, would support them in their attempts to police what they saw as a worsening law and order situation?

5. How could he be seen to be getting tough very quickly as the Conservatives had promised in their election campaign?

6. What did 'the rule of law' mean anyway, and how did one set about restoring it?

7. How could all this be done without incurring an inordinate increase in government expenditure?

In an attempt to resolve these problems Whitelaw introduced the 'short sharp shock' regime to two detention centres and delegated the drafting of the *Young Offenders* White Paper to Leon Brittan, an ex-barrister who was then a Minister of State at the Home Office. He was aided and abetted in this task by Robert Sims, formerly of the Council of the Magistrates' Association and Personal Private Secretary to William Whitelaw.

The White Paper and the subsequent bill were drafted in a hurry since the legislation was eagerly awaited by the government as its major law and order initiative. Law and order was important because even in 1980 the government was being conspicuously unsuccessful in its other political endeavours. This legislative endeavour initiated a repoliticisation and moralisation of juvenile crime, the restoration of the power of the bench, an attempt to restore some prisoners to the community, the imposition of the prison on the community and the annexation of human and material resources by a law and order crusade.

Repoliticisation and moralisation

The 1979 Thatcher administration not only repoliticised crime and punishment but dramatised it to the point where it came to assume an importance in the political bestiary akin to that previously only granted to the Warsaw Pact and the National Union of Mineworkers. Patrick Jenkin (1979), paraphrasing the Duke of Edinburgh, at a conference on IT in July, directed the attention of participants to: 'the avalanche of lawlessness threatening to engulf our civilisation'. This apocalyptic vision clearly justified the introduction of tougher penalties. One supporter of this move, James Anderton (1979), Chief Constable for Greater Manchester, remarked in June of that year that we needed: 'penal work camps where through hard labour and unrelenting discipline they (young offenders) should be made to sweat as they have never sweated before and remain until their violence has been vanquished by penitent humiliation and unqualified repentance'.

It is interesting that from 1979 onwards senior police officers appear to have been freed from the usual constraints which require public servants to keep their opinions to themselves, and are allowed to emerge instead as moral commentators on behalf of the new right. William Whitelaw always seemed embarrassed by the hysteria and vulgarity of supporters like Anderton and some of his cabinet colleagues but in the interests of unity he soldiered on until the 1981 Conservative Party conference where he was booed from the stage by a powerful and confident radical right wing for his alleged liberalism.

The Thatcher government's sabre-rattling rhetoric was necessitated in part by a need to make concessions to the party's right wing, but was only the surface manifestation of a more profound change. Thatcher's administration embraced classicist social and economic doctrines with the uncritical enthusiasm of the newly converted. This new doctrine drew heavily on ideas developed by an emergent right-wing intelligentsia in the 1970s which began to contest the left/liberal assumption that Keynesian economic interventionism and a gradualist policy of redistribution of wealth and resources were the only ways in which liberal democracies in advanced industrial societies might be regulated.

The new right believed that if the 'hidden hand of the market', currently tied behind the back of the 'body politic', could be released, and an interfering state 'rolled back' then prosperity would be achieved, the virtuous rewarded, the cheats and idlers (the mob, organised labour, and criminals) would get their just economic deserts. In a similar vein in the sphere of crime and punishment, we see the emergence of the 'new realists', the 'intellectuals for law and order' and a genre of social critique, peculiar to the 1970s and 1980s which is fiercely, and indeed often vindictively, classicist. It reintroduces 'wickedness' into the discourse on crime and punishment. Platt and Takagi write:

> There is a general agreement among the new realists that 'wicked people exist. Nothing avails except to set them apart from innocent people. And many people, neither wicked nor innocent, but watchful, dissembling, and calculating of their opportunities, ponder our reaction to wickedness as a cue to what they might profitably do. We have trifled with the wicked, made sport of the innocent, and encouraged the calculators.' There is also general agreement that the criminal justice apparatus is chaotic and ineffective. For Van den Haag, this is the result of a 'worldwide decline in punishment and therewith a respect for law', for Wilson it's a combination of ignorance and soft-heartedness; for Morris and Hawkins it's the federal government's failure to understand 'predatory crime' as the most potent threat to the American way of life. (Platt and Takagi, 1981: 46–7)

The search for the causes of crime is abandoned and the focus for reform moves even further away from the social, familial or psychological factors which predispose people to deviation. It moves towards an exploration of the range and nature of penalties necessary to regulate potentially deviant populations. It is interesting that it is these highly educated intellectuals for law and order who articulate an anti-intellectual position as a rejoiner to the 'pretensions' of liberal reformers and social work professionals. They celebrate instead the superiority of the 'commonsense' amateurism of ordinary people. Geoff Pearson, in a droll review of *Can Social Work Survive?* by Colin Brewer and June Lait, two 'no-nonsense' British right-wing intellectuals, writes:

Social work is unnecessary and pretentious. It is a treason of the clerks against ordinary people and their humble attempts to come to terms with life's trials. A professional treason that has been committed, moreover, without even so much as a glimmer of professional competence or expertise. So explaining to readers of the *Daily Telegraph* (9/2/78) what happens 'when trendy methods fail to cope with juvenile delinquents', Mrs Lait concluded that the whole business of childcare should be taken away from permissive educationalists and do-good social workers, and placed instead 'in the hands of ordinary people who have rejected pretentious, self indulgent and unscientific theorising in favour of their own good sense'. (Pearson, 1981: 115)

Always this appeal to the common sense of the common folk. It is the failure of common sense, the triumph of liberal intellectual modes of child rearing, which has led to:

the spread of what could be called a delinquent syndrome, a conglomeration of behaviour, speech, appearance and attitudes, a frightening ugliness and hostility which pervades human interaction, a flaunting of contempt for other human beings, a delight in crudity, cruelty and violence, a desire to challenge and to humiliate, and never but never, to please. (Morgan, 1978: 13)

Here Morgan offers us the syndrome to which Warren Hawksley's 'provocative language' and flogging was the commonsense response which ordinary people would understand.

Here was the real backlash against the 1969 CYPA. This was no modification or non-implementation — it was a rout in which the gains achieved by 'welfare' in 1969 were to be reversed and a new era of 'the rule of law' was to be brought into being. Welfare and treatment all but disappear, delinquency management in as much as it is understood remains in disconnected pieces while the reversion to due process of law is set in train. Ivan Lawrence QC MP put his finger on what was happening when he said of the 1982 Criminal Justice Bill:

One of the most important steps in the bill, which I strongly welcome, is the reflection of public opinion which says that we are fed up with letting sentences be decided by social workers rather than the courts ... encouraged by wet socialist intellectuals from all over the place. (Rutherford, 1986: 64)

These important steps take us away from professionalism, away from intellectualism, and back to a reliance upon the good commonsense amateurism of juvenile court magistrates.

It is interesting that the right wing at the time of the election of the first Thatcher government was unanimous in its view that crime in general, and juvenile crime in particular, was a subversive activity promoted in no small part by the insidious and corrosive influence of left-wing teachers and social workers. When in 1981 some black and white young people chose to describe nationwide rioting as a political uprising the government angrily replied that this was nonsense and that they — the rioters — were merely common criminals.

The restoration of the power of the bench

In the sphere of juvenile justice the government's determination to re-establish the rule of law was expressed through the restoration and extension of the powers of juvenile court magistrates. As we have already noted, the magistrates had resented what they saw as the erosion of their powers and the extension of the powers of social workers occasioned by the 1969 CYPA. In 1972 Sir Keith Joseph had promised an agitated juvenile bench that something would be done. The House of Commons Expenditure Committee, convened in 1973, containing two ex-magistrates, one ex-approved school head, and no representatives of social work, recommended in its report of 1975 that magistrates be given the power to send a juvenile directly into local authority care. The election, in 1974, of a Labour government meant that this change did not occur, but it was clear that a form of 'secure care order' was high on the legislative agenda of a future Tory government.

The 'secure care order' was a resuscitated Approved School Order (ASO). The ASO disappeared with the advent of the 1969 CYPA. The Act had meant that the approved school system, a system of residential schools approved by the Home Office as suitable establishments in which young offenders could serve their sentences, had been broken up and control over the schools had passed to local authority social services departments. Not only did social workers, and not magistrates, have the power to decide whether a child should be sent to what were now called 'community homes with education' (CHEs) but the heads of these CHEs, not magistrates, would decide whether to accept the child as a 'pupil' or not.

While the question of the 'secure care order' was first and foremost a question of the power and supremacy of the bench, it was also a question about the desire of central government to exert control over the apparatus of justice and juvenile incarceration, in the face of a disseminated system in which the power resided in the hands of local authority social services department personnel. The Thatcher government wished to vouchsafe the operation of the juvenile justice system to a juvenile bench which had shown itself to be the tried and trusted ally of Conservative governments and could be relied on to 'do the job'. Thus while it was unwilling, and probably unable, to resume control of the approved school/CHE system, the implementation of a 'secure care order' offered to give the bench powers to require local authority social workers to act in the ways that central government wanted. Thus the 'secure care order' held the promise for central government that it could utilise substantial local government resources in its law and order campaign, and in so doing begin to reverse one of the most radical shifts effected by the 1969 CYPA, namely the decentralisation of power in the juvenile criminal justice system.

Section F of the *Young Offenders* White Paper (HMSO, 1980) states that the government intends to seek approval for changes:

> Where a juvenile already in the care of a local authority as an offender is found guilty of a further imprisonable offence, power for the court to add a *residential care order* with the effect that for a fixed period not exceeding six months he is not to be allowed to remain at home.

The residential care order went some way to solving two political problems. It restored power to the bench and it gave central government both a symbol of toughness and greater control over the means whereby they could actually get tough. There was however a very serious logistical problem to be overcome.

The reconviction rates for young people who are the subjects of a care order under the offence condition of the 1969 CYPA is about 36 per cent (Cawson and Martell, 1979). We know that those actually in residential care have a higher reconviction rate than those 'at home on trial'. In an exercise undertaken in Lambeth in 1981 it was estimated that the introduction of the 'residential care order', or 'charge and control condition' as it was actually called in the Act, would result in an increase in expenditure of between £650,000 and £1,100,000 in Lambeth alone. This calculation was made on the assumption that the young people who re-offended but were living at home would be shifted to non-secure community home provision at a cost of £300 per week, while the re-offenders in non-secure residential provision would be shifted to secure provision at a cost of £610 per week. This calculation was made on the assumption that adequate secure and non-secure residential provision existed, which it did not, and that no additional capital expenditure would be necessary, which of course, it would. It also assumed that each re-offender would only re-offend once a year, which was optimistic (Cornish and Clarke, 1975) and it further assumed that local authority residential social workers would be prepared to deal with this massive influx of new and reluctant clients, which was similarly optimistic since those interviewed said that they would not (Pitts and Robinson, 1981). The government had set aside only £20,000,000 to meet the extra costs which would be incurred by all the local authorities in England and Wales as a result of the introduction of the 'residential care order'. The government, or more specifically Leon Brittan, had given no thought to the implications for capital expenditure on secure provision if this measure were to be taken seriously by the bench. The Association of Metropolitan Authorities, the Association of Directors of Social Services and Professional Advisers in the Home Office and the DHSS had all warned him of the dangers which lay ahead. Brittan however was one of the new breed of politicians on whom the Thatcherian sun had shone. His peculiar distinction was that where other mortals took warnings to mean that one should reconsider one's course of action, Brittan took them as a challenge. This is possibly the reason why his career as a cabinet minister was so brief. The juvenile court magistrates worked out fairly quickly that they had been short-changed by Brittan and the charge and control condition has more or less fallen into disuse.

The 1982 Act had two major objectives. The first was to strengthen the law relating to juveniles and young offenders aged 15–21 in England and Wales. The second was to limit the use of imprisonment for this age group. One way of limiting imprisonment, a way favoured by most liberal reformers, is simply to stop locking people up. To do this would require legislative and administrative changes which reduce penalties for offences which currently attract prison sentences. Alternatively one might follow the example of Holland and set a limit on the number of prison sentences which can be imposed by the courts. This limit is determined by the number of prison places. Even if courts impose custodial sentences they cannot be executed unless the government is prepared to grant a reprieve to those currently in prison. In this way governments can exert control over the judges and can of course reduce the prison population still further by reducing the number of prison places (Junger Tas, 1984).

In Britain in 1982 the first option, a reduction in penalties, was not politically viable because the Act aimed to 'strengthen' responses to adolescent offenders, not weaken them. The alternative option of limiting the number of prison sentences which could be imposed was however politically unthinkable because it would have involved the Thatcher government in what Conservatives have always tended to describe as 'an unwarranted violation by the state of the independence and impartiality of the courts'. The fact that this argument is fundamentally flawed, since its logical outcome would be that Holland, possibly the most liberal nation in western Europe, was a totalitarian dictatorship, does not stop law and order Tories using it as a rationale for either doing what they want, or doing what they cannot avoid doing. The commitment to the restoration of the powers of the bench meant that another method had to be found in order to limit imprisonment. Thus Brittan and Whitelaw developed a plan to get the same, or indeed increased, numbers of offenders through the system more quickly. The 1982 Act was to penal politics what the F-plan diet was to the slimming business. But first they had to lay the ground for this endeavour.

Overcrowding in British prisons is localised. While in 1982 there were empty places in high security category A prisons, borstals were bulging at the seams. The crisis of overcrowding in prison was a crisis brought about by the influx of 15–21-year-olds, a crisis precipitated in no small part by the non-implementation of the 1969 CYPA.

The borstal was created in 1929 by Alexander Patterson as an alternative to imprisonment for young people aged 16–21. Modelled on the British public school and staffed by ex-public school housemasters, it attempted to offer deprived young offenders the kind of opportunities their more privileged counterparts would receive as a matter of course. Should we be tempted to grin knowingly about the naivete of Patterson's philanthropic vision we might reflect on the fact that throughout the 1930s the reconviction rate of ex-borstal boys remained constant at around 30 per cent. In the 1960s the Home Office prison department attempted to effect a closer integration of the borstal into the mainstream of the prison system. This involved a change from a recruitment policy in which staff opted for work in a borstal to one in which they were drafted in randomly to what many saw as a backwater in which careers tended not to develop. Possibly as a result of these changes the reconviction rates in the 1960s and 1970s crept up to around 70 per cent for the borstal population as a whole and 79 per cent for 15- and 16-year-olds.

The Home Office account of these developments predictably attributed the abysmal reconviction rates to the 'poor quality of receptions', harking back to a golden age when they were being sent a better class of burglar, but as Little (1962) demonstrated, the decline in the effectiveness of borstal training 'holds true for receptions of a similar quality'.

The 1982 Act gave the final kiss of death to Patterson's dream by repealing Section 3 of the 1961 Criminal Justice Act which restricted the powers of the courts to imprison young adult offenders in the mainstream of the prison system. The return of borstal staff to uniform in May 1983 with the implementation of that part of the Act which redesignated the borstal as a Youth Custody Centre was not just 'get tough' law and order window-dressing. It signified the final absorption of the borstal into the mainstream of the prison system. It meant that young people in the prison system could be placed in any part of the system if overcrowding dictated that this was necessary. The principle which had informed the prison system for over 50 years, that 15- to 21-year-olds should be dealt with differently and in a different place from adult offenders was abandoned. The related principle that 15- to 21-year-olds committed to prison department establishments should all receive some form of trade training and education was also ditched. From May 1983, 15- to 21-year-olds could be committed to imprisonment pure and simple.

With the advantage of hindsight we may say that the history of the borstal is the history of a 50-year endeavour by governments to confound, and then annihilate, any traces of progressive reform in the custodial treatment of adolescent offenders. These changes made it possible for the Home Secretary to move 15- to 21-year-olds around the prison system in order to unblock any bottlenecks which might be created by excessive sentencing. It was a move which suggested an uncanny prescience on the part of the Home Secretary and it made the day-to-day management of prisons much easier.

The other major consequence of the repeal of Section 3 of the 1961 CJ Act was to give power to juvenile court magistrates to impose prison sentences on adolescents without the need to remit them to crown court for sentencing. Farrington observed that:

> In a clear movement away from welfare and towards retribution, the indeterminate borstal sentence was to be replaced by determinate youth custody 'so that the court can mark the seriousness of the offence by the length of sentence they impose' . . . This represents a considerable increase in power for magistrates since they will be able to pass a youth custody sentence of up to the maximum for juveniles (one year, if the juvenile has committed two offences) rather than remanding juveniles to the crown court for borstal sentences. It is also likely to lead to increasing institutionalisation of juveniles. When juveniles were remanded to the crown court with a recommendation of borstal training, only about 65% (in 1981) were actually given borstal. This is partly because some juvenile offences that seem relatively serious to magistrates seem relatively trivial to crown court judges. When the magistrates can pass youth custody sentences, the 35% who currently benefit by going to crown court will also receive youth custody. (Farrington, 1984: 86)

Between the end of May and the end of July 1983, the first two months after the implementation of youth custody sentences (YCS) the borstal/youth custody population rose from 5892 to 6839 (approximately 12 per cent). By the end of its first full year of operation, the increase was 65 per cent. Clearly more were going through but they were not going through as quickly as had been planned. Many juveniles were receiving the maximum sentence of six months or, indeed, two consecutive six-month sentences. Even with the possibility of one-third of the sentence being remitted the log-jam in the system kept growing, causing first embarrassment and then panic in the Home Office. Latchmere House, a remand facility in London, was hastily given over to young offenders serving shorter sentences of youth custody. They were locked in cells for up to 23 hours per day, no training, no education, and in some cases no exercise, were offered. Within months youth custody had assumed all the worst features of the mainstream of the prison system.

The indeterminate borstal sentence of six months to two years had allowed borstal governors and the Home Office a partial means whereby they could control overcrowding. Prior to the implementation of the Act the average time spent in borstal had been reduced to between nine and eleven months. Now the Home Office reluctantly realised that they had effectively relinquished what little control they had ever had over the size of the 15- to 21-year-old prison population.

The plan was not working, and it wasn't working because it was based on the erroneous assumption that one could give additional powers to juvenile court magistrates and then persuade them to use these powers sparingly. The government had attempted to limit custodial sentencing by requiring that before a young person could be sentenced to custody it must be stated in open court and recorded in the court register than no other sentence is appropriate because either the defendant is unwilling or unable to co-operate with a non-custodial sentence, or the offence is of such a serious nature, or the offender is so dangerous, that a custodial sentence is unavoidable. Burney (1985) has shown that magistrates and clerks have interpreted these vague conditions in remarkable ways, and in many cases the decision in favour of custody is reached by the magistrate and the clerk who then work out how the safeguards can be avoided. In some juvenile courts magistrates don't even pretend to be taking the safeguards seriously.

Nonetheless, the government tried, and continues to try, to persuade the bench that if they will only keep the errant adolescents' sojourn behind bars brief, then they, the government, will make this sojourn memorable. It is the short sharp shock of the revitalised detention centre which is to make the memory linger on.

At the Conservative Party conference in October 1979 William Whitelaw announced the introduction of a new experimental regime at New Hall and Send detention centres. The centres were opened in 1980. In March 1981 Patrick Mayhew, Minister of State at the Home Office, announced that the experiment was being extended to two more centres, and significantly, that a number of borstal places were to be converted to the new regime. *Tougher Regimes in Detention Centres*, published by the Home Office Young Offender Psychology Unit, appeared in 1984. It concluded that at New Hall and Send:

> 8.24. The purpose of the pilot project was to assess whether young offenders can be effectively deterred from committing further offences by spending a period of weeks in a detention centre with a more rigorous and demanding regime.

> 8.21. The introduction of the pilot project regimes had no discernible effect on the rate at which trainees were reconvicted. (HMSO, 1984: 243)

On 6 March 1985 the new regime was extended to all detention centres in England and Wales.

Just prior to the implementation of the 1982 Act (in 1983) the Home Office sent a circular to detention centre governors, alerting them to an anticipated increase in the 'throughput' of their establishments of 40 per cent. What the government had hoped was that magistrates would be attracted by the shorter DC sentence, as little as 3 weeks, if it was backed by a tough regime. Brittan's decision, to extend the regime to all DCs in 1985, was taken in the face of research commissioned by Whitelaw and undertaken by Home Office personnel which demonstrated that the short sharp shock didn't work. It was Brittan's final desperate attempt to change the behaviour of the juvenile bench and he failed. At present Douglas Hurd is contemplating the introduction of suspended sentences for juveniles in an attempt to limit incarceration. This, as Heath found to his cost, could have disastrous results, and could project even more young people into the prison. It will be a disaster if it is tried because whenever juvenile court magistrates are given new powers they use them to exert greater control over lesser offenders rather than less control over more serious ones.

The restoration of the prisoner to the community

On 26 January 1983 the DHSS published Local Authority Circular LAC(83)3. It stated that:

> Under Section 64 of the Health Services and Public Health Act 1968, the Government makes grants to voluntary bodies to support the introduction of intermediate treatment facilities that complement those provided by local authorities. New money has been made available for those grants from 1983/4 in order to help the development of more intensive IT programmes designed specifically for those young people who would otherwise go to borstal or detention centre. These resources can also help authorities to bring forward plans which are dependent upon the release of resources currently tied up elsewhere, e.g., in residential provision earmarked for re-deployment. (DHSS, 1983)

The amount in question was £15,000,000 to be spent over three years and it constituted an unprecedented infusion of resources into intermediate treatment. The 1982 Act had introduced a strengthened form of intermediate treatment, the Supervised Activity Order, which gave the juvenile bench the power to specify the duration and content of IT. The government hoped that by increasing the magistrates' control over, and hence confidence in, IT, and by establishing a network of alternatives to custody of the type described by the PSSC working party as IIT, it would be possible to limit imprisonment for juveniles.

This infusion of resources was styled the 'New Initiative' and Leon Brittan, in the foreword to *Criminal Justice*, a Home Office working paper published in May 1984, expressed the hope (HMSO, 1984) that it would create '4500 additional community-based places for the more serious offenders by 1985/6'. While it would be churlish to doubt the government's commitment to easing pressure on the prison and residential child-care establishments one cannot escape from the central irony of the 'new initiative'.

The Home Office anticipated that as a result of the implementation of the 1982 Act the DC population would rise by 40 per cent, or 2500 prisoners a year. Research commissioned by the DHSS and the Home Office indicated that the introduction of the Residential Care Order could lead to the reception into residential care of an additional 1100 children or young people per year. The Home Office prison building programme indicated that provision was being made for an additional 900 Youth Custody prisoners by 1990. These projections were, of course, wrong but the anticipated increase in the numbers of children and adolescents who would be subject to residential care or custody as a consequence of the changed sentencing powers of the juvenile bench, 4500, is exactly the same as the projected number of places in alternatives to residential care or custody which were to be brought into being by the introduction of the Supervised Activity Order backed by the 'new initiative'.

Here was confusion on a grand scale. One piece of legislation which simultaneously promoted two diametrically opposed responses to the same behaviour by the same group of people. Whatever Brittan thought he was doing he was in fact creating 4500 'alternatives to custody' with no assurances from the juvenile bench that they would use them as he intended, a growing body of evidence suggesting that they would not, and as we have seen, no effective legal safeguards to prevent the abuses which the evidence suggested would inevitably occur. Beyond this Brittan was deliberately opening up the possibility that a further 4500 children and young people could be locked up and he was doing this in a period in which the juvenile crime rate had remained virtually static for several years and the proportion of adolescents in the population was beginning to decline.

In the event the Youth Custody population did not grow by 15 per cent between 1983 and 1990, it grew by 65 per cent between May 1983 and May 1984. The DC population did not grow by 40 per cent, it declined. The Residential Care Order all but disappeared. It was all a terrible mess, someone had blundered, and this mess was handed over to intermediate treatment.

The courts were locking up larger numbers of less problematic offenders for longer periods. IT had to confront a situation in which young people who before the Act would not have been considered for an 'alternative to custody' project were now in desperate need of one. Once again welfare in the form of IT was handed one population to 'rehabilitate' while justice in the form of the juvenile bench punished another. And here again was the dilemma that although the 'new initiative' threatened to impose the prison on the community, the absence of the alternatives financed by the 'new initiative' could lead to even higher levels of youth imprisonment.

The imposition of the prison on the community
The 1982 Act made it possible for a juvenile court to impose a Community Service Order on a 16-year-old defendant. Described by some as 'an opportunity to make meaningful reparation to an aggrieved community' and by others as 'the chain gang', community service is about as close as you can get to being in prison without being in prison. As we have seen, community service from its inception has tended to be imposed upon those who would otherwise have received a less serious non-custodial penalty rather than upon those who would otherwise to go prison (Pease et al., 1975). The government had no reason to assume that a different pattern would emerge if community service were applied to a younger age group. With the introduction of community service into the juvenile criminal justice system we saw yet another means whereby quasi-penal control and surveillance could be imposed on the community.

'Night restriction' or the curfew forces parents to supervise their own children in their own homes. As such it reflects an abiding Conservative preoccupation with the idea that lawlessness is promoted by the abdication of responsibility for control and discipline by teachers and working-class parents. The curfew requires that the child or young person remain at home between 6 pm and 6 am for a period of three months. This effectively turns the home into a prison and the parents into gaolers. It does of course help to 'keep the family together', which Mrs Thatcher feels is very important if standards are to be maintained. It remains a moot point, of course, whether in forcing a bored adolescent to stay in an overcrowded flat, we are punishing the young person or the parents. As Howard Parker (1974) has shown, large low-income families, living in overcrowded accommodation, depend on their older children spending their leisure time out of the house in order to make 'family life' tolerable. It is a question of space and material resources. The curfew was to be supervised by social workers and probation officers, thus exhuming the spectre of the Younger report's (1974) 'screws on wheels'.

The other way in which parents were to be made responsible for their children's behaviour was by making them ultimately responsible for fines imposed upon their children by a juvenile court. Should parents be unable or unwilling to do this they could then be prosecuted in the magistrates' court for non-payment of fines, and if necessary, imprisoned. Thus the attempt to improve the quality of working-class parenting threatened to land poor, but innocent, parents of juvenile offenders in jail.

Annexation

In a speech given by Patrick Jenkin in July 1979, when he was Secretary of State for Social Services, he said: 'The government is prepared to regard child care services as part of the national pattern of law and order services and to have the priority which that accords it.' We have already seen how the charge and control condition strove to annexe residential child care provision in order to transform it into part of the junior penal system. The curfew attempted to annexe social workers and probation officers into the policing, surveillance and containment of young offenders in their own homes. For this reason the National Association of Probation Officers instructed its members not to co-operate with the Night Restriction Order and so, some might say to its eternal credit, did the Camden branch of the National Association of Local Government Officers (NALGO). The strengthening of the juvenile magistrates' control over IT was a further manifestation of the attempt within the 1982 Act to move control of the apparatus of juvenile justice away from social workers and back into the hands of the bench and the judiciary.

This annexation strove to mobilise the resources, skills, initiative and energy of a range of local authority and voluntary sector welfare professionals for purposes defined by central government. This was attempted, as we have seen, in two ways. First, by introducing legislation which changes the power relationship between social work and the bench and local and central government. Second, by redesignating, or transferring, money from one area to another. The life of the Thatcher government has seen a steady erosion of government financial support for the voluntary sector of social welfare. Government grants given to allow voluntary organisations or settlements to experiment with new services or new ways of working with people in need have dwindled to virtually nothing. Yet the government has repeatedly expressed its support for the voluntary sector. The reality is that it will support the voluntary sector to the extent that the voluntary sector is prepared to do what the government tells it, and to do it more cheaply than the government could. Thus that part of the voluntary sector which is financed by manpower services and the new initiative thrives. A substantial part of the income of organisations like NACRO, the Apex Trust, Save the Children

(UK), Dr Barnardo's, and some of the settlements, is contingent upon these organisations running employment projects and providing part of the apparatus of the juvenile criminal justice system.

As Davies (1982), among others, has argued, while the youth service, education, the health service and large areas within the voluntary sector have become more and more impoverished, those parts of statutory and voluntary welfare which meet the government's needs are inundated with embarrassingly large amounts of money.

An ideological victory

The performance of the Thatcher government in the sphere of criminal justice may have been a strategic and administrative disaster but it must be counted a political and ideological victory. The government entered vowing to arrest the slide into lawlessness but within three years was presiding over scenes of civil disorder on a scale never previously witnessed in mainland Britain. The spring of 1981 saw rioting, looting, and arson in every major British city. With that peculiar ability Margaret Thatcher has to persuade us that the unintended consequences of her policies are merely instances of the pressing need for those policies, she presented the 1981 riots as a vindication of her strategies on juvenile crime, unemployment and policing.

The government characterised itself as a cleansing crusade which would restore Britain to economic and moral health. The infidels were the usual suspects — left-wing subversives in education and welfare, miners, gays, black people, social security claimants and the unemployed. Identified in this way the crusaders took the battle deep into the enemy's territory.

Operation 'Major', the mass entrapment, by agents provocateurs, of social security claimants at Oxford in 1982 signalled an assault on scroungers but it also marked a radical movement beyond what had previously been regarded as reasonable police behaviour. None the less it was presented, and largely accepted, as an assault by the crusaders on behalf of the poor but virtuous who had always paid their own way. The introduction of the Nationality Act was resisted by some black people and some left-wingers but few people dwelt on the fact that it actually robbed all of us of our previously inalienable right to domicile in Britain. Under the Thatcher government the interests of the prime minister and her inner cabinet confidants and the national interest became merged in political rhetoric. Misleading the House of Commons was presented as a patriotic duty while the prosecution and imprisonment of civil servants who revealed these misdeeds was presented as an assault on political subversion. The police were granted new and more flexible powers in order to free them to get on with the job of rooting out the cancer of crime and disorder. The major objections to this came from black people, left-wingers and, interestingly, the Police Federation which complained that the Police bill was vague and allowed police officers far too much leeway in interpreting its meaning. The young homeless discovered one morning in 1985 that if they lived in lodgings by the seaside or in a major city then they would only be allowed to stay there for 6 weeks before their dole money was cut off. This was a sop to those who were in work but wanted to be at the seaside. It was all vindictive, petty, but corrosive stuff which left its mark on popular consciousness and desensitised the public to the illegalities and excesses which were being perpetrated in its name.

Who killed Angus Boyd?

On 17 February 1984 Angus Boyd was found dead in his cell at Glenochil Young Offenders complex in Clackmannanshire. Angus Boyd's death was the fifth at Glenochil in three years. All of the boys had hanged themselves. In the year prior to the death of Angus Boyd 171 young men had been placed on strict suicide observation at Glenochil.

Glenochil was the prototype and the model on which the new 'short sharp shock' regimes of the detention centre were based. The extension of the tougher regime to all detention centres in Britain in March 1985 was undertaken in the knowledge that it made no difference to reconviction rates but that where it had been in operation for some time five young people had killed themselves.

In April 1985 police were called to Aldington detention centre in Kent to investigate allegations of brutality to prisoners. The brutality was revealed anonymously by probation officers. Their anonymity was, they believed, necessitated by the fear that in revealing criminal offences perpetrated by prison officers against prisoners they would be branded by their own employers, and prison personnel, as trouble-makers:

> Another probation officer from South London produced case note details of a black youth who had been in the centre for a burglary offence between October and November last year.
> As soon as he arrived he said he was subjected to racial abuse and slapped in the face with a ruler. A prison officer then punched him in the stomach and took off his belt and slapped him around the face with it. (*The Guardian*, 26 April 1985)

In August 1986 allegations of brutality were made by the mother of a prisoner at Send detention centre in Surrey who had seen her son punched and kicked as he was being taken away from the building in which their visit had taken place. This boy was the son of a naval officer and had been imprisoned in Send for his first offence of stealing a bicycle.

At the time of the Aldington investigation, Leon Brittan (1985), writing in *Community Care*, claimed: 'Some commentators have caricatured the new regime as harsh and brutal. This is not so, we have taken steps to ensure that it strikes the proper balance.' The government, in its pursuit of political credibility for its law and order policies and a pragmatic concern to manage the penal population more effectively, was prepared to introduce a regime which required prison officers to act in a more coercive, controlling and forceful manner. It was prepared to take a chance with the rights, civil liberties, and lives of children and young people in order to achieve its political and administrative ends.

Labour MP Martin O'Neil has campaigned consistently for a public enquiry into the Glenochil deaths but the government has refused. In the light of the clamour surrounding the deaths of Jasmine Beckford and Tyra Henry at the hands of their parents we are faced with a strange paradox. The demand that the professional social workers responsible for the well-being of these children should be called to account, occupied the front pages of the tabloids for weeks. Meanwhile the issue of Angus Boyd, the other four boys at Glenochil, and the young people at Aldington and Send, all victims of non-accidental injury and all under the supervision of penal professionals simply disappeared from the public eye. Tyra Henry and Jasmine Beckford will never be forgotten but Angus Boyd and the other boys were forgotten by the public as surely as the Argentinian young people who died in the Falklands were forgotten, and this is the true measure of the Thatcher administration's ideological victory.

Harold Wilson had presented juvenile offenders as a pathetic anachronistic proletarian residue which could be restored to the *conscience collective* by the judicious application of welfare and treatment. Edward Heath had presented juvenile offenders as the 'something for nothing mob' who could be made to shape up if they were managed correctly and the right people were given the right amount of treatment or punishment. Margaret Thatcher presented juvenile offenders as part of a more pervasive 'enemy within'. She established them as a force threatening to subvert 'our way of life' and in doing so legitimised and turned a blind eye to any response, however extreme, which the body politic or its professional representatives deemed fit in order to preserve 'law and order'. The Thatcher administration chose to draw no distinction between the 'rule of law' and 'law and order', but as Stuart Hall (1985: 55) has argued: 'The rule of law is not the same thing as law and order. Law and Order is about effective policing and what it says is if you can deliver the goods I am not going to ask too many questions about how you do it. We must conclude that ultimately Send, Aldington and Glenochil were a price that the Thatcher administration was prepared to pay in its attempt to restore 'the rule of law'.

4 The professional response 1: the era of optimism

They start as crusades ...

Howard Becker

It is ironical that governments which want more law and order usually want to spend less public money. They are usually particularly keen to spend less public money on welfare services but come reluctantly to realise that if they want more law and order then they actually have to increase expenditure on welfare. A further irony is that this results in the creation of more jobs for people who either do not share their views, or are actively engaged in attempts to subvert their policies. The problem for these governments is to re-shape welfare in such a way that it may complement their law and order policies. The problem for radicals is to keep the space they inhabit sufficiently flexible and ambiguous in order that they can develop radical initiatives within it.

The tensions between the ambitions of governments and the ambitions of those charged with the care and control of children and young people in trouble finds expression in the practices which evolve in the wake of legislative or policy changes. This tension is nowhere more evident than in the field of IT. From 1969 to the present day IT has provided the stage upon which the tensions, conflicts and absurdities in the politics of juvenile justice have been played out.

The most important thing that ever happened to IT was something that did not happen. As a result of the non-implementation of key sections of the 1969 CYPA IT did not replace the Attendance Centre and the Detention Centre, and young people aged 15 to 17 were not prevented from being sentenced to borstal training. In 1969 a Labour government had placed IT at the centre of its abolitionist juvenile justice strategy. By 1971 IT had lost all its political support, all its power, and most of its friends. If IT was going to take children and young people out of residential and penal institutions then it would have to do this on the basis of influence alone. But as Spencer Millham pointed out, the politics of influence were unlikely to shift IT's most intractable adversary, the residential tradition.

I would stress to you that the residential tradition is very strong. It has been going for nearly 300 years and it is not going to be shifted by a few murmurs about Intermediate Treatment, particularly when children are often popped into institutions by an administrative elite who have been educated in similar places and whose idea of adolescent heaven is a whiff of Lifebuoy soap and sweaty socks. Nor will it disappear just because you can demonstrate the abilities of IT. In the old approved school system demonstrations that the failure rates were enormous or that the institutions had a host of other difficulties were irrelevant for policy, simply because residential institutions have one enormous advantage over community care. Behind their walls the children are not visible, and if they run away and cause trouble, they are obviously extremely difficult — a view which justifies institutional practice. In contrast, if an offender placed on a community project misbehaves, people see this as your fault. Far from justifying your position, the problems which the adolescent poses reproach the intervention. I think this is a very important difference between institutional care and intermediate treatment. (Millham, 1977: 23)

Non-implementation had left IT without a power base. It had no legal, political, or administrative purchase on the key decision makers in the juvenile criminal justice system. IT emerged from the 1969 CYPA as an empty space somewhere between probation and incarceration in which somebody, who could imagine what IT could do and be, was hopefully going to do something. Unlike more established practices within social welfare, which were merely required to adapt their existing practices to the requirements of the 1969 Act, IT's first job was to invent itself.

On one hand, IT did not look a very good bet for those wishing to embark on a career in social welfare. On the other hand, however, it provided the perfect vehicle for those who could imagine what IT could be, and for those who saw in the poorly-defined nature of IT a perfect opportunity to effect radical social change. The subsequent history of IT began with an internal struggle between groups of IT workers to define the aims and objectives of IT practice. This internal struggle came to assume secondary significance in the mid-1970s as it was eclipsed by an external struggle between IT and field and residential social work in which IT attempted to gain greater power within local authority social services departments in order to exert greater control over the operation of the juvenile criminal justice system at a local level.

Like most people or movements with identity problems IT has often shown a tendency to edit its own history in order to demonstrate that what it is doing at the moment is an advance on what it did in the past. IT is prey to a partial but convenient amnesia and a preoccupation with novelty which means that many contemporary accounts of the early development of IT tend to be simplified and misleading.

It is therefore necessary to correct the misapprehension that all early forms of IT consisted of therapeutic groups in which politically naive Freudian disciples made unwarranted incursions into the lives and liberty of juvenile offenders by translating normal youthful misbehaviour into social pathology. The endeavour was in fact more diverse, more confused, and much less dogmatic than this popular caricature suggests.

If there was a dominant intellectual or ideological influence on the development of IT in the early 1970s it was not one which derived in any straightforward way from social work's psychoanalytic inheritance. An equally significant influence was derived from the critical theory and the critical politics which emerged from the new left and the 'alternative society' in the mid- to late 1960s. This influence did not simply take the form of the application of a new and better set of curative techniques or 'practice theories' to the obvious, essential, and timeless phenomenon of juvenile delinquency. Early IT developed within an intellectual climate, a paradigm, which offered no specific injunctions for action, but rendered traditional conceptions of the problem and traditional formulations of the solution problematic. Pearson identifies the core of this new understanding:

> We must make here a similar pronouncement: all claims to talk of the politics of personal distress, the politics of deviance, and the politics of the machinery of the welfare state within which personal distress is handled must come to terms with the scandalous imagination of the counter-culture. For it is there that the relationship between what is personal and what is political finds some articulation. (Pearson 1977: 80)

We must remind ourselves about what was happening to welfare and social work during this period. As Pearson again points out:

> At this time also, of course, we find the emergence of welfare client groups (or groups of potential clients) who pose traditional welfare problems as politics: Claimants' Unions, Gay Liberation, Women's Liberation, Mental Patients' Unions, Child Poverty Action Group, various community and neighbourhood control movements, squatters, Preservation of the Rights of Prisoners (PROP), and in the United States the Mental Patients' Liberation Front and the Insane Liberation Front. (1977: 95)

It was clearly not the case that more traditional conceptions of the problem of, and the solutions to, 'juvenile delinquency' were completely supplanted by the adherents of an 'appreciative' misfit paradigm. New movements co-exist with traditional practices. A single social work agency may contain practitioners, administrators and senior executives who understand the problems they confront and the solutions to these problems in radically different ways. What is the case, is that in the early 1970s, it was the ideas which emerged from new left politics and the alternative society, ideas brought to the Seebohm departments by the great influx of new professional workers who had been participants in the turbulent politics of the 1960s, which gave the impetus to some of the most significant innovations in work with children and young people in trouble with the law.

In the period 1969 to 1975 the practice of IT was largely influenced and shaped by political and professional movements beyond social work. While some had a direct and obvious impact on the practice of IT others were more oblique, lending a way of seeing and understanding young people and their offending rather than a prescription for action. What they shared was an optimism about the possibility of effecting positive betterment as a result of intervention in the lives and neighbourhoods of the socially disadvantaged. They were: radical welfare; the alternatives movement; social facilitation and normalisation and welfare and treatment.

Radical welfare

By 1969 in Britain, the brief economic boom was ending causing unemployment in general but youth unemployment in particular to rise. The idea that youth unemployment was now a permanent feature of British economic life rather than a recurrent but temporary problem related to fluctuations in the trade cycle was gaining currency in government circles. Meanwhile the attempt to reduce poverty through the expansion of the personal social services and educational opportunity had yielded little obvious success.

The problem confronting the government in 1969 was like a Chinese box in which each door which is opened reveals another one. There was a problem of youth unemployment but within this was the problem that it was economically and educationally disadvantaged young people who were most likely to be unemployed. Within this was the problem that there was a disproportionate concentration of economically and educationally disadvantaged young people in the blighted inner cities where unemployment levels were highest. Within this was the problem that a disproportionate number of these economically and educationally disadvantaged unemployed inner-city young people were black. Within this was the problem that in the disadvantaged, unemployed, multi-racial, inner city, juvenile crime rates were highest. Indeed, had it been possible to eradicate the crime perpetrated by children and young people in the twilight zones of the major British cities, then statistically at least, Britain would have emerged as a virtually crime-free society. What was needed was a practicable point of entry to this complex web of inter-related problems.

The Wilson administration was having American nightmares and American dreams. Enoch Powell had predicted 'race riots' in his infamous 'rivers of blood' speech and many influential commentators held that it was precisely the conditions noted by Powell which had led to the riots of 1967 and 1968 in the American inner cities. On the other hand, the Kennedy administration had apparently devised a solution. Harold Wilson's solution to crime, unemployment and poverty in the inner city in Britain in 1969 was based on the definition of the problem and the recommended remedies devised in the early 1960s by the architects of the US poverty programme.

Juvenile crime became a major political issue in the USA in 1960 because it contained within it the two most pressing political problems with which the Kennedy administration had to deal. They were: the problem of the unequal position of black Americans, and a level of unemployment, unsurpassed since the Great Depression, which had led to staggeringly high levels of joblessness among black American and Puerto Rican young people in the ghettos of the northern cities, the areas where crime rates were highest. The massive 'March on Washington' by black and white civil rights campaigners in 1963 was for 'Jobs and Freedom' and increasingly black activists insisted that the demand for equal civil rights and the demand for equal economic and educational opportunity were indivisible.

In 1961 John F. Kennedy established the President's Committee on Juvenile Delinquency and Youth Crime and appointed his brother Robert, the attorney general, as Chairman. One of the most influential and persuasive members of the Committee was Lloyd Ohlin of the Columbia School of Social Work. The Committee was profoundly influenced by a book published in 1960 and written by Lloyd Ohlin and his colleague at Columbia, Richard Cloward. The book was called *Delinquency and Opportunity* (Cloward and Ohlin, 1960). It is undoubtedly the case that this work gave the intellectual rationale not only for the 'Mobilisation for Youth' which was Ohlin's specific concern, but for the entire poverty programme. A theory was developed which, explicitly and implicitly, informed the politicians who developed the US and the British poverty programmes and the administrators and activists who tried to make them work.

Cloward and Ohlin argued that in the United States the dominant culture, mediated via the press, television, and the educational system, presents all citizens, irrespective of their social or economic position, with universally valued success goods. This culture suggests moreover that these goals may be attained by all on the basis of hard work and individual endeavour. It is as if everybody can make the journey from the log cabin to the White House if they have a mind to do so. The reality which belies the 'American dream' is that the opportunity to achieve these success goals is not distributed equally. Down at the bottom of the social heap among the young people of the ghetto such legitimate opportunities hardly exist at all.

This presents the lower-class residents of the ghetto with something of an ontological problem. If they are unable to achieve socially valued success goals then either they are failures or something else is going on. They have, Cloward and Ohlin suggest, three options. They may avoid blaming themselves by banding together with other young people in a similar predicament in order to redefine the situation as one in which the system conspires to keep them down. Thus, in the manner of Durkheim's functional rebels, they may innovate by adopting illegitimate opportunity structures (that is, crime) in order to achieve the valued goals. This is only possible however if they have access to a milieu, 'the organised slum', in which the activity is culturally supported and a sufficiently sophisticated criminal infrastructure, into which they can be absorbed, is in existence.

If however they live in a 'disorganised slum', the new housing projects in which, characteristically, Puerto Rican or black American émigrés from the southern states are housed, and in which no reliable illegitimate infrastructure has had a chance to develop, they can still collectively avoid self-blame. They can do this by sidestepping universal success goals in favour of an alternative status system based on toughness and bravery, demonstrated in gang fights. In this alternative status system the ceiling of one's aspirations is established by the size of the milieu in which one gains one's reputation.

For those who are denied legitimate opportunity, have no access to the criminal 'goings on' of the organised slum, and cannot fight their way out of a paper bag, the prospects are bleaker. They will continue to accept socially valued goals but they must also accept that they have failed as individuals to achieve these goals, and so they come to blame themselves. This, Cloward and Ohlin argue, accounts for the retreatism, the withdrawal into alcohol and drugs, which is so common among lower-class ghetto youth.

Cloward and Ohlin point out that the organised slum is characterised by close relations between criminals in the illegitimate opportunity structure, the police, local government officers, and local politicians. Not to put too fine a point on it, 'the fix is in'. As a result of this the organised slum is a milieu subject to tight social control in which conformity is demanded of the young. Nobody in the organised slum wishes to attract too much 'heat', nobody 'rocks the boat'. The organised slum is an intricate social system built on a complex web of favours and tacit understandings, and a firm commitment by all participants to keep things the way they are. Nobody riots in the organised slum. Cloward and Ohlin are ambivalent about the organised slum because what they describe is so obviously capitalism with a human face, operating slightly to one side of the straight and narrow. It is as if they are saying with the character in the film *Prizzi's Honour*, 'They saw a chance to make a buck and they took it, it's the American way.'

What is so intriguing about *Delinquency and Opportunity* is that the illegitimate opportunity structure of the organised slum is not presented as a problem. On the contrary, it is presented as a blueprint for the solution to the problem of the disorganised slum. Cloward and Ohlin's book is not about how juvenile crime can be stopped. It is about how juvenile crime might be contained at an acceptable level and rioting averted. The organised slum was doing all right on its own but if violence, rioting and social mayhem were to be avoided then the disorganised slum had to get a lot more of what the organised slum had in abundance, and that was organisation.

'Don't agonise, organise'

The major thrust of what came to be called the 'War on Poverty' was the involvement of the residents of the disorganised slum in the planning and implementation of programmes which would create opportunity for children and young people in those areas. The job of the professional workers was to mobilise the 'indigenous leadership'. Problems in local communities were to be defined by local people, young and old, and campaigns were to be launched. Discriminatory practices in local industries were to be challenged. Barriers to educational access and achievement were to be bludgeoned down by a politically aware community using a combination of community action and compensatory programmes for educationally deprived youngsters (*Sesame Street* meets the Weathermen). Local welfare bureaucracies were to be called to account. Robert F. Kennedy speaking of the existing social welfare structure said:

> They plan for the poor, not with them. Part of the sense of helplessness and futility comes from the feeling of powerlessness to affect the operation of these organizations. The community action programs must basically change these organizations by building into the program real representation for the poor. This bill calls for 'maximum feasible participation of the residents'. This means the involvement of the poor in planning and implementing programs, giving them a real voice in their institutions. (Moynihan, 1969: 90–1)

The war on poverty seemed to offer the possibility of the state-sponsored subversion of state agencies by the people. The proponents of a radical welfare through community action, a welfare designed by the people, for the people, were set against traditional welfare in the belief that the process whereby the residents of the disorganised slum would 'get out from under', would enable them 'to develop the degree of social organisation', and hence social stability, which would allow residents to create and utilise opportunity. The organisational structures developed during the political struggles would serve the same purposes that the inter-relations of local government officials, police, politicians and community leaders had in the organised slum. The disorganised slum would be grafted back on to the body politic.

The poverty programme in Britain and the US contained the central ambiguity that in as much as it seemed to offer a political voice to the poor it also offered to 'cool out' genuine dissent, among the poor, by deflecting their attention away from issues of structural social inequality towards questions of how a finite quantity of welfare resources was to be distributed. Beyond this the poverty programme seemed to offer a more pervasive form of social control in the guise of social improvement. Harold Wilson handed responsibility for the British poverty programme to Derek Morrell and Joan Cooper (the architects of the 1969 Children and Young Persons Act) who showed an awareness of the more insidious aspects of the proposed endeavour:

> Miss Cooper (Chief Inspector, Children's Department, Home Office) said that in both the British and American plans there appeared to be an element of looking for a new method of social control — what one might call an anti-value rather than a value. 'Gilding the ghetto' or buying time, was clearly a component in the planning of both CDP and Model Cities (the US Poverty Programme). (Community Development Projects, 1977)

Nevertheless, Derek Morrell saw in the Community Development Projects the possibility of developing a new tier of representative local government, the 'neighbourhood council' as a means whereby the marginalised and disenfranchised residents of the poorest parts of society could make their voices heard:

> The Chairman (Mr Derek Morrell) said the general context (of the discussion) was in his view the liberal democratic process. It would be possible to discuss programmes and policy on the assumption that we had lost faith in this process, but he himself believed it had a highly creative future potential . . . The whole process . . . involved practical problems of the transfer of power from the 'haves' to the 'have nots' — power, in the sense of the ability to effect or resist change. (Community Development Projects, 1977: 56)

The British poverty programme was composed of the Urban Programme (urban aid), Educational Priority Areas, Community

Development Projects, Inner Area Studies, Quality of Life projects and hundreds of more modest endeavours located in local authority social services and housing departments, settlement houses, and other voluntary organisations.

Cooper and Morrell's 1969 CYPA strove to humanise social reaction to children and young people in trouble. Cooper and Morrell's poverty programme attempted to strike at the root causes of juvenile crime by orchestrating a political assault on poverty at a local level. It is hardly surprising then that Cooper and Morrell's intermediate treatment, which had been reduced to an ambiguous and poorly defined entity drifting somewhere between the borstal and deprived inner-city children hanging about on a street corner, should eventually find itself caught up in the radical welfare practices of the British poverty programme.

Whereas the ways in which the poverty programme were formulated by the British government left open the question of whether poverty was in fact the fault of the poor, the practitioners of radical welfare were in no doubt that it was not. The final report of the Coventry CDP asserted that:

> 2.0. We can no longer accept that the problems of Hillfields can be satisfactorily explained primarily as the result of:
> (i) inadequacy, pathology, deviancy or any other personal character-istics of its residents;
> (ii) apathy or failure to participate in community activity;
> (iii) low take-up of personal support services or poor communication between fieldworkers and residents; or
> (iv) technical incompetence or failures in planning, management or administration of local government.
> 2.1. Few of the problems (except redevelopment) experienced by individuals in Hillfields are different in kind from those experienced by large sections of the working class in other parts of the city, or indeed the country as a whole (e.g. precarious incomes, insecure housing, etc). They must be treated therefore as part of that class, not as a separate minority sub-group. (Benington et al., 1975: 63)

The endeavour was unequivocally concerned with social need, but constitutionally opposed to ideas of individual pathology. Radical welfare is the attempt to effect localised political change through the participation of socially disadvantaged people. Whether practised in the family, a tenants' group, or an entire city, it assumes that socially disadvantaged people encounter, experience and are oppressed by problems which are an unavoidable by-product of the recurrent economic crises endemic to an advanced capitalist society. This assumption may be right or wrong but it leads inevitably to a position in which intervention is not directed towards the attitudes, feelings, or behaviour of the disadvantaged subject because this would mean falling into the same trap as traditional social work. It would involve 'blaming the victim'.

In the late 1960s and early 1970s practitioners of IT and community work did not seem unduly concerned that they lacked a discreet, respectable and sacrosanct professional identity with its attendant body of theory, knowledge and expertise. The involvement of IT in radical welfare took the form of the participation of IT workers and the investment of what vestigial amounts of IT money existed, in tasks which complemented broader local anti-poverty strategies. These tasks were seldom called IT because what things were called mattered less than how the central problem of poverty, which offered the key to all the other problems, could be assaulted. Thus, working with groups of young people, some of whom had a substantial involvement in crime, in order to devise ways of achieving better leisure services, was regarded as a perfectly legitimate use of IT time and resources because it addressed the issue of the powerlessness of the poor. Dave Robins and Philip Cohen give the flavour of this type of endeavour:

> At a meeting in August 1973, the Open Space Committee was finally overthrown in a bitter coup, and a new and comparatively inexperienced group of tenants were democratically elected as the official Tenants' Association. This was done with not a little prodding from local Community Organiser, Gerry Stern, a young man working for the Home Office-backed Community Development Commission . . .
> While the Tenants' Association Committee was suffering its birth pangs, the Youth Group was faced with the possibility of increasing youth militancy around the issue of a disco club for the Black Horse pub. It will be remembered that the haphazard youth alliance had suffered a heavy defeat at the hands of the Open Space Committee. Subsequently there had been talk of storming the place and occupying it, with vague threats from some boys of putting the place out of commission if they weren't given what they wanted. However direct action was rejected by the Youth Group — why march yet another youth army up yet another futile hill? So with the demise of the Open Space Committee and ascendance of the new Tenants' Association, the Youth Group decided to embark on the tactics of careful patient negotiation. (Robins and Cohen, 1978: 40, 42–3)

Radical welfare addressed the relationship between the disadvantaged and those state institutions which have the power to offer, or withhold, goods and services from them. The state institution which has the greatest impact on the life chances of children and young people is the school. There were many initiatives, some of them orchestrated via the Educational Priority Areas programme, which strove to make education accountable to its local community. In this sphere IT resources were used to promote work which tried to reconcile the needs and desires of deprived young people with the demands of the school. Roger Evans illustrates an approach to this work:

> ... they came to see that the incidents had common elements as between individuals and individual schools. We asked the boys what they could do about these injustices which, on their evidence, had a basis in fact. Their common opinion was that to complain as individuals just led to further trouble. After a lively discussion on this point it was proposed that a film depicting scenes in school should be made. If shown to teachers this might both protect individuals as it came from the group and it might open up a dialogue with the local schools involved. As far as the staff were concerned the general aims of the video were: firstly, to increase collective consciousness about incidents in school and start making an analysis of them during the making of the film, secondly to explore alternative ways of handling situations both on the part of the boys and the teachers and in terms of challenging and changing school organisation ... (Evans, 1982: 34)

The identification of the school as a site for intervention had a very respectable theoretical pedigree. A.K. Cohen (1956) had demonstrated the ways in which the school promoted status frustration by presenting its pupils with unattainable social goals. In 1967 David Hargreaves had shown how bright working-class boys moved steadily down from the A stream in the first year of secondary modern school to the C stream in the fourth year, as a result of their social class orientation rather than their intellectual ability. Most importantly, in 1967, Michael Power discovered large differences in delinquency rates between ostensibly similar secondary modern schools which could not be explained in terms of the delinquency rates in the areas from which the schools drew their pupils. It was on this basis that the concept of the delinquescent school, a school which generated high levels of delinquency, was developed (Power et al., 1972). Intervention in the delinquescent school using community action techniques has a much stronger empirical and theoretical justification than intervention with individual offenders or their families. Early IT in the guise of radical welfare made this important theoretical connection and developed models for intervention in the school.

Radical welfare chose to enter the juvenile criminal justice system only in the role of advocate and it did this, as often as not, with the backing of an urban aid-funded law centre. The ethos of radical welfare, drawn from contemporary revolutionary politics, indicated that to get inside the system and away from one's political constituency, who were the 'victims' of that system, was bad ethics and bad politics. Radical welfare would normally rather challenge a practice than collude with it in the hope that the practice might be modified.

The endeavour of radical welfare was ultimately to move the class struggle out of the factory and into the community. It strove to politicise personal suffering. In the community action approach it saw a way of developing a 'pedagogy of the oppressed', a radical do-it-yourself political education. It had remarkable political ambitions, sometimes believing that it could be the means whereby the capitalist state could be destabilised. It was unrealistically optimistic in believing that an £80,000,000 war on poverty, using welfare as the heavy artillery, could effect substantial and lasting social change. Yet, all this said, the analysis of the problem, developed by Cloward and Ohlin, and many of the solutions, devised by the poverty warriors, remain more plausible responses to the phenomenon of juvenile crime in the inner city than the theories and interventions which preceded them and most of the theories and interventions which came after.

The alternatives movement

The 1960s saw the rise of the alternative education movement in the United States and western Europe. In *Deschooling Society*, written in 1971, Ivan Illich drew attention to the ways in which the hidden curriculum of formal schooling systematically inhibited learning. In his view:

> The hidden curriculum is always the same regardless of school or place. It requires all children of a certain age to assemble in groups of about thirty, under the authority of a certified teacher, for some 500 or 1,000 or more hours per year ... What is important in the hidden curriculum is that students learn that education is valuable when it is acquired in the school through a gradual process of consumption; that the degree of success the individual will enjoy in society depends on the amount of learning he consumes; and that learning about the world is more valuable than learning from the world. (Illich, 1973: 13)

The alternative education movement, which was inspired by the ideas of Ivan Illich and Paulo Friere, attempted to 'liberate' children and young people from the oppressive structures of formal schooling by providing them with 'Free Schools' geared to learning through dialogue with others and an exploration of oneself and one's relationships. Friere describes this process:

> There are many among them (oppressed people) that flee from freedom. Oppression is such a deep strong reality that it produces fear of freedom. Fear of freedom exists when one sees a threat even in talking about it. Freedom is never a gift. It is something difficult because nobody can give freedom to somebody else and nobody makes himself free either. Men are made free in communion with others through a situation we have to change. We have to make our freedom together, with others — 'We' not 'I'. (cited in Dale et al., 1976: 227)

In Britain the rise of the alternative education movement had been paralleled by a process of spontaneous 'de-schooling' in which truancy rates in the third, fourth, and fifth forms of inner-city secondary schools had risen as high as 40 per cent. This was causing more than a little embarrassment to local education authorities and head teachers. By 1970 the alternative education movement, which aimed to subvert formal education, was being offered funds by local education authorities to deal with its truanting and disruptive pupils. It was not that education authorities or head teachers had undergone a miraculous conversion to the libertarian gospels of Illich and Friere, it was rather that they knew it made sense. The free schools demonstrated an ability to work effectively with children who were irretrievably lost to formal education. Small groups, a high adult-child ratio, the absence of academic competition, and the individual attention, concern and support offered to children with learning or emotional difficulties, had the effect of drawing these lost children back into education. The names of children who attended free schools usually remained on the register of their secondary school of origin whose truancy rates consequently improved. The agreement between the education authority and the free school usually contained a statement to the effect that the objective to be achieved by the child's attendance at the free school was an eventual return to formal schooling. This appeared to place the free school in the role of a therapeutic unit. Since, however, the education authority, head teachers and free school workers all knew that this caveat was a face-saving nicety whereby the education authority could have truck with renegade educationalists without appearing to accept their damning critique of formal education, nobody was too worried that few if any children would in fact return to school.

For the free school, these children and young people were Friere's 'oppressed', whether they came with local authority money or not. This was not simply left-romanticism in which non-conforming children, whatever their motivation, are seen as nascent revolutionaries. The oppression was in most cases all too real and the children who attended the free schools were as much the victims of the 'delinquescent school' as of their chaotic or impoverished family circumstances:

> Reynolds and Murgatroyd found that attendance rates were worse in schools with a high use of corporal punishment; Heal found that misbehaviour was worse in schools with formal punishment systems; and Clegg and Megson noted that delinquency rates tended to be highest in schools with a great deal of corporal punishment ... the trend was for more misbehaviour and more delinquency with high levels of punishment; and this trend was significant in the case of particular forms of punishment

(unofficial slapping and cuffing of children and a disciplinary style in the classroom which involved frequent checking and reprimanding). (Rutter and Giller, 1983: 308–9)

The free school was enormously attractive to IT for a number of reasons. Practically it offered a form of day care which provided the full-time education required by the 1944 Education Act. Free schools had staff and premises whereas IT was only empowered to fund the participation of individual young people in existing statutory or voluntary provision. The other important benefit the free school offered IT and the social services departments was its willingness to work with long-term truants who were also offenders. By far the highest proportion of children and young people in CHEs were there as a result of their persistent truancy rather than their offending. As we have already noted the 1976 White Paper specifically addressed the assumption that persistent truants should be placed in residential care and it did this because of pressure on central government from local authorities which could no longer afford this remarkably expensive and ineffective response to non-school attendance. The free school offered the possibility of averting reception into care, thereby saving the social services department a great deal of time and money.

The free school was so important to education authorities and social services departments in their attempts to manage their troublesome young people that they all but annexed it. The free school was one of the great successes of the late 1960s and early 1970s and it is no surprise that the IT day care centres and the off-site educational units, established later in the decade, bore more than a passing resemblance to it. Staffed jointly by teachers and social workers, who sometimes owed their first allegiance to their employing authority rather than a philosophy about how young people can be freed to learn, the freedom of the free school was often lost in translation.

The alternatives movement had an impact in psychiatry where the work of Bateson, Foucault, and Laing and Esterton challenged a medical model of madness and sanity. It gave the intellectual rationale for the community arts movement. The rise of the adventure playground was in no small part a consequence of the radical shift in the perception of children championed by the alternatives movement. From being perceived as no more than the product of the socialising and controlling endeavours of parents and other grown-up authority figures, the image of the child was redrawn to depict a resourceful, self-managing, choice-making, creative being who, given the appropriate materials, freedom and responsibility could learn to grow up and be quite a nice person at the same time.

One aspect of the 'alternative' vision, epitomised in the contemporary slogan 'steal yourself', stressed the importance of individuality and individual liberation. The other aspect placed an emphasis on communalism and the identification of a shared predicament. Paul Senior writes of a probation day centre in which this sharing is attempted:

> From this group sharing comes the realisation that what traditionally have been seen as 'personal problems' in fact have social and political bases and solutions. Seemingly complex analytical issues such as power and its use can and should be examined within personal situations. Consciousness-raising deliberately locates thinking in everyday experience and arises from the ability to translate those experiences into altered perceptions of the same reality ... Friere offers a different insight in relation to the same dilemma. Examining education, he argues that it cannot be seen as a neutral process and, of necessity, means political activity. He refers to the idea of conscientisation as 'A permanent critical approach to reality in order to discover the myths that deceive us and help to maintain the oppressing dehumanising structures'. Again there is an emphasis on collective discovery and collective action, on not pre-determining goals but encouraging congruity between personal and political dimensions. (Senior, 1985: 116–17)

One sometimes had the sense that the alternatives movement was a greenhouse where citizens for the new society were being grown. There was an implicit faith that if we could increase the numbers of people with the new consciousness then that quantitative change would transform itself into a qualitative change in the social order. It was as if the alternative schools, psychiatric refuges, arts, playgrounds and shops would eventually, by a process of steady incremental expansion, come to engulf that other world to which they were the alternative. Timothy Leary posited precisely this model of how social revolutions happen when he suggested a short cut which involved putting LSD into the New York water supply in order to 'turn on' the entire city and with this first taste of personal liberation, effect an overnight social revolution.

Radical welfare saw new human beings emerging as a result of experiences gained in the political struggle to change the external world. In this conception human beings emerge as simultaneously transforming and transformed in a perpetual dialectic between personal identity and political action. The alternative movement, by contrast, built human-sized, human-oriented alternatives run on humanistic principles to produce more fully human beings who would, hopefully, come into their own when the world came to its senses.

Social facilitation and normalisation
One lesson we can learn from a consideration of the history of IT is that the professional practices which develop into orthodoxies tend to

be those which can be most readily adapted to serve as vehicles for the achievement of particular political goals at a particular time. They must moreover be fairly easily accommodated within, or adaptable to, pre-existing administrative categories and bureaucratic structures. Like theories of deviant behaviour, their popularity, or acceptability to governments, policy makers, and bureaucrats is not contingent on their offering an accurate account of the problem or a demonstrably effective response to it. Good ideas and apparently effective practices often evaporate through a lack of political punctuality and their administrative and bureaucratic inconvenience. They are forgotten and history gets written around them, not about them.

Here is a remarkable observation about the impact of a delinquency prevention project which operated in Manchester between 1966 and 1969:

> From January 1966 to July 1969, one year after the end of the social work programme, controls had been sentenced to and received a total of 909 weeks of residential training. Seven boys were still undergoing training and, calculating on the basis of an average length of borstal training of 18 months, were expected to receive a further 153 weeks during the following twelve months giving an overall total of 1062 weeks. By July 1969 participants had spent 169 weeks in such training and were expected to receive a further 13 weeks giving a total of 182 weeks. Correcting for the differences in size of the two groups we would have expected the participants to have spent an extra 593 weeks in training had they followed the pattern of the control group. (Smith et al., 1972: 255)

Put another way, participants in the project were expected, on average, to spend 3.5 times longer in custody than they actually did. The project made a significant impact on participants' offending, but it was as a method of intervention which diverted young people in trouble from custody that Wincroft has an obvious claim on the attention of IT. It seems strange then that in 1972, when the results of Wincroft were published, IT did not set about translating the lessons of Wincroft into the practice of IT lock, stock and barrel, since it appeared to offer IT a way of doing what it was originally invented to do, namely to keep young people out of prison. In the current literature on IT and juvenile justice there are few if any references to Wincroft.

A discussion paper produced in 1965 stated the objectives of the project as follows: '(a) To work with young people in need of help, and assist them in finding a dynamic adjustment to society, and thereby among other things to control delinquency; (b) To develop methods of working with difficult young people in an unstructured setting' (Smith et al., 1972: 6).

Wincroft's rationale suggested that in certain neighbourhoods in large cities we will find areas with unusually high levels of juvenile delinquency. These areas will tend to be run-down, one-class inner areas characterised by all the usual indicators of urban deprivation. In these areas we will find a disproportionate number of young people with whom urban schools, youth clubs, and welfare agencies will find it hard to make and sustain contact. These will be the youngsters who get suspended from schools, thrown out of youth clubs, and whom social workers and probation officers find most resistant. They will be the young people who get arrested and sent to community homes and borstals, not least because nobody has a good word to say about them.

These people are of course Patrick Jenkin's (1979) 'avalanche of lawlessness', *A Future for IT*'s (1977) 'persistent delinquents', *The Expenditure Committee Report*'s (1975) 'hard-core' (1975) and modern day IT's 'heavy end'. The Wincroft Youth Project described them as 'participants'. Wincroft, having identified the 54 boys most 'at risk' in the chosen area proceeded to contact them by using 'detached work' methods of the type developed in the street gang work undertaken by the New York City Youth Board. This involved using, in the three years of the project, 156 students and volunteers as detached social workers who made contact with the peer groups in which the target 'clients' were located. The workers worked with 600 young people in order to be able to work with the 54 target clients in groups. They recognised the importance of the peer group and the more extensive local adolescent networks as a potential generating milieu for juvenile crime. The role of the worker was to enable those natural groups to identify their needs and wishes and to facilitate problem solving and the development of social, educational or recreational activities with them. The worker was there to facilitate culturally deprived young people in their endeavour to achieve goals and to take opportunities normally only available to more privileged youngsters. The emphasis was upon opening up access to normality. There was an assumption in the project that much of the apparently disturbed behaviour of the target clients was a function of cultural deprivation — a frustration born of an absence of opportunity, permission, and the tools and materials with which to develop their own interests and fulfil their own needs.

One of Wincroft's most remarkable achievements was that it made and sustained contact, over a three-year period, with young people who were selected because other professional workers had found this insuperably difficult. The project had dispensed with premises since the common experience of youth workers and others trying to deal with difficult young people in premises designed to attract them was that the need to protect and defend these very premises from them constituted a very serious barrier to contact. The other feature of the project which seemed to promote success was its commitment to 'permissiveness' and the absence of negative sanctions:

> One further aspect of the method of working in Wincroft deserves some comment, since it has been widely misunderstood, this is the use of permissiveness as a technique and must be distinguished from permissiveness as an ideology. Permissiveness is a technique to keep open a relationship where the client can and will break it off if he is subjected to the disciplines that normal adolescents would accept. It has particular value to the withdrawn child who may need to be encouraged to act out some of the aggressive feelings that he normally conceals because he is fearful of the consequences, and also to the child who tests adults out in order to prove that they will punish him and do not love him. (Smith et al., 1972: 264)

Wincroft had an important impact on youth work, offering as it did the most comprehensive account of British detached youth work available. Its impact on IT was more oblique. Some projects adopted the detached work method pioneered by Wincroft, but on a smaller scale. Others benefited from the guiding assumptions of Wincroft about the nature of juvenile crime in slum areas. Yet others derived important ideas about monitoring, evaluation and research. But given the obvious applicability of Wincroft to IT we are still left with the question of why Wincroft was the first project of its kind in Britain and also the last.

In the mid-1960s social welfare and social work seemed set for a period of rapid expansion. The probation service, the children's departments, education welfare, and mental welfare were poised to pool their resources and expertise in a new 'family service'. The newly professionalised youth service was developing as a community work agency and this coincided with a growing desire on the part of mainstream social work to use a community development approach address social problems. The new Certificate of Social Work courses developed curricula which had considerable points of overlap with the curricula of youth and community work courses. Preventive work, research, experimentation, and the use of volunteers were in the ascendant. It seemed that a convergence of ideas, efforts, professional orientation methods and theories would result in a unitary personal social services agency which would deploy the most effective and scientifically respectable interventions available to resolve social problems. This was the climate of optimism in which Wincroft developed and the projected structure in which the lessons of Wincroft were to have been elaborated into a routine social welfare practice.

By the early 1970s the political and administrative picture was very different. A Conservative government, through the 1972 Criminal Justice Act, had injected substantially increased resources as the probation service in order that it could develop as a community correctional resource geared towards reaction to, rather than anticipation of, juvenile crime. The new social services departments were short of social workers and in a state of disarray because of the non-implementation of key sections of the 1969 CYPA. The Educational Welfare Service was professionalised and expanded but was quickly consumed with the problem of policing the rapidly-rising levels of truancy in inner-city schools. The youth service, resisting attempts to implicate itself in IT and the statutory surveillance of youth, committed itself to a community development approach and to discrimination in favour of the poor. This signalled the beginning of its decline as a social service.

There was nowhere for Wincroft to go. Its commitment to prevention was out of time with the dominant political thinking on crime which increasingly favoured reaction. Administratively Wincroft could not be fitted into any of the agencies concerned with social need, juvenile crime or community development.

Wincroft pioneered effective and original approaches to juvenile crime. It provided an important test-bed for sociological and criminological theories, but the most important lessons it had to teach IT were not learned. Wincroft's success in diverting young people in trouble from care or custody has been attributed to the fact that probation officers, social workers and juvenile court magistrates were aware that the project participants were in regular contact with a social work agency, and that they were also part of a 'delinquency reduction' experiment. As a result, it is suggested, courts were inclined to make non-custodial sentences and social workers and probation officers less inclined to recommend custody. This is an important observation because subsequent work in the field of juvenile justice has asserted that if the juvenile bench realises that the offender in the dock is already involved in a delinquency prevention or treatment programme which, by the evidence of the court appearance, has been unsuccessful, then the offender's progress into care or custody will be accelerated. This argument asserts that any attempt to anticipate delinquency or to prevent it by social work intervention must inevitably lead to stigmatisation and criminalisation and that such endeavours should be abandoned in favour of 'leaving the kids alone'.

The findings of Wincroft suggest that it was precisely because juvenile court magistrates *did* know that the young offenders who participated in Wincroft were the objects of professional intervention and research that they were treated leniently. The Wincroft participants were rescued from imprisonment by a combination of academic respectability, the aura of professionalism, and the Hawthorn effect. (The Hawthorn effect refers to a situation in which the presence of the researcher, if known to the subject or significant others in the subject's social milieu, will affect the behaviour of the subject, thus altering the phenomenon which is to be researched.) Magistrates, then as now, it seems, could often be persuaded to keep young offenders in the community if they could be persuaded that somebody competent was doing something sensible with them.

It is ironical that in the 1980s the results of projects which have attempted to help communities develop into 'safe neighbourhoods' by introducing measures to minimise crime all point to the need to intervene in the peer groups and the networks of local adolescents (Bright and Petterson, 1984). Recently a worker in an intensive intermediate treatment project funded by Leon Brittan's new initiative was asked by his colleagues to see if he could find out what a thing called the 'Wincroft project' had been.

Welfare and treatment

In 1971 the Manchester Youth Development Trust (MYDT) which had initiated the Wincroft Youth Project, established an experimental IT project. This was one of ten projects which were to be monitored by the DHSS. Like Wincroft, the IT project aimed to work with children and young people identified by social workers and teachers as delinquent and at risk of reception into care. The work focused initially on the school where project workers and teachers worked together with small groups of identified children and young people and their friends. The project was a product of Wincroft and it attempted to refine the technique developed initially by Wincroft in which the workers worked with the identified client within his or her 'natural' peer group. Over time the project was subject to growing pressure from the local authority social services department, which was providing the bulk of the funding, to abandon this model in favour of one in which it would act as a resource into which children and young people 'at risk' or 'in trouble' could be referred by social workers. This was more than an attempt to modify the project's referral procedures for it involved a change in the conception of the problem to be dealt with, a change in the target for intervention, and a change in the project's pattern of accountability.

Wincroft and the subsequent MYDT IT project located the genesis of adolescent crime or conformity in the interaction between a social world characterised by deprivation and a lack of legitimate opportunity, a peer group which attributed meaning to this world and devised prescriptions for action within it, and individuals who experienced themselves as failures in this world, and carried with them negative attributions placed upon them by powerful adults. The peer group was seen as a milieu which could contain or exacerbate the propensities of its members to violate laws or norms. For the purposes of their interventions they sought to mobilise the peer group as a source of social control, but also as a place in which the alternative to deviation could be explored and articulated in action.

It was an intervention in the 'here-and-now' dialogue of real life, not a form of treatment aimed at individual transformation. It located the ultimate problem in the chances and choices available to members of the peer group as a result of social class, geography, and history.

The attempt by the social services department to divert the focus of the project to the problems of individuals referred for treatment in a group setting, betrayed a substantially different set of assumptions about the aetiology of the problem. In this revised formulation the problem of juvenile crime was located squarely within the juvenile criminal. As a consequence the target for change shifted from the interaction between the individual, the peer group and the social world to the motivation, attitudes, beliefs and behaviour of the individual deviant. It was not that the initiatives pioneered by the MYDT had ignored the importance of the individual or the fact that some individuals seem to show a greater enthusiasm for social deviance than others in any social milieu. It was rather that it acknowledged the crucial role of the peer group in mediating individual behaviour, however ostensibly 'disturbed' or otherwise that behaviour might, at times, appear to be. This changed emphasis in the MYDT IT project precluded the possibility of intervening in what had previously been seen as the key intervening variable in the 'poverty causes crime' equation.

The MYDT IT project was developed as a means whereby natural peer groups of inner-city adolescents could participate in a social education project which might, among other things, prevent juvenile crime and help to divert participants away from care or custody. As such, it operated as a resource to its participants. As this original model was gradually supplanted by one with an explicit commitment to individual treatment the accountability of project staff shifted from participants to referring social workers. At its inception the MYDT IT project had seen itself as a subcontractor for the local authority, executing part of its preventive social work function. The local authority was to supply funds and sufficient information on the potential clientele, and other matters necessary to maximise the impact of the MYDT initiative. In the event the local authority effectively annexed the project.

What started out as an attempted solution to the problems of children and young people in a deprived inner-city neighbourhood became an attempted solution to the problems of inner-city social workers who had nowhere to place children and young people in trouble.

The transformation of IT into an appendage of family casework was common in the early 1970s. The family service was organised to deal with families. Each social problem, whether it fell into the category of mental health, mental handicap, physical handicap or juvenile offending, was located conceptually, and also administratively, within the family. Professional ideology and bureaucratic and financial arrangements presumed that the site of the problem, the focus for the intervention, and the genesis of the solution could be located within the family. The day centre, the community home, the assessment centre, meals on wheels and IT were conceptualised and organised as specialist diagnostic and therapeutic resources available to the post-Seebohm GP as she or he restored the body of the family to social health. While the family caseworker worked on root causes within the family, IT was required to offer 'compensatory' and 'corrective' experiences to the offspring of the caseworker's cases.

The primacy accorded the family 'case' by the local authority social services departments was understandable both in terms of the ideology which inspired the 'family service' and its organisational structure. It was by no means clear however that the problem of working-class juvenile crime was caused by, nor readily solved within, the family.

By puberty the family's major task in relation to its children, that of primary socialisation, is at an end. Similarly the family's potency as an agency of immediate social control is waning. Sociologists and psychologists of all political persuasions are agreed that by the onset of adolescence the young person is marginal to the family and increasingly susceptible to influence and pressure from the peer group and the subculture (Musgrove, 1964). Social scientists, parents and youth workers recognise that on a day-to-day basis adolescents are more open to the influence of unrelated adults than their parents.

The peer group and the school, and often the peer group within the school, have supplanted the home in terms of their impact on, and knowledge about, the lives of many young people by the age of 13 or 14 (Rutter et al., 1979). Youth workers and teachers are from time to time confronted with bewildered parents, staggered by the fact that their child has broken the law. For the youth workers, teachers and peers of this child the most bewildering thing is often that the parents are the only people who hadn't realised what the child was up to.

The peer group and the school are an obvious focus for intervention in the lives of young offenders and yet from 1971 the social services department, organised around a central concern with the family or 'case', carried this responsibility. The family 'case', shaped as it is by bureaucratic, legal and psychotherapeutic imperatives, served as a barrier to the development of theoretically informed responses to children and young people in trouble.

This is not to argue that the offending of some young people cannot be directly related to serious problems within the family. Most workers in the sphere of juvenile justice have met young people who would rather be in care or custody than at home. In certain 'cases' family work or family therapy can be effective in identifying some of the reasons for a youngster's behaviour and effecting changes which render this behaviour unnecessary. This type of intervention represents a somewhat esoteric tributary of work with young offenders rather than its mainstream, however.

The argument here is that effective intervention with young people in trouble is often most usefully directed at the point where a commitment to the deviant enterprise is either forged or discouraged and that for most adolescents this is no longer the home and the family; on the contrary, it is the school and the peer group.

The approach to IT developed within social services departments was to form groups of adolescents from aggregates of cases, and to work with them on the assumption that they were the victims of deprived and depriving families. In doing this social work developed forms of social group treatment which strove to find the source of delinquency in damaged and damaging family relationships. This may well have been the correct point at which to look for the ultimate causes of all sorts of socially deviant behaviour but it was not the point where the commitment to law-breaking was made, and to this extent, welfare and treatment tended to miss the point.

5 The professional response 2: the era of pessimism

> ... they end as bureaucracies.
>
> Howard Becker

By the mid-1970s, the academic debate about juvenile crime, in Great Britain, had effectively abandoned its preoccupation with the causes of juvenile offending in favour of an analysis of the ways in which the justice system compounded criminal careers and generated crime (Preston, 1980). This changing focus emphasised the ways in which the justice system selected and identified its subjects, how it processed them, and the consequences of this processing for personal identity and future offending. In the USA David Matza (1964) had chronicled the ways in which the juvenile court, by conflating the concerns for treatment, welfare, and justice, served to mystify the defendant. Aaron Cicourel (1969) had suggested that social class rather than law violation was the major determinant of prosecution in the juvenile justice system. Howard Becker (1963) had demonstrated how labels were attached to people and how people came to 'live the label', while Edwin Schur (1971) had advocated 'radical non-intervention' as the most efficacious response available to us in our dealings with young law-breakers.

This movement away from causation or the site of primary deviation, to a focus on social reaction, marked the conclusion of a 150-year endeavour to discover the genetic, biological, psychological or sociological determinants of deviant behaviour. In this new analysis it was the legal and disciplinary apparatus which was identified as problematic rather than the offender. The focus on social reaction in the USA tended to ignore, or take for granted, the role of the state, and alighted instead on the activities of police officers, social workers, and psychiatric nurses, the 'zoo-keepers' of deviance, the 'bad guys' who kept the 'underdogs' under (Becker, 1967).

In Britain the social reaction perspective developed both a radical and a technicist strand. The radical strand of the 'new criminology' set off to reconcile the Marxian dialectic with Meadian interactionism (Taylor et al., 1973). The technicist strand followed the lead of the theorists in the USA. These theories were adopted pragmatically into an administrative criminology which attempted to develop a technology of delinquency management which was more humane, rational, and cost-effective (Thorpe, 1980).

By 1976 this movement was having a serious impact on IT. These initiatives were opportunistic in as much as they traded on growing anxieties within government about the mounting costs of, and the impending crisis within, the British juvenile justice apparatus. The quest for a technology of human manipulation had given way to the quest for a technology of system manipulation. This technology eschewed considerations of the state, the causes of crime, and importantly the attempt to appreciate and understand the motivations of deviant actors which was at the core of earlier American social reaction theory. Administrative criminology reduced the offender to an inadvertent victim of low-level 'soft policemen', ignoring the radicals' claim that he or she might be a critic, albeit an inarticulate and misdirected one, of the social order. It was an approach which was nihilistic and hence forgetful. It appropriated theories but broke them at the stem leaving their ideological and political roots in the ground. The fact that Goffman's *Asylums* (1961) was also an allegory for the relationship between the state and the citizen was lost in the scramble to infiltrate and refurbish the state's controlling and socialising bureaucracies. The endeavour to do things to, for, or with the poor was being contested by a minimalist approach which envisaged no good coming from intervention in human lives, and enjoined us to do less harm rather than more good. 'Leave the kids alone' (Schur, 1971) it said.

It was in this changed intellectual and political environment that the 'back to justice' movement, 'delinquency management' and abolitionism began to change the shape of IT.

Back to justice movement
The 'back to justice' movement emerged in the mid-1960s in the USA in response to a disillusionment with the capacity of a juvenile justice system which fused 'welfare' and 'punishment' to deliver 'justice'. The watershed in the USA came with the Gault decision of 1967. In this case the supreme court ruled that where a juvenile faced incarceration as a consequence of offending, the juvenile should be entitled to the protection of due process of law in the same way as an adult offender. The implication of this ruling was that the period spent in an institution should be proportional to the seriousness of the

offence committed and not based on 'treatment'-infused considerations concerning the likelihood of future offending.

In Great Britain 'justice for children' and 'fair play' pioneered the justice model which was also advocated by Taylor et al. (1980) and by implication at certain points Thorpe et al. (1980). Social workers bear the brunt of the back to justice attack. Morris et al. (1980) write:

> Because we do not understand the significance of much juvenile 'misconduct', the various reports presented to decision-makers contain value judgements and unfounded assumptions. As a general rule, we do not know with certainty which factors refer to, or which situations indicate which form of treatment ... As such, these reports are useless guides to choosing dispositions, but these 'facts' then justify the form and content of intervention. These reports recast or reconstitute the child's identity as a 'delinquent', 'truant' or 'troublesome'. They are in essence what one American writer calls 'character assassinations'.

The proponents of a back to justice position argue that the juvenile court, by fusing 'welfare' and judicial considerations, offers the young offender the worst of all possible worlds. On the one hand it denies them the civil liberties available to adults while on the other it allows unbridled interference by agents of the state.

Parker et al. (1981) have argued that social workers are often identified as scapegoats in the juvenile justice system whereas in reality the magistrates and police are still the major power-holders. The back to justice stance, by minimising the complexity and difficulty of working in the best interests of the child in an era in which law and order concerns have come to the fore and resources for the poorer sections of the working class are shrinking fast, perpetuates this scapegoating. It identifies the problem as a consequence of false ideas held by social workers rather than as a function of radical changes in provision, expenditure and political ideology.

This raises the question of what it is that the back to justice campaigners actually want. Young (1979) writes: 'It is important to reflect on the contradictions of a position which all too frequently leads the radical criminologist simultaneously to demand formal equality in the field of juvenile justice and substantive equality for adults.'

The reality is of course that in the 1970s many minor adult and juvenile offenders were dealt with purely in terms of their guilt or innocence and as a result were committed to prison department establishments (Priestley et al., 1977). The juvenile court has increasingly used the penal institution in preference to social work or social service department provision and has become more and more punitive. The 1982 Criminal Justice Act met many of the demands of the back to justice lobby in terms of determinate sentencing and restrictions on the discretion of social workers. This resulted in an increase in the numbers of young offenders being locked up. It seems clear that in the current political climate a left or liberal back to justice lobby whose radical demands include decent legal representation for all juveniles, radical limitations in sentencing powers and judicial discretion is easily accommodated by a right-wing government which will grant the demands for a reversion to due process while ignoring the issues of the limitation of the powers of the bench and judiciary, and the need for a radical restructuring of penalties and penal institutions. We therefore confront a strange convergence in which left-liberal positions become conflated with those of the radical right.

The back to justice lobby criticise treatment and welfare in that they tend to individualise and personalise what are essentially social or structural problems. The irony is, of course, that, accurate though this critique might be, in place of treatment and welfare they pose a model of judicial procedure which, as Foucault (1972) has observed, not only served as the model, but made possible the conception of individualised responses to the phenomenon of crime. If the law is to be used as a means whereby a more equitable society is to be achieved, then government and the judiciary must, as Christie (1974) argues, abandon the eighteenth-century utilitarian ideology which currently underpins the system and permeates the back to justice stance, in favour of a morality rooted in ideas of social justice. If this is to happen then back to justice, which thus far has concerned itself with a manipulation of the existing rules to make them approximate more closely to this notion of an abstract utilitarian justice, will perforce have to get back to politics. This would require them to move beyond their bland dismissal of welfare and treatment to an analysis of the ways in which welfare resources gained in part as a result of class struggle come, in certain circumstances, to be transformed into oppressive procedures which militate against working-class interests. Such an analysis would raise the issues of extra-judicial conflict resolution and the abolition of major parts of the control system. Thus far only Taylor et al. (1980) have moved beyond this reformulation of the rules to a consideration of these broader issues.

As currently formulated the proposals of the back to justice movement lead us back to a rationalised prison divested of its trappings of treatment and rehabilitation, in which the legal subject is granted his or her right to punishment.

Delinquency management

Delinquency management is an approach which is more often practised than theorised. Put simply, delinquency management involves the attempt to change the behaviour of decision makers in the juvenile criminal justice system in an attempt to divert some young people out of the system altogether, and to minimise the institutionalisation of those within the system. These objectives are pursued by an analysis of existing patterns of decision making and discussion of this analysis with key decision makers in an attempt to get them to revise their objectives. Alongside this, intensive IT provision for young offenders is developed which offers sufficient control and containment to make it a viable sentencing option for the court. The IT programme maintains an exclusive focus on offending behaviour and excursions into questions of need or subconscious motivation are rejected in favour of hard-headed behaviour modification. Meanwhile, residential institutions are closed down or re-designated for another function.

This approach to juvenile crime is articulated most thoroughly by the Lancaster Centre for Youth Crime and Community (cf. Thorpe et al., 1980) whose work has had a considerable influence upon contemporary practice in IT. Their position draws its theoretical rationale from labelling theory and focuses on the functioning of the agencies and agents of the juvenile criminal justice system. They state:

> A complex process of definition, discrimination and decision-making must be undergone before any child appears before a juvenile court. When he does get there what happens to him depends largely upon what social workers and sentencers see as the range of choices open to them. It is in these areas — modification of the administrative processes which precede a court hearing and the development of credible alternatives to the sentencing options now available — that the possibilities of change are clearest and the prospects most hopeful. (Thorpe et al., 1980: 8)

They argue that much behaviour which is formally penalised is no more than a manifestation of a relatively innocuous working-class youth culture. In this picture of the world, the police and social workers misrecognise behaviour and attribute to it a greater significance than it merits. Thus intervention by social workers aimed at the 'prevention' of such behaviour is seen to be doomed to failure since it confuses culture and pathology. It is also dangerous because it tends to label certain youngsters and project them needlessly into the juvenile justice system. For Thorpe et al., professionals in the juvenile justice system seem to be constantly engaged in pre-emptive intervention and over-reaction to youthful misbehaviour. They say that we must make ' . . . an ethical and political choice about whose side . . . we are on'. They are on the side of the underdog offender and opposed to the professional system heavyweights who stigmatise and imprison them. There is, as we have seen, a tendency in this analysis to locate the responsibility for all this injustice with low-level operatives and to ignore the role of government in promoting the decline in the number of CHE places through the 1970s and the parallel expansion of detention centre, borstal and secure unit places. In the light of these developments it becomes necessary to consider the expansion of penal and secure provision as an indicator of shifting government priorities and the restructuring of state expenditure in favour of law and order services rather than as a simple consequence of bad decisions made by social workers or magistrates. Thorpe et al. tend to minimise the growing symbolic and actual importance of the penal institution in the juvenile justice system for governments anticipating the threat to social order occasioned by rapidly rising levels of youth unemployment. The delinquency management perspective largely confines itself to an analysis of the functioning of local authority social services departments and is silent on the issue of penal provision. It therefore fails to show why the closure of community schools (CHEs) should result in young offenders entering community facilities rather than penal institutions as has tended to happen to date. By ignoring the need to attack the youth custody centre as the pinnacle and backstop of the juvenile justice system it runs the risk of advocating administrative and procedural reforms which could well condemn even larger numbers of youngsters to penal dustbins.

The idea of the young offender as a randomly selected working-class youth whose idiosyncratic and culturally supported activity is dramatically criminalised by intrusive and arbitrary official labelling is also problematic. First, this view ignores the reality that youth sub-cultures are not always merely exotic features of a pluralistic society but are sometimes, quite understandably, organised around resistance to deprivation and oppression (Willis, 1977). To respond to these young people by a strategy of non-intervention, as Thorpe et al. seem to suggest, is not to replace pernicious state intervention with enlightened tolerance but rather to abandon them to the vagaries of a rapidly worsening social predicament. As Cohen (1975) has suggested, such liberal non-intervention is too often a form of 'benign neglect'. It is also the case that their behaviour may cause alarm to peers, parents and neighbours as well as the authorities, and that the victims of much juvenile crime are in fact other members of the working-class community. By adopting a position which advocates 'an ethical or political choice about whose side we are on' the question is raised, for example, about those side one takes in the case of youngsters involved with the British Movement who launch attacks upon Bengali families. This view of juvenile crime also fails to account for the overwhelming majority of working-class young people who are not engaged in serious or persistent delinquency.

The labelling perspective tends to steer us away from the site of primary deviation and the social and economic conditions which foster the least acceptable manifestations of juvenile crime. It is of course correct to identify interactions between the police and young people as a crucial determinant in the identification of certain youngsters as 'delinquents' but as Lee and Young (1984) have pointed out, this is a much bigger issue than policemen making the wrong decisions about the wrong children at the wrong time. It is simply not the case that the police merely misunderstand the phenomenon of juvenile crime and over-react to it, although this is obviously a component in the processes at work. The policing of inner cities, and those with large black populations in particular, has changed radically in the last decade. High profile policing or 'the policing of the unemployed ghetto', rooted as it is in the notion that the police should maintain an obvious and uncompromising presence in certain inner-city areas in anticipation of a growth in crime and civil disorder, has served to inflate juvenile arrests and channel growing numbers of juveniles to penal institutions. Strategies for policing the inner cities are increasingly formulated at the highest levels of the police bureaucracy and are not merely the sum total of decisions taken by individual police officers (Hall et al., 1978).

Thorpe et al. castigate social workers for their punitive recommendations and the unwarranted power they exert over clients, but tend to ignore the formidable constraints under which they work. Parker et al. (1981) have shown in contrast that the power-holders in the juvenile justice system are the police who frame the charges and the bench who in 1982 were handed even greater powers to sentence and control young people. This research also suggests that quite often the social worker in court is reduced to 'reading' the bench in an attempt to negotiate the least punitive response to youngsters in trouble.

By suspending considerations of political power and the relationship between the juvenile justice system and broader political and administrative changes in the state, the delinquency management approach has presented a prescription for change which leaves the major determinants of the present crisis in the system untouched. While this approach has done much to divert young people from the CHE and offers a salutary reminder of the problems created as a consequence of the subjective perceptions of agents of the juvenile justice system, it must move beyond its focus on attitudes and attitude change if it is to contribute to substantive system change.

The growing popularity of delinquency management is in large part attributable to the worsening economic situation and the financial constraints in which local authorities currently operate. As a pragmatic approach it remains unreflective about the roots of its own strategies and uncritical of an increasingly authoritarian response to young offenders by governments throughout the 1970s and 1980s. By viewing the provision of welfare as the thin end of the totalitarian wedge the point that in the wake of the 1982 Act, the thick end, the youth custody centre, is being driven deeper and deeper into the working-class community, is missed.

By the end of the 1970s the back to justice and delinquency management positions had, for the purposes of the practice of IT, become fused. The Association of Juvenile Justice was formed by IT workers who broke away from the National Intermediate Treatment Federation because the Federation retained its commitment to preventive work and welfare. It epitomised the minimalist radicalism, a self-styled 'politics of reality', which had emerged as an orthodoxy within IT by the late 1970s. This position can be expressed in the form of ten propositions.

1. *Juvenile crime is not a serious problem*
    (a) because, when we calculate the proceeds of the sum total of juvenile crime or the costs in terms of damage wrought by juveniles, this pales into insignificance against a backdrop of organised and corporate crime;
    (b) because the government, media, and public concern about juvenile crime is the result of a series of moral panics orchestrated by various moral entrepreneurs and media hungry for horror stories with which to sell papers. These groups are periodically aided and abetted by the police.

2. *The helping professions are the major source of hindrance to young offenders*
    (a) because it is in the nature of social work and social welfare that it will constantly search for new needs and new causes of deviant behaviour far beyond the time and place of the particular deviant act;
    (b) because social work by its equation of deprivation and deviance will intervene in the lives of non-adjudicated delinquents in an attempt to prevent delinquency. In doing this, it will serve to stigmatise new non-deviant populations and thus draw them into the juvenile criminal justice system through a process of guilt by association with social workers doing delinquency prevention work. This is often described as the application of a 'needology' which results in the 'spreading of the net';
    (c) because social workers in their Social Enquiry Reports (SERs), while ostensibly offering the court an opinion about the subject based on social and psychological scientific training,

are in fact mainly offering a character evaluation — a moral judgement. Thus SERs may be seen as either a pitch or a denunciation or, indeed, a character assassination.

3. *Placing young offenders in residential or custodial institutions is a bad thing*
   (a) because it fractures links with home, family and neighbourhood;
   (b) because it forces the subject to take on an 'inmate' identity, it spoils identity;
   (c) because it increases the subject's rate of offending and serves to project the subject into a deviant subculture, thus promoting secondary deviance and projecting the subject into a deviant career;
   (d) because it is costly and, in the light of (c) above, ineffective in achieving the objective of rehabilitation to a non-deviant mode of existence in the community.

4. *Placing young offenders in a community-based alternative is a better thing*
   (a) because it avoids all the disadvantages itemised above;
   (b) because it is less costly, and even if it is as unsuccessful as the residential or custodial institution in achieving rehabilitation, the failure is less expensive.

5. *Leaving the kids alone is the best thing — radical non-intervention is the most desirable response to young offenders*
   (a) because it avoids all the problems associated with the application of deviant labels by the heavy-handed agents of the state who serve to stigmatise the subject and worsen the problem to which they are purportedly the solution;
   (b) because much behaviour which is the object of intervention by the police, education authorities, social workers, probation officers and courts, is no more than a relatively innocuous expression of working-class youth culture which should be tolerated as a normal part of growing up;
   (c) because most interventions by powerful labellers tend to serve the professional interests of the labellers rather than the needs of the subjects, we must always be sceptical about the purpose of such interventions;
   (d) because it costs virtually nothing.

6. *Welfare considerations should be banned from the juvenile court*
   (a) because the consideration of deprivation, need and the determination of deviant behaviour by mysterious, intrapsychic or social forces serves to mystify the defendant and lay her/him

open to the possibility of the imposition of protracted treatments in residential establishments for offences for which an adult would receive a much less intrusive or restrictive penalty;

(b) because a consideration of guilt or innocence and the adversarial due process of law enables the greater possibility of proportionality, i.e. justice;

(c) because the child or young person has an innate sense of cause and effect and justice and (i) expects, and (ii) has the right to expect, punishment;

(d) because social workers are inept in their operations in court and lawyers, the police, magistrates and judges are not.

7. *IT must concern itself only with adjudicated offenders*

(a) because any excursions into work with girls as the objects of sexual abuse, non-school attenders, glue sniffers, etc, is welfare or social work and is not the concern of IT which works only to prevent adjudicated offenders being locked up;

(b) because such net-widening may suck new populations into the system while limiting the opportunities for adjudicated offenders to be offered the alternative.

8. *In IT programmes credibility with the courts is more important than what you do*

(a) because IT is first and foremost a strategic intervention to keep young offenders out of care or custody. Since courts put people into care or custody anything which looks like a plausible alternative, and this may often involve including a punitive or overtly controlling element in the programme, may be tried to achieve the decarcerating objective;

(b) because programmes which begin to concern themselves with issues other than offending are in danger of drifting into the metaphysics of needology and denying the essential unproblematic normality of the subjects of IT programmes.

9. *The job of science is to quantify how much less harm we can do or have done, not to explain crime or devise cures for it*

(a) because in the entire history of criminology no effective technology of behavioural change has been devised;

(b) because the problem is clearly social reaction and the task is to find it and neutralise it;

(c) because practitioners need a science they can use to get the job done, not irrefutable metaphysics and intellectual speculation about the nature of humankind and the nature of the social world.

10. *The state is run by unsophisticated, unscientific, deaf idiots, who for some reason, keep making mistakes at the levels of policy or implementation. This has the unintended consequence of locking up even more young offenders. Our job is to tell them how to do their job properly*
    (a) because politicians do not understand the dynamics of the juvenile criminal justice system;
    (b) because if they did they would then be able to turn their stated objective, i.e. the minimisation of custodial confinement, into a reality;
    (c) because if we can keep pumping them information about cost-effectiveness, and evaluations which show effectiveness in terms of individual behaviour and system change, we will win their hearts and minds.

This technicist orthodoxy elaborated the fullest and clearest account of the role and function of IT in the juvenile criminal justice system. Unlike some earlier theoretical and political perspectives on IT it gave practitioners something concrete and quantifiable that they could do. The problem for the other strand of thought influenced by social reaction theory, radical criminology, was to identify a practice and it was to this problem that Thomas Mathiesen (1974) turned his attention. Mathiesen's roots were in the 'new left' politics of the late 1960s and the attempt within this movement to devise a political praxis which would contest the power of the state.

Abolitionism

The abolition of the prison has been a minor theme in criminological debate throughout the twentieth century. Described by David Downes (1980) as the ultimate penal reform, abolition has been supported by, among others, H.J. Eysenck, George Bernard Shaw and Beatrice and Sidney Webb. It is surprising therefore that while the Justice for Children and New Approaches to Juvenile Crime pressure groups and the Lancaster Centre for Youth Crime and Community vigorously debated reform of the juvenile justice system, abolitionism was seldom mentioned. The abolition debate was rejuvenated in 1974 with the publication in Britain of Thomas Mathiesen's *The Politics of Abolition*. In this book Mathiesen spells out an abolitionist politics which offers to would-be reformers short-term goals, long-term objectives, and strategies for their achievement. He argues that reformers normally founder on the rocks of the 'reform versus revolution' problem. In demanding the abolition of the prison the reformer is asked to suggest what she or he will put in its place. In

Mathiesen's terms they are asked to offer a 'fully-formed' alternative which will meet objectives established by the prison system the reformers aim to replace. This, as Mathiesen points out, is a virtually impossible task for reformers who are then driven back to working on piecemeal reforms of parts of the prison system. The irony he sees here is that in working for 'positive' reforms, better educational facilities, better treatment programmes, colour TVs, etc, rather than hastening the demise of the prison, successful 'positive' reform merely serves to give greater legitimacy and credibility to the prison system. This then makes the eventual abolition of the prison all the more difficult. As Downes (1980) has argued 'the stage is set for penal reformers to end up hopelessly compromised with the system on the one hand or condemned to the irresponsible revolutionary role on the other'.

In the face of these problems Mathiesen argues that rather than opting out of the long-term goal of abolition and into piecemeal 'positive' reform reformers should pursue both simultaneously. This, he suggests, can be done if instead of 'positive' reforms they demand 'negative reforms', that in place of a 'fully-formed' alternative they offer an 'unfinished' alternative, and that crucially in their efforts, they form links, and work with, the 'expelled' institutional populations.

Negative reforms do not give greater credibility and legitimacy to the penal system. Thus Mathiesen would argue that to demand the cessation of solitary confinement in prisons, and child-care establishments, to oppose the forcible application of drug 'therapy', and to require the granting of full civil and legal rights to institutional populations would all constitute legitimate negative reforms. Their legitimacy resides in the fact that they require the system to relinquish its power and control over its subjects for the demands to be met. This diminution of power and control is part of a process of attrition in which the legitimacy and power of the system is worn away.

If, Mathiesen argues, a 'fully-formed' alternative to a penal system is proposed which stays within the objectives of that system, it is destined to piecemeal incorporation and will serve to strengthen that system. If, however, a 'fully-formed' alternative which requires a radical shift in objectives and practices is posed then it will be rejected because it offers no solutions to the problems decision makers in the existing system are trying to solve. He proposes instead of the 'fully-formed', the 'unfinished' alternative, which constantly confronts and heightens the contradictions and absurdities in the current structure and current practices while offering only a sketch or a hint of what might happen if current structures or practices are abandoned. In this approach to reform, the alternative is seen to emerge in the wake of abolition and in the space left by the defunct structures or practices.

This alternative Mathiesen argues may be shaped by the 'expelled' populations themselves.

Central to this theory is the idea that institutional populations, the 'expelled', will take increasing power in negotiating for reform. The populations of mental hospitals, children's homes, prisons and old people's homes, Mathiesen argues, are the unproductive and troublesome members of a society which routinely generates human waste but would rather not look at or be reminded of it. Thus these people are expelled, stripped of social status, and often legal and civil rights and the rest of us are not reminded of the real nature of the world we inhabit. He sees the task of abolitionism as one of reuniting the expelled sectors of the working class with the mainstream of the labour movement in order that the true nature of capitalist social relations is comprehended and changed. Thus he commends the establishment of links between the expelled populations on the inside and trade unions, ex-prisoners, political pressure groups, academics and journalists on the outside who will together constitute an abolitionist alliance.

Downes offers an analysis of the 'possibilities' and 'pitfalls' of abolitionism, pointing out that Norway has a relatively small institutional population, an established social democratic reformist tradition in the sphere of prisons, and a 'crime' problem which is far less significant than Britain's. He also shows that organisations like Preservation of the Rights of Prisoners (PROP) and Radical Alternatives to Prison (RAP) in this country have made headway only on issues of alternatives to prison which Mathiesen (1974) would see as a mere diversion from the real issue of abolitionism. In the light of Mathiesen's theory we are left with a problem concerning how we regard IT. Is it merely a mechanism whereby the existing institutional apparatus strives to legitimise itself as Millham (1977) once suggested? Or might it, as was originally intended (in the Children and Young Persons Act 1969), provide the space in which the 'unfinished' alternative might develop in the wake of abolition?

Within the sphere of IT the abolitionist position was articulated most clearly by the editorial collective of *Eureka*, the journal of the London Intermediate Treatment Association:

> . . . New approaches to Juvenile Crime for example is a marriage, or more accurately a menage, of convenience between a number of interested professional groups each of which is concerned to keep its 'solution', its capacity to manage the problem of juvenile crime, on the political agenda. The actual 'problem' of juvenile crime and the boundaries of the debate about it are largely defined by the government, the police and the magistrates' association. The problem this poses is that in order to keep their 'fully-formed' alternative in the debate they have to accept, in public

at least, the governmental definition of the problem as the starting point for their policy recommendations. The same would be true for the All Party Committee on Penal Affairs (chaired by Mr Kilroy Silk) whose recent report accepted the need for punitive responses to those who engaged in the type of 'hooliganism seen on the streets of Brixton and Toxteth'. In a similar way Justice for Children proceeds uncritically from the position that formal legality represents a desirable and just model of conflict resolution in a fundamentally unequal society.

An abolitionist strategy by contrast regards these bland orthodox assumptions about the nature of the problem as themselves problematic. It would contrast the social realities of Brixton and Toxteth and the bitter heritage of aggressive policing with Mr Kilroy Silk's 'hooliganism' in order to point up the absurdity of a punitive response to individual participants in a profoundly social conflict. It must constantly link its proposals for negative reform, police accountability, community control of policing, the decriminalisation of SUS, with a thorough-going analysis of the real nature of the problem. Thus, to use a time-honoured metaphor it must not merely propose a radical re-arrangement of the deck chairs on the Titanic but must ask of the captain and the owners why it is that the ship is being steered towards the iceberg in the first place. (Pitts, 1981: 30)

They observed that if it was true that 'alternative' responses to children in trouble must always be measured in terms of their potential for containment and control vis-a-vis the borstal, detention centre or other custodial provision, then only with the abolition of these institutions could IT stand a chance of becoming a creative 'unfinished' and major response to juvenile crime. In this case the only defensible rationale for the future development of IT was as a replacement for, and not as an adjunct of, punitive custodial provision and this led them to a position where they maintained that any further development of IT had to be paralleled by vigorous abolitionist action. Cohen (1979) identifies the three essential components of an abolitionist strategy.

1 . The demand for a 'total moratorium on all new prison construction' and the closure of existing institutions.
2 . Decarceration — all prisoners who can safely be released from the institution (usually estimated at 70−80 per cent) should be released. This, he argues, will make no difference to re-conviction rates and might actually lower them.
3 . Excarceration — we must stop putting people into penal institutions by decriminalising certain offences and placing severe limits upon the powers of the courts to impose custodial sentences.

Within the abolitionist strategy only those initiatives which diminish the power and contest the centrality of the custodial institution, i.e. negative reforms, are admissable. For IT this would mean that only those initiatives which can be conclusively proved to have taken young offenders out of institutions, or can demonstrate that they have kept out young people who would otherwise have been subjected to incarceration, should retain a formal link with the juvenile justice system.

Abolitionism is unique among the initiatives described here in that it addresses the parliamentary politics of juvenile justice rather than its administration or the practices of its professional personnel. It locates the problem in the relationship between the state and its surplus and unproductive citizens, the people Spitzer (1975) describes as social junk. Abolitionism is a minimalist theory and practice which attempts to erode, by a process of political attrition, the apparatus of penal control developed within advanced capitalist states. It attempts to reverse conventional social democratic political processes by championing an intervention by the socially disadvantaged expelled populations into the functioning of the state apparatus. The expelled are to contest and erode the power of the state by developing a politically powerful abolitionist alliance. Bill Beaumont, chair of the National Association of Probation Officers between 1981 and 1984 writes:

> In campaigning work, probation officers need to seek support and this involves making wider contacts than is usual in the job. We will need to contact local authority and government departments, MPs, councillors, campaigns, trade unions, tenants' associations and other community groups. Seeking out and making links is an important stage in campaign development. Alliances around limited aims are possible between quite disparate groups but caution is needed in avoiding allies who seek to limit goals, differ significantly on methods or arguments, or desert when the going gets tough. Effective lobbying in councils and parliament requires some detailed knowledge and considerable effort. With care good use can be made of local councillors and MPs, special interest parliamentary groupings and parliamentary debates, all of which can make news as well as contribute to administrative and legislative change. (Beaumont, 1985: 98–9)

The technique is of course remarkably similar to the community action strategies adopted by the practitioners of radical welfare. Their endeavour was to facilitate the political organisation of unorganised, and previously politically marginal, sections of the working class. Radical welfare, as it developed, adopted the same strategy as Mathiesen in which an attempt is made to link the concerns of the socially and economically marginal to the mainstream politics of the labour movement. Radical welfare and abolitionism both identify the problems of economic and social marginality as a manifestation of political marginality, and hence, powerlessness. Both identify the need to re-connect this 'reserve army' with the political process, but this has proved, in the sphere of juvenile justice reform, to be the hardest trick of the lot.

6 The politics of reform

The struggle around the prisons, the penal system and the police-judicial system, because it developed 'in solitary', among social workers and ex-prisoners, has tended increasingly to separate itself from the forces which would have enabled it to grow. It has allowed itself to be penetrated by a whole naive, archaic ideology which makes the criminal at once into the innocent victim and the pure rebel — society's scapegoat — and the young wolf of future revolutions. This return to anarchist themes of the late nineteenth century was possible only because of a failure of integration of current strategies. And the result has been a deep split between this campaign with its monotonous, lyrical little chant, heard only among a few small groups, and the masses who have good reason not to accept it as valid political currency, but who also — thanks to the studiously cultivated fear of criminals — tolerate the maintenance, or rather the reinforcement, of the judicial and police apparatus

Michel Foucault, *Power and Knowledge*

A politics of ecstasy

If the central political issue inside parliament, in the mid- to late 1960s, concerned which party had a legitimate claim to manage a prosperous, expanding, technologically sophisticated society, then outside parliament the issue was the legitimacy of parliamentary government and the social order it represented.

By 1968 a new generation of 'meritocrats' was locking their teachers out of the new universities and polytechnics and running their own courses. The texts they adopted were written by Fanon, Friere, Illich, Laing, Chomsky, Marcuse, and Karl Marx. In Grosvenor Square this new generation was asking 'Hey, hey LBJ, how many kids did you kill today?' In Paris in May 1968 students and workers fought on the streets with the police and it appeared, for a time, as if they might actually achieve a socialist revolution.

Earlier in the decade a newly prosperous younger generation were apparently beating each other senseless on the beaches of Margate and Clacton. By 1968 the 'tough mods' had transmogrified into the more menacing skinheads. Rock bands were breaking up their instruments in accordance with the injunctions of dadaism, but it was hard to get at the full gist of this particular endeavour since most of the people who were doing it had normally been smoking a lot of marijuana when they were asked about it. Commentators talked about a sexual revolution and although these young people hadn't invented sex they seemed to be the first generation which actually enjoyed it.

The well-educated beneficiaries of the welfare state were 'hip' and they were rejecting both the means and the ends of industrial capitalism in favour of hedonism or revolution. As the 1960s progressed the existentialists, beats, dadaists, situationists, hippies, yippies, and freaks had consolidated into the 'alternative society' or the 'revolutionary left'.

At its core the radical critique suggested that industrial capitalism in its voracious pursuit of profit violated both the human environment and the human spirit. It was a system built on the oppression of all but the powerful. This oppression was doubly pernicious because its subjects were manipulated into believing that they were its beneficiaries rather than its victims. The system worked because human beings were alienated from their natural environment, themselves, their creativity and their potentiality. The costs could be counted in the numbers of people driven into madness. The process could be observed in schools which merely produced the right amount of the right type of fodder for the machine, and in the factories which reduced human beings to mere appendages of the productive process. Whereas the parliamentary politics of the 1960s concerned the management of technological expansion, the critique developed by the 'alternative society' and the 'revolutionary left' repudiated a society which deified growth and productivity and subordinated human beings to it.

Beyond the parliamentary social democratic consensus this 'new' left politics rejected social democracy as the velvet glove clothing the iron fist of capitalist domination. Social democratic reform was regarded as a practice which conspired to delude and tranquillise the working class and mislead them about where their interests lay. If welfare and treatment were opiates, justice was a hallucination.

The irony is, of course, that a government which contained erstwhile members of the revolutionary left had abandoned an 'outdated' class politics in favour of a modern managerial style and now espoused a philosophy which suggested that it was possible, through the provision of opportunity, to transcend social determination and achieve freedom. Outside parliament a group of people who had been the beneficiaries of previously unprecedented educational and occupational opportunities espoused a philosophy which suggested that this side of a socialist revolution no change was possible and 'freedom' would remain a mystificatory illusion.

The 'alternative society' was at odds with the 'revolutionary left', not over the revolutionary goal, which always remained vague, but over the ways in which revolutions happened in mid-twentieth century Europe. R.D. Laing specified the ways in which the revolution of the alternative society would be realised:

> In our society, at certain times, this interlaced set of systems may lend itself to revolutionary change, not at the extreme micro or macro ends; that is, not through the individual pirouette of solitary repentance on the one hand, or by a seizure of the machinery of the state on the other; but by sudden, structural, radical qualitative changes in the intermediate system levels: changes in a factory, a hospital, a school, a university, a set of schools or a whole area of industry, medicine, education, etc. (Laing, 1968: 16)

The alternative society posed the possibility of incremental revolution initiated by doctors, teachers, managers, or social workers who held an alternative consciousness. The apparatus of the state could, it seemed, be used as an instrument to transform the state and bring into being a new era in which what was most human in human beings might be elevated and celebrated. For the revolutionary left, however, the practices of state personnel, however enlightened, were irredeemably tainted by the structures in which they took place. For them the problem was not the transformation of the state apparatus. The problem for the revolutionary left of the late 1960s was how they might most effectively 'smash the state'.

In 1970 the 'family service', the central pillar of Labour's assault on poverty and inequality was brought into being creating a vastly expanded social work apparatus and an unprecedented number of jobs for a generation of social science students committed to effecting radical social change on behalf of the poor through the medium of a social welfare.

As we stood, in 1970, on the verge of a new era in welfare, in which the development of the personal social services was supposed to complete the task initiated by the architects of the welfare state in 1945, doubts were looming. Could we, as the Fabian reformers had claimed, achieve social equality and usher in a classless society by the redistribution of wealth in the form of welfare resources and by the judicious application of treatment to deviants?

Or could we, as the alternative society implied, assume control of the welfare apparatus and then, audaciously, redefine the problem so that the ideas of the conventional and the powerful were rendered problematic, and the actions of 'deviants' could be revealed in all their rich rationality?

Or should we, as the revolutionary left enjoined us, infiltrate the state apparatus, identify, exploit and hence heighten its contradictions in order that it would eventually self-destruct as a result of its own intolerable internal tensions?

Were we to be therapists, consciousness raisers or guerrillas? As we pondered this dilemma Edward Heath's Conservative government was elected. Heath pledged his administration to the control of inflation, the unions, and crime. In the midst of strident argument, confusion, bitterness and dissent at all points left of the Labour Party, the first post-war law and order government came to power.

By the early 1970s the post-war social democratic consensus in British politics had given way to a sharp division between the right and the left. Within the labour movement the traditional alliance between the intelligentsia, the trade unions and the parliamentary Labour Party, having failed to achieve its main objectives, lay in disarray. The Wilsonian myth of the prosperous classless society had exploded in the face of growing evidence of poverty, social unrest, political dissent and an impending economic crisis.

During this period the new left found few points of contact with the traditional labour movement. They rejected both the means and the ends of parliamentary politics, arguing that a 'socialist government' in a capitalist society must inevitably betray the working class in its attempt to 'make a deal' with capital. They castigated the trade union movement as a self-seeking and politically impotent bureaucracy which had been incorporated into the capitalist state and served merely to legitimise wage restraint. Whereas an old left politics had seen the class struggle unfolding within the 'endemic' and 'historically necessary' conflict between capital, in the form of industrialists, and labour, in the form of the trade union movement, the new left found only collusion here, arguing that the real 'struggle' was now somewhere else.

Indeed, the new left found evidence of class struggle virtually everywhere except the workplace. Whereas a traditional reading of Marx had suggested that changes in the social structure were always and everywhere prior to, and the determining factor in, changes in political consciousness, the new left asserted that the relationship between material conditions and consciousness was a dialectical one in which each affected, and was affected by, the other. Thus by revising, or offering a more sophisticated version of, socialist doctrine it became possible to shift the site of the class struggle away from the moribund shadow-play of the workplace towards populations and conflicts where social oppression was both more evident and more keenly felt. The politics of gender, race and poverty came to supplant a more traditional politics of class struggle located within, and dominated by, those sections of the working class which were organised into trade unions. For the new left the quest was for the political in the personal and the personal in the political. Oppression, generated by an inequitable social order, could be identified and worked with in all personal relations, not simply industrial relations.

A politics from below
The new left had of necessity to seek an alliance beyond the traditional coalitions of the British labour movement. As an essentially middle-class endeavour new left politics had no roots in the labour movement and inevitably sought an alliance with those who were not organised by, and hence not subject to the protections of, the labour movement. The new left attempted to forge an alliance with the socially, economically, and politically marginal populations of the inner city.

For the new left the newly expanded social welfare apparatus offered a base and 'radical welfare' the means whereby the class struggle could be fought out. Put another way, finding no point of accommodation with the proletariat, the new left, composed of members of the non-commercial bourgeoisie, attempted to form an alliance with an unorganised non-industrial lumpen proletariat. Engels had once unkindly remarked:

> The lumpen proletariat, this scum of the depraved elements of all classes, which establishes its headquarters in the big cities, is the worst of all possible allies. This rabble is absolutely venal and absolutely brazen ... Every leader of the workers who uses these scoundrels as guards or relies on them for support proves himself by this action a traitor to the movement. (Engels, 1874: 646)

Sweeping and bigoted though Engels' condemnation is he does alert us to an important division within the working class between the 'respectable' and the 'disreputable'. The choice to align oneself with the 'disreputable' is also a choice to distance oneself from the respectable, but of course the respectable, in the guise of the mainstream of the labour movement, had offered the new left little choice.

There were three central problems attendant upon this alliance between the new left and the newly discovered poor. First, there was no pre-existing organisational structure which could be utilised by the poor to articulate their demands. Second, the politics of the poor (the elderly, single-parent families, the intermittently employed) was grounded in their day-to-day experience. As a result they were inclined to say that they wanted another job rather than a socialist transformation, a winter coat for the baby rather than a popular uprising. Third, some of the activities of the very poor, predatory juvenile crime not least among them, made some elements of this population harder to market than others when attempting to develop a political voice which would be heard and taken into account by those with the power to effect change.

It is notable that two of the most effective organisations which emerged from the new left of the early 1970s, the Child Poverty Action Group and the Low Pay Unit, succeeded in large part because they were able to present those who had previously been viewed as culpable or negligent, as either innocent by virtue of age, or industrious but wronged. Their success lay in their ability to ideologically prise away certain sections of the previously 'disreputable' and represent them as 'respectable' but previously misunderstood. Similarly the plight of the elderly and the psychiatric patient could be addressed by offering a potentially sympathetic public the means with which to identify with their plight. It was perhaps for this reason, among others, that radicals working with young offenders in the 1970s chose to present juvenile crime as either an inconsequential spin-off of poverty or an unintended consequence of official intervention, but seldom, if ever, as juvenile crime.

The new left endeavour was to reinstate the marginalised populations of the run-down inner city into the political process by transforming the images of the poor and getting their concerns on the right agendas at the right time. Thus a previously oppressed population was to arise and take its rightful place in the political process. This was achieved, where it was achieved, by demonstrating that it 'wasn't their fault'.

A politics from beyond

This proved to be an enormously difficult task even where one could effect the necessary redistribution of blame. Young offenders proved to be less amenable to such a dramatic social metamorphosis since most potential audiences, including the poor themselves, insisted on believing that juvenile crime was the 'fault' of juvenile criminals.

The new left's ambivalence didn't help since in as much as they argued that juvenile crime was a pathetic consequence of deprivation or an invention of heavy-handed agents of 'social control', they also hoped, and sometimes believed, that young people in trouble might be proto-revolutionary Robin Hoods engaged in activity which anticipated the imminent post-revolutionary redistribution of wealth. To this extent those members of the new left who chose to concern themselves with juvenile crime entered the ideological ghetto in which young offenders were themselves trapped.

It is no doubt true, as Muncie asserts, that:

> ... sections of youth are all too readily defined as deviant or criminal and thus are continually feared on the streets and in the schools ... there is as much 'trouble' created for the youth of today through the processes of media and public reaction as youth itself may create for its critics. (Muncie, 1984: 28)

Yet quite clearly the fear and disapproval of juvenile crime by a potentially victimised citizenry, irrespective of social class, is a social reality. It may be fed by, but it is certainly no mere creation of, a sensationalist media. What the new left was unwilling to confront was the fact that those who are most likely to be victims of crime, the very poor, also tend to take a dim view of it:

> At about that time I happened to be supervising the survey described in Chapter 1 and noted the striking fact that when asked what was the biggest problem facing large cities, black respondents were more likely to mention crime and juvenile delinquency than any other issue. (Wilson, 1975: 65)

The problem for the new left was that through a process of denial and romanticisation of juvenile crime they left no route open to the places where the power to make things change resided. As 'radicals' they located themselves 'outside' the system, only entering it as advocates and critics. They were concerned either to develop the alternative to existing structures or to bombard those structures with the rhetoric of change. Whereas the new left made remarkable advances in the spheres of psychiatry, welfare rights and community work the issue of 'children and young people in trouble' was fumbled because the activists isolated themselves politically, in the same way that the children and young people they strove to help were isolated.

To say this is not to say that the experimental work developed in the free-school, alternative youth projects, the adventure playgrounds and community arts had no value. These were, and remain, some of the most exciting, and arguably the most effective, interventions with inner-city young people in this century. The problem was that in the sphere of juvenile crime, the new left lost any political purchase it might have had on the issue because it misunderstood the actual and symbolic political significance of juvenile crime. It ignored the victim of juvenile crime, and it never had a clear view of what the 'state' was beyond a notion that it was alive, oppressive and existent within every formal structure. This was, however, a distinction it shared with most of the other actors who attempted to effect reform in the juvenile criminal justice system in the 1970s.

The politics of reality: reframing the problem by framing the problem solvers

In the mid-1970s the protagonists of 'delinquency management' and 'back to justice' developed an explicit critique of social workers and their involvement in the juvenile criminal justice system and an implicit critique of the prescriptions for change offered by the new left.

The failure of government to implement key sections of the 1969 CYPA left social workers with some unpalatable choices. Would they simply attempt to bring some unspecified 'welfare' to those children who were patently not faring well or would they attempt to bury the contradiction implicit in their new role beneath a professional rhetoric which reconciled care and control as related and legitimate activities of 'responsible parents', and presumed that those responsibilities and activities might be discharged by a range of state institutions, and state professionals?

While the first option involved a certain denial, optimism and romanticism, the second involved a very serious psychological mistake for it developed analogies between the uses of rewards and punishments by parents in the process of childrearing, and the functions of the normalising and coercive institutions of the state. Primary and secondary socialisation were not to be squared so neatly and the random deployment of welfare resources designated for crime control soon revealed a nasty propensity towards the moral contamination of those they touched because in the act of deployment lurked the imminent possibility of stigmatisation.

Both options opened up the possibility of self-defeat. Both options, couched as they were in the positive, determined as they were to effect positive change and adjustment, or positive reform, ultimately ran into the limit set by the non-implementation of the 1969 Act. Both options, predicated as they were on a hope of the possibility of individual salvation and change, threatened to transform the state-employed solution into part of the state-inspired problem. So how then was it to be possible to effect the desired and desirable goal of the deinstitutionalisation of young offenders from the 'inside' when to be inside was to be part of the problem? Was it possible to be a subversive insider simultaneously accepted and oppositional?

Here was the juncture at which eighteenth-century utilitarianism, 1960s labelling theory, abolitionist politics, microcomputer technology and the patter of the used-car salesman united 'delinquency management' and 'back to justice' in the 'politics of reality'. This foray into the intellectual supermarket brought together the ideas and approaches it did in the way that it did in order to find a way out of the strategic bind which confounded would-be reformers within the welfare apparatus. Despite its devastating critique of social work, the 'politics of reality' grew out of, and was sustained by, social work and social workers who were its audience and its market. The eclecticism of the approach was strategic and pragmatic. Each element of this new coalition of ideas addressed a different aspect of the problem. Ironically it did what governments had always done with theory. It wove ideas together into a vehicle which would take it where it wanted to go, irrespective of the purity, form or coherence of those ideas.

If the practice of social work in the juvenile criminal justice system had previously proceeded on the assumption that it was bringing scientifically informed practices to bear on the problem of criminality then the 'politics of reality' indicted this endeavour as a major cause of criminalisation. If social welfare personnel had dreamt that they were helping the offender, the 'politics of reality' fractured that dream by citing them as a source of hindrance. The traditional oppositions of a legal and penal apparatus struggling with a welfare apparatus for the body of the accused were rendered problematic by a new idea that together the penal, judicial and welfare apparatus stood in opposition to the interests of the accused. But this reversal was even more radical for it suggested that legal professionals, magistrates and judges, might in fact, if separated from welfare, become the real defenders of the young offender, the people who would protect them from the voracious ambitions of welfare professionals. If all of these people had previously believed that the problem was located within the psyche, morality or activity of the individual offender and that the remedy should also be sought there, the new orthodoxy pointed to a system which delivered outcomes at stark variance with the stated aims of justice, social well-being, and morality articulated by professionals within the system.

Yet in all this, the apparent radicalism of the critique notwithstanding, was a central assumption about how change might occur. This assumption was that the chaotic and unjust outcomes of the juvenile justice system arose by mistake. They arose it seemed out of false ideas, mistaken assumptions and a misplaced professional entrepreneurism. The solution lay in control and information, gatekeeping and feedback. It was in this way that the system would return to optimal functioning. Thus the problem was not the system itself, not the structure, not the legitimacy of the process, but rather the mistakes, inefficiency, stupidity and professional greed of its operatives. The 'politics of reality' strove from its inception to restore the system to optimal functioning. It did this in the implicit belief that the system in equilibrium with all the anomalies ironed out, would deliver formal and social justice. This essentially liberal endeavour saw its central task as that of closing the gap between the rhetoric and the actuality of the juvenile justice system. It strove to make the system live up to its promises by exposing the irony in its functioning. Yet in choosing to believe this account of events the possibility that the mistakes identified so clearly were not in fact inadvertent, irrational and arbitrary was denied, for to accept this possibility meant that the technology of delinquency management would become instantly redundant.

So the other strand of the 'politics of reality', the fit between its ideological coalition and its technology, was revealed. It was a technology whose viability was contingent upon the world being in fact a pluralistic and ultimately benign one. It relied on the hope that technological rationality would eventually triumph over vested interest. An alternative analysis which suggested that the juvenile criminal justice system might be yet another battleground on which a class struggle was being enacted threatened to render the technology irrelevant. 'Do-ability' required the politics of reality to locate itself within a pluralistic paradigm. Being located within a pluralistic paradigm meant that some of the most striking anomalies identified by the technology could only be understood as human errors and not as indicators of profound political conflicts lying beyond the juvenile criminal justice system. Thus the question arises as to whether the 'mistakes', 'anomalies' and outright absurdities identified by the technology were in fact 'problems' or whether they were manifestations or 'symptoms' of other deeper, more intractable problems which lay beyond the understanding of this ideological coalition and the reach of its technology.

The new left had struggled to develop a base within the working class. The coalition which spawned the 'politics of reality' had no political base but a central political idea. It was a coalition developed in the university with an implicit commitment to the minimisation of state intervention in the lives of citizens. To that extent it remained unselective about those elements of the state and those activities of its professional personnel which might be defended and those which might be condemned. It was committed to a pragmatic social science and the development of technologies which would minimise bureaucratic intrusion into personal lives and to that extent its programme coincided with that of the radical right. It had no strong objections to the existing social order and betrayed an enthusiasm for the unfettered operation of free market forces when it came to peddling its cost-cutting computer technology to hard-pressed local authority social services departments. It claimed to be 'on the side' of the young offender and against clumsy social reaction. It chose not to discuss juvenile crime because it was wedded to a conception of labelling theory in which social reaction was seen to generate crime. It launched its assault upon the activities of social workers in the social services departments where it had marketed its equipment. And as the attendance centres, the detention centres, and the borstals grew fuller and fuller with less and less problematic offenders throughout the 1970s, the protagonists of a 'politics of reality' could only suggest that social workers or policemen or magistrates seemed to be making a lot of mistakes. They could not account for the growth of the prison and offered no strategy with which to address it. They did not address the reality of social inequality or the reasons why new forms of juvenile offending, like street crime or heroin abuse, might rise to prominence at a particular moment. They had nothing to say about any relationship which might exist between poverty, offending, and control, dismissing such concerns as 'needology'. They therefore repudiated the very possibility of a political dimension to their essentially technological and administrative project. Like the new left, they ignored the victim and remained vague about the nature of the 'state' seeing it as a large, inept but potentially benign bureaucracy which could be made to operate efficiently if offered the right sort of information. By the late 1970s the 'politics of reality' had developed into an 'administrative criminology' concerned with problems of the more efficacious dispersal of criminal bodies, rather than a confrontation with a criminalising and criminogenic world.

The politics of entrepreneurism
While the endeavours of the protagonists of a 'politics of reality' were opportunistic in as much as they traded on a growing scepticism within government about the efficacy of social intervention and a pressing need on the part of local authorities to cut expenditure, they did alert us to the phenomenon of professional entrepreneurism in the sphere of juvenile justice. There is an adage in local government circles which suggests that politicians understand buildings and equipment much better than they understand procedures and practices. Thus if you wish to ensure a future for your procedure or practice you are advised to try to get as many buildings, and as much specialised equipment in which, and with which, to proceed with your procedures and practise your practices. It is also extremely important to spend all of your budget if not more, lest the councillors should come to believe that you will need less next year. Survival in a local authority, it is suggested, is contingent on acquiring buildings and equipment which you may not need and spending far more money than is necessary. It is also the case of course that if you do this you will then need more staff. More staff will lead to greater responsibility and a consequent extension of your span of control. As a result of this

your post will be regraded and you will gradually rise in the hierarchy, projected upwards by the empire which is inflating below you.

What the usual critiques of professional entrepreneurism miss is that this activity, where it can be observed, may or may not be a reflection of the incumbent's desire for self-aggrandisement but it most assuredly is an example of the best way to get a new solution to an old problem established in a welfare bureaucracy. The fact is that if a very able senior social worker runs IT and a very inept assistant director runs children's residential establishments then the chances of IT replacing the CHE as a solution to juvenile offending will remain slight. The internal politics of local authorities dictate that your success will be gauged by your rate of expansion and the velocity of your ascent through the hierarchy. You have done the job if you have done more things to more people in more places. For the purposes of evaluation in the informal power structure of the social services bureaucracy, meals on wheels and IT are regarded similarly. Both are innovative, both respond to the needs of rate-payers and while the efficacy of the former is calculated on the basis of prunes down throats the efficacy of the latter is calculated on the basis of bodies up mountains.

Power is achieved in the process of expansion. The irony for professionals who wish to implement a non-interventionist strategy with young offenders is that in order to achieve the requisite power it is necessary to expand the means whereby one can intervene in the lives of young people.

While it is generally recognised that more than enough community-based provision exists to decant the entire CHE, detention centre and youth custody population into the community, the role of IT as a political base from which to exert influence on local authority child-care policy requires it to keep growing.

This need for perpetual growth is fuelled by the nature of the funding of IT provision. Much IT provision has been jointly developed by the voluntary and statutory sectors and local and central government, and it is therefore subject to the requirements placed on it by funding agencies, both governmental and voluntary. The funding agencies are usually enthusiastic about innovation and tend to be unimpressed by projects which just keep on doing the same thing to the same kinds of young people just because it works. They want to put their money into something new and innovative, something, one suspects, for which they will be remembered. This places IT workers who want to keep doing what they already do because it works, in something of a dilemma. They therefore come up with something new, innovative, exciting and based squarely on what they already do so that what they already do is not jeopardised. Thus in order to achieve sufficient political influence, and in order to retain existing provision, projects must grow and change. Growth and change involve intervention in new, previously unreached populations.

The motivation of those embroiled in the politics of entrepreneurism may be pristine but once at the wheel of the IT juggernaut very delicate steering is necessary in order to avoid transforming what started out as an attempt to restore the prisoner to the community into a means whereby the prison, in the form of expanded intensive IT provision is imposed on the community. What we do know about control systems leads us to believe that where space exists it will be filled irrespective of levels of crime or levels of social need.

To argue that the structure of local authority social services departments and the requirements of central government and voluntary funding have tended to push IT in the direction of opportunism is not to suggest that IT is unique in this. Radical welfare and delinquency management as movements of professional academics and welfare workers operating within the educational and welfare apparatuses were equally opportunistic. Each had an investment in suppressing inconvenient bits of social reality and emphasising others. Each set out to get more power and more money in order that its solution would triumph over other people's solutions. Each sought to establish its definition of reality and demolish other definitions. Each was ultimately limited in its reforming endeavour by the position it came to occupy in the welfare apparatus.

Politics and ideas

The politics of reform in the juvenile criminal justice system in the period from 1969 to date has been a politics elaborated by radical professionals within the system rather than political activists beyond the system or groupings of the clients or subjects of that system. Attempts to elaborate reforming alliances beyond the system like 'new approaches to juvenile crime' or 'keep out' have invariably met with failure. NACRO and the Howard League speak up if an excess or anomaly is reported in the press, while PROP and RAP can barely function through lack of money and support.

The ideas and activities of these radical professionals have undergone a remarkable transformation over the period. Commentators on juvenile justice have maintained that the emergence and popularisation of new ideas in this field is an example of a theoretical 'survival of the fittest' in which theories and ideas, by the sheer force of their explanatory power or practical relevance, elbow their way to the fore. This Darwinian explanation, had it been pursued to its logical conclusion, would however have suggested that ideas and theories, like species, survive because they adapt to a changing and sometimes worsening environment. It is not necessarily the explanatory power of the theory which ensures its popularity but its adaptability to a changed political environment which encourages the emergence of some theories and the suppression of other, equally plausible, ones.

The development in the early 1970s of a practice of radical welfare found its intellectual rationale in ideas and assumptions derived from the 'opportunity theory' developed by Cloward and Ohlin (1960). There were a number of possible 'readings' of this theory. It could have been read as a remarkably fatalistic account of the structural barriers to any significant redistribution of wealth and opportunity in American society. It was read by would-be social interventionists, however, as an injunction to apply community action methods in order to help lower-class communities get themselves organised into an additional tier of local government so that their discontent could be channelled via the formal political process. This was certainly the reading of the Wilson government and it served as the rationale for the creation of the Community Development Projects and the Educational Priority Areas. Workers in these projects who held new left sympathies read opportunity theory as an injunction to help the lumpen proletariat mobilise for the struggle which was to hasten the demise of a corrupt capitalist social order.

Opportunity theory did a lot of things for a lot of people but in both Britain and the USA it was adopted in the first instance by governments as a solution to the problem that the existing social and political order was facing in its attempt to retain credibility and legitimacy with the politically marginalised and potentially disruptive residents of the inner city. The fact that other theorists had levelled serious criticisms at Cloward and Ohlin's formulations was completely irrelevant in terms of the co-option of the theory by governments which needed a plausible do-able academically respectable solution.

Adopted in this way opportunity theory in its endlessly vulgarised versions described what ought to be done and what central and local government was prepared to spend money on. Radicals 'radicalised' opportunity theory but worked within its intellectual parameters because that was where the work was. They worked on a government-defined problem, operationalising a government co-opted theory, implementing a government-defined solution, financed by government money. The new left did not invent 'radical welfare', they adapted it from the community action approach commended to them by the government.

The usual accounts of the historical emergence of particular theories also ignore the issue that for the radical professional the first prerequisite of professional survival is to stay relevant. For professionals to be taken seriously it is necessary for them to annexe a body of theory which supports their claim to specialist knowledge and skills unknown and unavailable to non-professionals. A problem arises however if, as happened during the 1970s and 1980s, the Home Office, the probation service, and local authority social services departments in their dealings with young offenders begin to distance themselves from traditional social work responses and to speak of 'hard-headed', 'no-nonsense', usually a euphemism for behavioural, approaches to young offenders. It certainly seemed by the mid-1970s, with the rise of a right-wing intelligentsia and the 'decline of the rehabilitative ideal' in criminology and penology, that the days of traditional social work, based on a diluted version of Freudian psychoanalysis, were numbered. This shift was fuelled by financial cutbacks in social welfare budgets which meant that there were fewer and fewer workers to undertake traditional social work. This was of course the era in which 'brief focal work' and 'contracts' gained currency in the social work vocabulary, for these innovations, neither of them new, offered the possibility of dealing with more people, more purposefully, and hence more cheaply. Two messages were passed down the line from government to the probation service and local authority social services departments. The first was that the government wanted to see more control being exerted over young offenders by social workers if social work was to retain any relevance in the juvenile criminal justice system. The second was that local authorities should reduce their expenditure on residential care. The minimalist assumptions of the back to justice movement and the technological cost-cutting pragmatism of delinquency management offered the possibility of ideological acceptability. The time for a politics of reality had arrived.

Whereas traditional social work had offered intervention, the message of the politics of reality was 'radical non-intervention'. Their project was to minimise formal intervention in the lives of young offenders. They wanted less government, a diminished social work, and hence a less pervasive welfare state. Their theoretical mainstay was labelling theory.

Now as every sociology student knows, one of the problems with labelling theory is that it does not tell us why people choose to deviate in the first place. What they also know is that labelling theory gives us an inadequate account of the sources of social reaction suggesting as it does that the problem of social reaction is dealt with if we stop welfare professionals, psychiatric nurses, and police officers saying bad things about people. Labelling theory does offer an interesting, albeit speculative, account of why some people may deviate on a subsequent occasion if bad things are said about them. The problem is that the available empirical evidence suggests that although the dramatic official labelling involved in a court appearance may serve to project some defendants into a future deviant career, the majority of young offenders only appear in court once and this could suggest that such official intervention, or labelling, actually prevents the development of a deviant career.

On the face of it then, labelling theory, which is not without its merits, seems to offer a shaky set of premises from which to market the solution to the problem of juvenile crime on a national and indeed an international scale. Its explanatory power was not great but it gave a professionally respectable theoretical underpinning to an endeavour which fitted well with the ideological and political imperatives of the time in which it was launched. Similarly we see the politically timely emergence of a revitalised Pavlovian behaviourism in the 'correctional curriculum' of the contemporary intensive IT programme. If the response to young offenders is to resemble a sentence of the court, eschew considerations of social need, and fit into a classical justice model, it must be based on a time-limited intervention which assumes that its subjects are motivated by the pursuit of pleasure and the avoidance of pain, and effect rational choices about their own behaviour. This is abominable sociology, poor psychology, but a good example of a political initiative which attempts to placate an increasingly predatory bench and government.

It seems clear that in these circumstances theory is adopted pragmatically in order to achieve a rationale for a necessary movement in a necessary direction. The movement is necessitated by the need to remain indispensable. Continuing indispensability in a rapidly changing world requires speed and flexibility. Continuing professional credibility requires a knowledge base which professionals can claim for their own. Change indispensability and professional credibility mean that theories must be adopted and dropped with equal alacrity. Thus the emergence of a 'new' theory does not signify a further step in a progression towards a new enlightenment, it may signal no more than the fact that 'radical professionals' and 'radical' welfare academics have effected a different adaptation in a changing political climate in order to ensure their continued relevance and presence in a law and order discourse which seems to be attempting to emancipate itself from social work.

The structure of the politics of reform
Radical professionals have striven to achieve a 'radicalisation' of face-to-face practice at certain points. In *Working with Offenders*

(Walker and Beaumont, 1985), a collection of articles by socialists working within the probation service, most of the contributors seem to be arguing that the job of socialists in welfare is to (a) humanise service delivery, (b) minimise authoritarianism, and (c) give clients an experience of participatory (socialist) forms of working:

> Being treated in a normal humane manner is often a pleasant surprise for these clients who have been previously treated to the exigencies of the 'deep' case worker. This style of working is also a positive antidote to another pressure that bears upon the officer- client relationship — the need to encourage conformity to a set of values promulgated by the criminal justice system. (Kirwin, 1985: 39)

These are laudable professional objectives but they do not, in themselves, constitute exclusively 'socialist' responses. The radicalism, indeed the courage, of these initiatives, resides in their espousal of humanitarian values in an authoritarian era. The irony is apparently compounded as the contributors discuss the radicalisation of practice in the court, in the prison, and in the day training centre because they advocate an internal radical practice for an expanding system of authoritarian control which the editors identified and bemoaned in their previous volume (Walker and Beaumont, 1982).

These socialist probation officers annexe, rework and give a radical edge to ideas and practices developed in the mainstream of the profession. This is necessary because it is difficult, if not impossible, to derive specific practices from the vast and contradictory body of Marxist writings. It is primarily necessary however because, as I have argued above, the population to be dealt with and the range of possible interventions and resources available to deal with them is given by the political, administrative, and bureaucratic imperatives which structure the service. Practitioners do have a degree of professional autonomy but they are not free to specify the goals to be achieved by the service. They have the freedom to impose a radical style on their practice rather than to develop a full-blown radical practice because a precondition for a radical practice would be that political and administrative imperatives would be changed to reflect socialist, and hence in the current political environment, oppositional and indeed subversive goals and values.

The question is raised then, whether it matters if the practitioner is an anarchist, a black separatist, or a Seventh-day Adventist. The answer seems to be that to the client it probably matters but it matters somewhat less to employers and governments. It matters less because the importance of an expanding control system lies in its capacity to exert more control and surveillance over more people. The style of that control is of less political significance than the extension of the state's machinery of control which allows it to 'keep an eye on', and exert control over, more wrong-doers.

> The bourgeoisie is interested in power, not in madness, in the system of control of infantile sexuality, not in that phenomenon itself. The bourgeoisie could not care less about delinquents, about their punishment and rehabilitation, which economically have little importance, but it is concerned about the complex of mechanisms with which delinquency is controlled, pursued, punished and reformed. (Foucault, 1977: 102)

Working with Offenders describes not merely a style of work, but a much more audacious attempt by socialist probation officers to transform practice as a step towards the achievement of a socialist transformation. The sophistication of their approach, and what distinguishes it from other approaches described, is that it attempts to operate at the levels of face-to-face practice, administrative change and parliamentary politics simultaneously. In this way it addresses the potential contradiction in which the reformer merely serves to legitimise and soften the image of repressive systems. At the moment socialists hold political power in the National Association of Probation Officers (NAPO). NAPO has the distinction among groupings of professionals in welfare that it is simultaneously a professional association, a trade union, and a penal pressure group. Its members occupy a strategic position in the justice system and have been able, as we have seen, to resist the extensions of control into the community proposed by the 'reinforced supervision' of the Younger report (HMSO, 1974) and the 'curfew' of the Criminal Justice Act 1982. In these instances NAPO has used its muscle as a trade union to exert negative control on behalf of, and in the interests of, its actual and potential clientele and arguably the entire community. NAPO's major struggle through the 1970s was to resist pressure from central government and the upper echelons of the probation service itself to become a community correctional service and assume a more controlling and coercive role in relation to its clients. NAPO's industrial action has slowed and modified these developments but it remains the case that the radical practices advocated in *Working with Offenders* are to be practised in the new institutions, and as facets of the new work roles created by this extension of the apparatus of control. It is this realisation which has taken NAPO over the threshold of the politics of abolition. Bill Beaumont writes:

> A fundamental criticism of social casework is its failure to tackle economic and social problems faced by clients. Campaigning work offers one way of overcoming that limitation. It may produce reforms which make a more significant widespread and long-term contribution to the welfare of the

client group than individual assistance ever could. Thus for PROP, if the removal of imprisonment were brought about, it would at a stroke remove the need for hundreds of mopping-up operations . . . There is considerable potential for campaigning work to become an integral part of probation work, routinely drawing upon the experience of practice to press for relevant change. (Beaumont, 1985: 90–1)

Whereas for the NAPO practitioner/activist attempts to resist the spread of control are pursued on the basis of the collective action of trade unionists applying pressure on behalf of their clients, for the 'delinquency managers' such action is initiated by the upper echelons of the welfare bureaucracy and is imposed on practitioners from above by administrative fiat. If the actions of NAPO in the sphere of reform can be described as radical collectivism, those of the delinquency managers could be described as radical authoritarianism. The approach is determined by the political assumptions of those with the power to impose their solutions. Socialist welfare professionals will try to create a lateral political alliance, seeing the collective action of practitioners as a solution. The radical liberalism of the delinquency management approach will locate the problem in the unfettered opportunism of welfare professionals and find the solution in an alliance with a senior management group which has an interest in cutting expenditure.

Whereas NAPO has resisted the concentration of power in the hands of senior management, delinquency management actively promotes such a concentration and yet both claim to do this to protect the client from unwarranted surveillance and control. The delinquency management and back to justice perspectives assume that a concern for social need must lead inevitably to an extension of control. It is for this reason that they are only prepared to countenance responses to offending which are effectively sentences of the court and in which the exclusive focus is on the offence. Socialists in probation by contrast would argue that a concern for social need rather than individual criminality should remain at the centre of any intervention with clients. They argue this because they see the attempt by management to push them towards an exclusive focus upon offending as an attempt to implicate them in the extension of control. They also see an aspect of the need of the client as the need to be afforded protection from the incursions of the apparatus of control by the probation officer. This need is addressed through the development of an internal radical practice linked to industrial action which attempts to resist the transformation of the service into a 'community correctional' apparatus. Over and above this the attempt by NAPO to enter the law and order debate by developing an abolitionist alliance from its base in the trade union movement has been a successful one, in which NAPO has added a radical voice to an issue previously dominated by the Prison Officers' Association (POA). This indicates that the requirements for a radical socialist practice, that it should operate simultaneously at the levels of political change, administrative change and face-to-face practice are beginning to be addressed.

NAPO is a particular and peculiar case but it offers an interesting model of a potential politics of penal reform which overcomes some of the limitations of the new left radical welfare initiatives and the endeavours of delinquency management and back to justice. Probation is an intrinsic part of the justice system, its practitioners are officers of the court and the court could not function without them, they are relevant and necessary. The centrality of probation to the justice system means that probation officers are not ideologically ghettoised with their clients. These are structural advantages. What the NAPO initiative has and what the early politics of the new left and the 'politics of reality' lacked is an analysis of the state which moves beyond its bland representation as either an omnipotent malevolent force or a potentially benign but inept monolith harbouring greedy professional entrepreneurs.

The abolitionism developed within NAPO is at odds with the abolitionism developed by Mathiesen (1974). The struggle for Mathiesen lies beyond finding the right kind of accommodation with a law and order state. It is far beyond the development of an internal radical practice, which he repudiates in favour of a politics of attrition to be mobilised in the struggle to minimise the power and effectiveness of the state apparatus. At this point, Mathiesen's minimalist politics of abolition coincides with the politics of reality of delinquency management and back to justice. He repudiates all radical humanitarian practice as merely serving to legitimise an intrinsically repressive state apparatus. While negative reform might be the key to a socialist abolitionist strategy, in its repudiation of all state activity it is also naive.

In the late 1960s and early 1970s the new left attacked the educational and welfare bureaucracies as the velvet glove masking the iron fist of the capitalist state. When in the mid-1970s the capitalist state began to dismantle the educational and welfare bureaucracies a, by this time slightly more sophisticated, left attempted to defend these services against the government axe. This was neither pure pragmatism nor protest for its own sake, because by this time the left was beginning to recognise that the state was a more complex phenomenon than had previously been assumed. The realisation dawned that if the, admittedly vestigial, welfare state was merely a mask for the conspiratorial intentions of the board of directors of 'capitalism UK' then either the state was acting against its own best interests in dismantling services during a time of economic recession or there was more to the welfare state than a shabby bit of political legitimation. The realisation dawned that the welfare state grew out of a struggle between the labour movement and the owners of capital in which, in the interests of social stability, and the creation of the necessary social and economic conditions for capital accumulation, concessions were granted (see Saville, 1957). Thus, the contradictions notwithstanding, the welfare state grew out of and remained a site upon which the class struggle had been and could be enacted (see Rowbotham et al., 1979). This same ambiguity, these same contradictions, were also seen to a lesser extent to characterise the justice system. It therefore became possible to be 'in and against the state' (London–Edinburgh Return Group, 1977) and to maximise the benefits and minimise the oppressive aspects of the welfare state on behalf of the poor.

If this analysis was correct then Mathiesen's, admittedly brilliant, formulation was too bland, and abolitionism in the form of the demand for negative reforms could in fact be squared with the maximisation of benefits and responses to the needs of disadvantaged offenders. This is what the NAPO initiative attempts to do. Their 'neo-abolitionism' emerges as the most sophisticated and thoroughgoing reforming initiative to be developed by radical professionals.

NAPO is effective because its organisational structure and its range of functions are similar to those of other groupings which are trying to gain some political leverage in the adult justice system. As an organisation it has adapted well to its political environment. The POA, like NAPO, is a trade union, a professional association and a political pressure group. The Magistrates' Association may represent amateurs but as a defender of a closed shop and restrictive practices it puts many trade unions into the shade. It is certainly the case that the Magistrates' Association, as a pressure group, exerts considerable influence on Tory governments. The Police Federation as a professional association and political pressure group has had a considerable impact on law and order policies. NAPO is the least powerful of the four groups but it holds some power by dint of the indispensability and centrality of the probation officer within the adult justice system.

Statutory or voluntary workers within the juvenile criminal justice system may belong to NALGO, NUPE or ASTMS, none of which has an exclusive interest in social work, let alone the concerns of social workers and IT workers working with young offenders. They may be members of the social work's professional association BASW but

BASW only has a subcommittee dealing with juvenile justice issues and this is not a permanent feature of the association. They may support the pressure group activity of the National IT Federation or the Association for Juvenile Justice or the Howard League or the NCCL but each of these has a slightly different view of what the main issues are in the juvenile justice debate.

The role of the social worker in the juvenile criminal justice system is neither central nor indispensable. IT remains an optional extra in the range of juvenile court disposals and even then the bench has to be persuaded of its usefulness. It is for these reasons that social work and IT have been fairly ineffective participants in the politics of reform. The radicals in NAPO have demonstrated an ability to carry the bulk of the membership with them on a range of issues because NAPO has been able to relate the radicalism of its policies to the professional and personal interests of probation officers. By contrast, social work with young offenders and IT is characterised by dissension and factionalism. Regional IT associations are periodically devastated by feuds between those who wish to do 'preventive work' and those who maintain that IT must only work with adjudicated offenders. IT workers attack social workers as the cause of the problem. Social workers sometimes indict IT workers as irresponsible anarchists who tacitly condone the bad behaviour of their clients but are unprepared to take any responsibility for them or to exert any control over them.

If an effective reforming alliance is to be constructed in the juvenile criminal justice system it might usefully consider what lessons can be learnt from the experience of NAPO. There appear to be six central principles which characterise the NAPO initiative. An effective alliance will act simultaneously to:

1. represent the interests of workers in its role as a trade union;
2. represent the interests of its clients in its role as a pressure group;
3. promote the development of a radical practice in its role as a professional association.

This radical practice will operate at three different levels simultaneously:

4. by developing an internal humanitarian face-to-face practice;
5. by attempting to effect administrative and bureaucratic change, either by initiating a systems management initiative controlled by basic grade officers, or by industrial action against management;
6. by developing an external abolitionist politics which contests current penal and judicial policies and the rhetoric of law and order through the construction of political alliances within and beyond the mainstream of the labour movement.

The politics of victimisation

What the politics of the new left, the politics of opportunism, the politics of reality, and the more sophisticated new left politics of contemporary NAPO do not address and what parliamentary politics in the 1980s and the 1990s must inevitably address are the causes of juvenile crime and the plight of the victims of juvenile crime. This preoccupation will inevitably steer political attention towards the inner city, it will inevitably focus on the black populations of the inner city and it will do this because it is these populations who, on the face of it, produce an inordinate number of victims, and an inordinate number of perpetrators, of juvenile crime (Lea and Young, 1984). The questions will concern the origins of predatory juvenile crime, the conditions which lead to victimisation and the origins and nature of social reaction in areas characterised by high levels of juvenile crime.

Radical professionals who have, by and large, been able to ignore causes and victims for a decade, will have to rethink their reforming project if they are to stay in the business of reform. If they wish to rethink their reforming project then they might usefully consider the Brixton Triangle.

7   The Brixton Triangle

To the right wing, 'law and order' is often just a code phrase meaning 'get the niggers'.

Gore Vidal

Today Brent — tomorrow Soweto.

Paul Boateng, 1987

The Bermuda Triangle is an area in the Caribbean bounded by the Bahamas, North Carolina, and Bermuda where people in boats and aeroplanes mysteriously disappear. Scientists using all the tools available to them are unable to account for these disappearances.

The Brixton Triangle is an area in south London bounded by Clapham Common, Tulse Hill and the Oval where young black people who commit offences, or are suspected of being about to commit offences, mysteriously disappear. Criminologists using all the tools available to them are unable to account for these disappearances.

Where did they go?

In 1982 an assistant governor at Wandsworth jail monitored the daily intake to that prison by colour and discovered that 23 per cent of the intake was black. Of the broader picture Martin Kettle (1982) wrote:

> In April this year according to the Home Office 50% of the population of Ashford remand centre was black. Brixton (another remand prison) and Aylesbury prisons were between 25% and 35% black. So were Rochester, Dover, and Hewell Grange borstals and Blantyre House detention centre. Others with more than 10% black inmates were Wormwood Scrubs, Parkhurst, Albany, Wandsworth and Reading prisons and Wellingborough, Bulwood Hall and Feltham borstals.

As we move down the age range so the proportion of black inmates confined in custodial institutions increases. While the Home Office contends that the Afro-Caribbean population in the penal system constitutes only 8 per cent of male and 12 per cent of female prisoners a recent RAP report maintained that the overall black population in the prison system was in fact nearer 20 per cent but that in young prisoners' wings this figure rose to 37 per cent and as Kettle has noted in some borstals (now youth custody centres) the figure is as high as 50 per cent. When we recognise that the proportion of black people in the population of the United Kingdom is somewhere between 3 and 4 per cent this over-representation begins to appear ominous (*Statistical Bulletin*, 1986).

These facts are stark enough, yet the fastest-growing section of the penal population is the 15−21 age group which in 1984 constituted 20 per cent of those in prison. Indeed the 1982 Criminal Justice Act was in large part a response to this fact, and its apparent commitment to the development of community alternatives to prison is explicable in that the 'crisis in the prison' is nowhere more acute than in the institutions for this age group. If we recognise that young black people will over the next few years constitute an ever-increasing proportion of this population it becomes clear that a significant component in the crisis in the prison is the increasing confinement of young black people. On 1 November 1981, the TV programme *Skin* televised a feature on young black people in borstal in which it suggested that if current trends continued, by 1991 50 per cent of all black males under 25 would have spent some time behind bars.

Why conventional administrative criminology cannot find them

The mystery of these disappearances persists because criminologists working in the sphere of juvenile justice have operated within a paradigm which relegated all identified anomalies to the category of 'mistakes' perpetrated by low-level decision makers within the system itself. They have therefore been unable to explain 'the basic triangle of relations which is the proper subject matter of criminology — the offender, the state and the victim' (Young, 1986). What happens in the Brixton Triangle can only be explained in terms of this criminological triangle. The Brixton Triangle must be explained if progressives in the field of juvenile justice are to break out of the political ghetto, which they share with their subjects, and enter the politics of 'law and order' as serious contenders.

Throughout the 1970s criminologists only asked the question of the relation between crime and the state in terms of the relation between particular offenders and particular 'soft policemen' — social workers or probation officers, and the impact of the actions of the latter upon the former. The possibility of understanding changing patterns of juvenile crime, and state reaction to it, in relation to the radically changed political landscape of Britain in the 1970s and early 1980s was therefore abandoned. The bland acceptance within the conventional criminological endeavour of an oversimplified version of Durkheim's observation, suggested that since juvenile crime, like the poor, is always with us, then its form need not tax us unduly. By accepting juvenile crime as an undifferentiated monolith to be managed more humanely it becomes irrelevant to ask why in a particular place at a particular time particular people choose, are impelled towards, or are implicated in the transgression of particular laws. Similarly changes in state reaction to particular groups of offenders tend to be attributed to the emergence of scientifically-targeted policing strategies, while the incursions which these strategies may make into the lives and liberties of citizens merely serve as indicators that the strategy may need further refinement. On the margin are a few rotten apples who are irrational, bigoted, unscientific and a source of embarrassment to the rational core of senior police officers and politicians whose first priority is to deliver rational policing. As for the victims, Chubb locks, resident caretakers, video surveillance and the hope of better luck next time are the best that conventional administrative criminology can offer them. As a result the massive over-representation of black children and young people in child-care and custodial institutions, the disproportionate criminal victimisation of black citizens and the peculiar nature of the policing of the black community can only be explained as a series of technical errors rather than the logical consequence of broader political, economic and social determinants.

The political economy of the Brixton Triangle

Marginalisation

The Caribbean colonies existed on the margins of the British Empire. One-crop islands peopled by ex-slaves, they served initially as a source of inexpensive raw materials and as a market for manufactured goods. Subsequently they became a source of inexpensive labour for a metropolitan economy locked into the logic of perpetual expansion. When, in the 1950s, Caribbean people were welcomed 'home' by the British government to what Salman Rushdie (1982) describes as the 'last colony of the British Empire', they found that once again they were forced to the margins. In the twilight of the British Empire they came to live in the twilight zones of the chronically ailing inner city.

The Caribbean people who came to Britain in the 1950s came to fill jobs vacated by the indigenous white working class. The post-war economic boom had brought with it a bonanza in highly-paid skilled and semi-skilled jobs in the 'new' industries and white workers moved rapidly into these new work roles. The demand for labour was outstripping the supply and dirty, inconvenient, unskilled, poorly paid, un-unionised jobs in the 'old' industries in the inner city were abandoned by white workers in favour of new industries and new homes in the new towns.

The economic boom of the 1950s and 1960s was a white economic boom played out before a black audience. The 'embourgeoisement' of substantial sections of the white labour force was achieved at the expense of the 'lumpen proletarianisation' of black labour. As the expectation of perpetual prosperity became lodged in the minds of the white working class and the educational and occupational means of achieving these expectations expanded, black citizens had to reconcile themselves to a set of economic circumstances which looked worse and worse when set against the steadily improving circumstances of whites. The experience of lack of access to occupational and educational opportunity, and its consequences for earning power and social status, has been an enduring one for black Britons and the backdrop against which the events enacted within the Brixton Triangle have unfolded.

In the 1950s and the early 1960s black people were offered low-level jobs but they retained high hopes for their children. As workers they were marginalised because they had no power and no voice within the trade union movement. As citizens they were marginal to the major political parties and a parliamentary politics which had no place on its agenda for the hopes and fears of black people. It was a politics moreover which responded to the racist hopes, fears and fantasies of white people by the implementation of policies which sought to limit immigration from the black commonwealth and colonies by constantly redefining the category of 'British subject' more narrowly. The marginality of Britain's black citizens was compounded by this barely concealed political hostility.

To occupy the margins with hope of future centrality can make marginality more tolerable but by the mid- to late 1960s such hopes were dashed as it became clear to black parents that their children, irrespective of educational attainment, were being offered the same kinds of menial jobs as they had:

> A check of the London Youth Employment Offices by a correspondent of the *Observer* showed that white youths in the 'deprived' areas of black settlement such as Islington, Paddington and Notting Hill were almost five times more likely to get skilled jobs than coloured youngsters. Of the 147 firms dealing with the Youth Employment Offices, nearly half had stated 'No Coloured', or were known to be 'unlikely to accept them'. (Hiro, 1971: 75)

As the 1960s turned into the 1970s it became increasingly apparent that black young people were to be in the front line again as the British economy responded to the economic recession by laying off labour. Hunt and Mellor write:

The second generation's labour power is no longer needed. So Britain caught in the heritage of her colonial past, is now faced with a population of young black Britons culturally alienated by racism and disillusioned, initially by the type of work they were offered and more recently by perpetual unemployment. Their predicament exposes contradictions inherent in the immigrant's position from the outset. (Hunt and Mellor, 1980: 62–3)

These contradictions were not lost on a rising generation of black Britons experiencing levels of unemployment without precedent in British history. Black youth unemployment in Brixton is currently running at over 60 per cent. In Moss Side and Handsworth the figure is in excess of 80 per cent. By the late 1970s an entire generation of black young people had become, to all intents and purposes, marginal to the productive process (Guest, 1984; Hunt and Mellor, 1980).

Alienation

The economic recession of the 1970s and 1980s has been accompanied by a growing concern within government and among the upper echelons of the police about the threat to 'cultural integrity' and 'social order' posed by the black inhabitants of the 'unemployed ghetto'. These concerns have resulted in the reorganisation and concentration of police resources on the black community on the one hand, and a contraction in the numbers of people who may now be regarded as British subjects, with a consequent expansion in the numbers of people who may now be regarded as aliens, on the other.

In his written evidence to the Royal Commission on Criminal Procedure in 1978, Sir David McNee of the Metropolitan Police called for new police powers to allow them to 'finger-print whole communities in certain circumstances on the order of a High Court Judge'; 'powers, to be legalised and formalised to stop and search everybody'; and 'powers to search the homes of all persons who are arrested and taken to the police station on whatever charge'. In a similar vein the Select Committee on Race Relations and Immigration Report (1978) recommends that:

> the police, the Immigration Service Intelligence Unit and other authorities should be afforded substantially more resources to trace over-stayers and tackle all aspects of illegal immigration. We recommend that the Department of Health and Social Security introduce without delay new procedures to tighten up identity checks and to improve the issuing of national insurance numbers to new applicants. (Hunt and Mellor, 1980)

Margaret Thatcher expressed the prevailing mood in government and policing circles very clearly in 1979 when she spoke of 'our culture' being 'swamped'. Thatcher's strategy was not a new one, the attempt from the Heath government onwards to transform the economic crisis ideologically into a moral one had the effect of locating the Afro-Caribbean, and to a lesser extent the Asian, populations as parasitic and potentially subversive to cultural integrity and social order. Thus in the second half of the 1970s the police did not just make a mistake or over-react in their policing of black neighbourhoods. They were deployed as a response to crime but also in order to recapture 'illegals' and forestall anticipated violent social disorder. These important decisions about the deployment of manpower and resources were made at the highest levels of the police bureaucracy (Hall et al. , 1978). The state was not benign nor crime meaningless, and the police and the black community understood this much more clearly than orthodox criminology. The borderland between policing and the black community was 'sus' and the successive indiscriminate sweeps of black areas by special squads of police. The consequences of such policies were effectively to transform all black people into suspects and all police officers into racists, irrespective of the wishes or intentions of individual citizens or police officers.

The effect of these policing and immigration policies has been to freeze the black British citizen in political rhetoric and racist folklore as a subversive and potentially dangerous alien who haunts the streets of the inner city ready to mug, riot or rape. If this alien population cannot be dealt with by immigration control or a Nationality Act there are other means whereby their insidious impact may yet be neutralised.

Expulsion

Thomas Mathiesen writes:

> In our society 'productivity' is to a considerable and increasing degree geared to activity in the labour market. At the same time, our social structure probably increasingly creates groups which are 'unproductive' according to this criterion. A social structure which does so must rid itself of its unproductive elements, partly because their presence creates inefficiency in the system of production, it 'throws sand into the machinery' and partly because the 'unproductive' brutally remind us of the fact that our productive system is not so successful after all. A society may get rid of its 'unproductive' elements in many ways. One way is to criminalise their activities and punish them by imprisoning them. This may be done towards a sub- category of the unproductive. In this perspective the rulers of the prison system are merely the executives of the expurgatory system of society. (Mathiesen, 1974: 77)

Research undertaken by the Policy Studies Institute showed that black young people were the prime targets for police stop and search operations (Smith, 1983). Figures collected by probation officers in the Midlands indicate that the second highest category of offences for which young black people are charged arose out of confrontations with the police on the streets. These offences, 'criminal attempts', assault and threatening or insulting behaviour, did not occur until the police arrived (Pitts, 1986).

John Dennington (1981) notes that 'The offence of "Criminal Attempts" offers the police a more flexible instrument than the 1824 Vagrancy Act ('sus'). The "criminal attempts" bill was welcomed by the *Police Review* in an article entitled "Let's Have a Loophole" and the *New Law Journal* explained that the new offence could be useful "where firm dishonest intention cannot be established" .' The 'sus' controversy concerned the use of the law as a means of harassing black young people but 'sus'/criminal attempts has other consequences. In Lambeth, for example, a young person charged with 'sus' would seldom, as a matter of local practice, be offered the opportunity of being referred to the juvenile bureau which, if the charge is admitted, is empowered to issue a caution. Young people charged with 'sus' were normally charged immediately as a matter of course which meant that they had to appear in court. In court the complainant and the witnesses were almost invariably the police. On conviction the young person's name would be added to the 'recidivists' list which meant that if at some future date he or she was apprehended for whatever charge no referral to the juvenile bureau could be made and the young person would be charged immediately. This had the effect of projecting those young people so charged deeper into the juvenile criminal justice system and further up the 'tariff' of penalties.

Landau's study (1981) noted that 'sus' was the offence for which there was the greatest difference between races. He discovered that white young people were up to 50 per cent more likely to be referred to the juvenile bureau for this offence than their black counterparts. While it might be argued that this discrepancy could be accounted for by the fact that black youngsters so charged had a larger record of previous offences, Landau shows that black first offenders were subject to an immediate charge decision significantly more often than whites. The only area in which 'sus' was used more than in Lambeth was in Toxteth in Liverpool. Landau also noted that the police tended to see black young people as more antagonistic to them than whites and suggests that this may be a significant factor in the decision whether to charge immediately or refer to the juvenile bureau. In conclusion he writes: 'As to ethnic group, the main finding was that blacks involved in crimes of violence, burglary, and public disorder are treated more harshly than their white counterparts.'

Black young people are subject to more intensive policing than any other section of the population. Such policing generates further offences, and on apprehension black young people are less likely to be diverted out of the mainstream of the system to the juvenile bureau and this appears to be related to the threat that they are perceived to pose to public order and the authority of the police.

It is usually at the point of the court appearance that the young black defendant will first encounter a social worker or probation officer. Here a difference between white and black defendants appears, for there is growing evidence that a majority of young black people who become involved in the juvenile criminal justice system do so at a later stage than their white counterparts. Whereas many white juvenile defendants and their families may have been known to welfare agencies for many years, the involvement of young black people tends to start around the age of 14 or 15. Put another way — a distinctive feature of the 'criminal careers' of many young black people is that they are not characterised by prior involvement with welfare agencies concerned with other social or family problems. They are not in the main drawn from families who have previously been a cause of concern to welfare agencies. Observations of young black people in penal establishments tend to support this in that they appear to be more socially and academically able than their white counterparts. They are also much more likely to be drawn from 'respectable' rather than 'disreputable' families (Pitts, 1986).

What we are not seeing here is the apparently inexorable unfolding of a criminal and institutional career which may be traced back, sometimes over generations, but rather a rupture, a departure, from a previously conventional mode of existence by a group of young people, many of whom had until shortly before their first arrest been successful conforming schoolgirls and schoolboys (Pitts, 1986).

Wendy Taylor has shown that in the crown court black defendants are two to three times more likely to receive a custodial sentence than whites. These custodial sentences have very little to do with the nature of the offence but correlate most closely with whether the defendant is homeless, jobless, or was previously the subject of a care order. As a consequence of institutionalised racism, young black people experience extremely high levels of homelessness, they are much more likely than whites to be unemployed and their predicament is seriously worsened if they have previously been the subjects of a care order (Taylor, 1981). This inequitable sentencing is not simply reducible to the racial prejudice of particular judges since unemployed homeless offenders, black or white, have always been particularly vulnerable to imprisonment. These defendants are victims of structural inequalities which affect the black population in general but Afro-Caribbean young people in particular. They are being sentenced three times over. First for their offence, over which they have some control, second for a set of social, economic and cultural circumstances which have dramatically limited their options and over which they have no control, and third because there exist few, if any, legitimate means whereby they might escape from these circumstances.

Black young people tend to identify the magistrates' court as the place where the most blatantly prejudiced judgments are handed down. In a study undertaken in the West Midlands only 11 per cent of white young people charged with indictable offences opted for trial by jury in a crown court, whereas 43 per cent of black young people did. They claimed that the magistrates' courts were 'police courts' and there you only got 'white man's justice' and they hoped that in a crown court one of the jury might be black (Taylor, 1982).

When black young people enter child-care or penal institutions their problems are compounded. Many CHEs operate a racial quota system which attempts to prevent the proportion of black residents rising above 20 per cent. The quota system is, it is argued, necessitated by the problems of management posed by Afro-Caribbean young people when they are together in substantial numbers. This parallels exactly the complaints of the police, prison officers, and to a somewhat lesser extent, field social workers and probation officers. 'They band together', 'They speak their own language' and 'They intimidate other residents or members or prisoners' (WLIHE, 1982).

When staff in an institution feel threatened, devalued or misunderstood, they will often develop collective defences in which the inmates are attributed all the characteristics that most threaten the staff and so a vicious circle of which the quota system is both a cause and a consequence develops. The quota system has created a log-jam of young black people in remand and observation and assessment centres, the institutions which assess young people for placement in community homes (with education). Indeed Stamford House, a large remand and assessment centre for young offenders in West London, frequently holds a black population of 60 per cent.

The Home Office Prison department shares similar concerns to those expressed by some of the staff of the CHEs. Staff are concerned that the increase in the numbers of black people in prisons has led to changes in the relationship between the institutions of control and their black inmates. Cook (1982) writes of the Home Office seminar on ethnic minorities in prison:

> The seminar heard that frequently the superior physical and intellectual abilities of many black people have led to a growing black hold on traditional prison rackets like extortion and hoovering — taking food away from weaker inmates ... But the department has failed to establish the point at which the growing proportion will become a danger to stability.

The spectre of the black deviant who poses special problems of control looms again. Institutions which, it is suggested, were quietly getting on with the job, the erstwhile white-dominated rackets notwithstanding, are suddenly confronted by a new and threatening phenomenon. The response to the problems has two aspects. On the one hand the Home Office, in a spirit of enlightened pluralism, has ruled that Rastafarians will no longer have their locks removed by the prison barber, while on the other, black 'subversives' and 'ringleaders' are identified and dispersed around the prison system in an attempt to forestall anticipated 'race riots'. Thus it is that black young people are expelled from the unemployed ghetto into prisons where their ghettoisation is reproduced and the responses of the powerful are similarly fearful and short-sighted.

The phenomenology of the Brixton Triangle

Beliefs
This account of the political economy of the Brixton Triangle describes the objective constraints placed on its inhabitants by their economic and political predicament. The subjective experience of these constraints, the meaning imposed on them by those who experience them, will vary from person to person, and from time to time, and will as a consequence evoke very different responses. The political and economic circumstances which conspire to loosen the commitment of some people to the legal and moral order may well serve to reinforce that commitment in others. George Jackson writes:

> You know our people react in different ways to this neoslavery. Some just give up completely and join the other side. They join some Christian cult and cry out for integration. These are the ones who doubt themselves most. They are the weakest and hardest to reach with the new doctrine. Some become inveterate drinkers and narcotic users in an attempt to gain some mental solace for the physical deprivation they suffer. I've heard them say 'there's no hope without dope', some live on as janitor, bellboy, redcap, cook, elevator boy, singer, boxer, baseball player or maybe a freak at some sideshow and pretend that all is as well as possible. They think since its always been this way it must always remain this way, these are the fatalists; they serve and entertain and rationalise.
>
> Then there are those who resist and rebel but do not know what, who, why or how exactly they should go about this. They are aware but confused. They are the least fortunate because they end where I have ended. By using half-measures and failing dismally to effect any real improvement in their condition they fall victim to the full fury and might of the system's repressive agencies. (Jackson, 1971: 70–1)

If the deprived believe that their deprivation is deserved and unavoidable they are likely to respond with stoicism and sadness. If, by contrast, they believe that their deprivation is an undeserved but unavoidable tribulation they may attempt to transcend it by spiritual means:

> The otherworldly posture accounts for the doctrinal importance of the beatitudes in the ideology of saints. By diverting their attention in a heavenly direction and explaining away the real objective causes of their predicament, the doctrine of the beatitudes helps saints cope with their sense of alienation and powerlessness. This expectantly otherworldly focus is responsible for the charge, sometimes levelled against them, that they are 'so heavenly-minded, they are no earthly use'. (Pryce, 1979: 211)

If however, they believe their deprivation to be undeserved and avoidable then they are likely to respond with anger, challenging the rules and practices which appear to compound their deprivation. It is this belief which propels the subject into a critical confrontation with the prevailing legal and moral order. The manner in which this critical confrontation is expressed will be determined by opportunity.

Opportunity

If we disagree with laws, rules and practices we may, if the opportunity exists, enter the political process and attempt to change them. Alternatively if we believe that laws, rules and practices compound the deprivation of our people because of the discriminatory manner of their application we may aspire, if the opportunity exists, to become lawyers, teachers and business administrators in order to ensure their just application. If we are politically marginalised and denied educational and occupational opportunity and we believe that the laws, rules and practices which are applied to us merely compound our deprivation then we can live silently with the pain and frustration or break the rules. Our beliefs will then become manifest in our actions. Dodd states the matter thus:

> The welfare state is seen on the street as another means of keeping blacks helpless and dependent. It leaves nothing to risk and provides no structure for action — except in designing schemes to manipulate it advantageously. It is just another white man's game for which the black man must as always invent his own response. The problem is how to construct a serious identity outside the roles that are offered — a problem of meaning as well as survival. Well, there is meaning in ganga and there is meaning in crime. For increasing numbers of black youth these are the only real options. (Dodd, 1978: 25)

To suggest that to hold certain beliefs about one's predicament makes crime an option for young people, who, with different beliefs and different opportunities, would shun the option, is not to suggest that crime becomes either inevitable, or central to their way of life.

Crime is an option which comes, in certain circumstances, to exist alongside other, conventional options:

> The available accounts clearly show that few young blacks confront a clear choice between the options of hard labour and crime, and settle permanently for one strategy or another. One of the precipitating factors is precisely a difference in attitude to the problems of survival between the two generations . . . All the evidence suggests that the numbers now forced to survive in these ways on the margin of the legal life are increasing directly in line with the numbers unemployed and that the age limit of those involved is dropping. (Hall et al., 1978: 358–9)

The bond which ties these young people to the conventional world is loosened as they grow more marginal to social and economic life. Their commitment to the dominant moral and legal order is conditioned by their stake in the dominant social and economic order. Put simply, 'when you've got nothing, you've got nothing to lose'.

The black children and the young people who inhabit the Brixton Triangle feel cheated. Their parents had hoped for a better life for their children. They had hoped that their children, like the children of previous waves of immigrants to the United Kingdom, would achieve material success and enhanced social status. Their teachers in the Caribbean had assured them that in the land of the mother of parliaments, and the fairest police force in the world, every citizen of the British Empire would be equal before the law and free to succeed. Instead the experience has been one of downward social mobility, material failure, and eventual ghettoisation. Immigration to Britain in the past 100 years has been characterised by a first generation with low social status and a relatively high crime rate which is transformed by a process of absorption and dispersal into a second and subsequent generation with higher social status and a low crime rate. The low-status immigrant group simply disappears into the existing class structure. In contrast the first wave of Afro-Caribbean immigrants was a remarkably law-abiding section of the population (Lambert, 1970). In the subsequent thirty years, however, levels of crime among Afro-Caribbean people have risen to, and in certain categories exceeded, the crime rates of the indigenous populations.

Black people in Britain have not disappeared into the existing class structure in the way that the Huguenots, Poles, Jews and Italians did and in Britain racial invisibility is a prerequisite of social mobility. The residents of the Brixton Triangle cannot achieve social mobility because they are black and hence racially visible. Their economic and political predicament has transformed these black British citizens into a beleaguered black underclass trapped in the unemployed ghetto of the Brixton Triangle.

The economic and political predicament which generates higher levels of crime also generates higher rates of victimisation, Lea and Young note:

> . . . a young black male (aged between twelve and fifteen) is twenty-two times more likely to have a violent crime committed against him than an elderly white woman (over 65), and seven times more likely to have something stolen from him. Thus the objective likelihood of serious crime occurring to a person is sharply focussed by locality and by the social characteristics of a person. (Lea and Young, 1984: 26)

In Britain and the United States black men and women are at much greater risk from crime than white men and women. Whereas deaths of white males by homicide in the USA are 9.2 per million, deaths of black males by homicide are 52.6 per million. Similarly a poor black woman in the USA is almost six times more likely to be raped than a rich white woman. Both serious and trivial crimes will tend to be perpetrated by young working-class men and it will be intra-class and intra-racial. Poor young white men tend to steal from and hurt poor white people. Poor young black men tend to steal from and hurt poor black people. Most juvenile crime is in this sense ghettoised. It is usually neither a political act in which the poor reappropriate the wealth of the rich nor is it a tightly organised conspiracy of feckless predators against the virtuous. It is sadder and more self-defeating than either of these crude political stereotypes suggests. It is usually episodic, unplanned, opportunistic and, often, a complete shambles. In central Lambeth the most likely perpetrators and the most likely victims of street crime will be young black men aged between 10 and 18 (Pratt, 1980). If you live on an inner-city housing estate the chances are that the person who burgles your flat will live in the same, or an adjacent, block of flats and you will probably have known them prior to the burglary.

The effect of these high levels of victimisation in the Brixton Triangle is corrosive and cumulative. James Q. Wilson writes:

> Predatory crime does not merely victimise individuals, it impedes, and in the extreme case, even prevents the formation and maintenance of community. By disrupting the delicate nexus of ties, formal and informal, by which we are linked with our neighbours, crime atomises society and makes of its members mere individual calculators estimating their own advantage, especially their own chances for survival amidst their fellows. Common undertakings become difficult or impossible, except for those motivated by a shared desire for protection. (Wilson, 1975: 21)

Wilson describes the conditions which promote a 'ghetto mentality', as does Harrison:

> But it is not just the facilities that suffer: it is the solidarity of the community itself. Redevelopment, migration and the rapid turnover of people seeking

better accommodation means there is precious little of that to start with. But crime dissolves it even further. The climate of fear engenders a defensive egotism of survival, in which everyone looks after themselves. A new code of ethics emerges: that thy days may be long, thou shalt not question strangers on the stairs; thou shalt not look if thou hearest screams or shattering glass; thou shalt not admonish youths for vandalism; thou shalt not admit to witnessing a crime; thou shalt not help the victim of an attack. (Harrison, 1983: 282)

So it is that levels of reported crime are lowest in areas where victimisation is highest. The police response has been to intensify their military-style policing which serves only to alienate the population so policed still further (Lea and Young, 1984).

What reformers might learn from the Brixton Triangle is that if we are serious in our wish to defend the children of the poor we must also address the conditions which make it necessary to defend them from each other. Black children and young people are the victims of a predatory and unjust system of justice and punishment but they are also the victims of predatory and unjust crime perpetrated against them. The perpetrators and the victims have been inserted into the social script of the Brixton Triangle in which individual choice plays only a minor part in determining the role they will act out in the drama. Any strategy which simply attempts to manipulate the justice system and leaves the social, political and economic factors which contrive to abandon a generation of black children and young people in the Brixton Triangle untouched, will inevitably fail. The problem is one of a profound social dislocation which cannot be met by yet another ineffective attempt to manipulate the law or the practices of a group of police officers or a particular juvenile bench. Reformers must address those profound structural social factors which precipitate the crime, victimisation and mundane misery of life in the Brixton Triangle. Saul Bellow states the problem with characteristic bleakness and clarity:

We are talking about a people consigned to destruction, a doomed people. Compare them to the last phase of the proletariat as pictured by Marx. The proletariat, owning nothing, stripped utterly bare, would awaken at last from the nightmare of history. Entirely naked, it would have no illusions because there was nothing to support illusions and it would make a revolution without any scenario. It would need no historical script because of its merciless education in reality, and so forth. Well here is a case of people denuded. And what's the effect of denudation, atomization? Of course, they aren't proletarians. They're just a lumpen population. We do not know how to approach this population. We haven't even conceived that reaching it may be a problem. So there's nothing but death before it. Maybe we've already made our decision. Those that can be advanced to the middle class, let them be advanced. The rest? Well, we do our best by them. We don't have to do any more. They kill some of us. Mostly they kill themselves . . . . (Bellow, 1982: 205)

8 Thinking about theory

Mirek is as much a rewriter of history as the Communist Party, all political parties, all nations, all men. People are always shouting they want to create a better future — it's not true. The future is an apathetic void of no interest to anyone. The past is full of life, eager to irritate us, provoke and insult us, tempt us to destroy or repaint it. The only reason people want to be masters of the future is to change the past. They are fighting for access to the laboratories where photographs are retouched and biographies and histories re-written.

Milan Kundera, *The Book of Laughter and Forgetting*

Back to the future

The history of the theory and practice of juvenile justice in Britain from 1959 is, to a considerable extent, a history of the perpetual and apparently random repudiation and replacement of one set of ideas by another. It is a process in which yesterday's theory or practice is attacked, dismantled, buried and, if the attacker is lucky, forgotten. Theoretical and practical orthodoxies are periodically recycled in a slightly different guise. For a time they hold sway, and then collapse in a hail of ridicule all too often emanating from erstwhile adherents who abandoned the position when they realised that its days were numbered. It is a process in which today's great new idea is often yesterday's idea standing on its head.

The examination of the intimacies of the mother-child relationship is abandoned in favour of opportunity theory. But opportunity theory, an expression of Durkheimian and Mertonian structuralism, is jettisoned within a few years in favour of a labelling perspective for which the concept of 'social structure' is effectively non-existent.

Social work intervention in the lives of children and young people in trouble which aims to help them improve the quality of their relationships with their families and adult authority figures is out. 'Radical non-intervention' is in. Yesterday's social worker was a human resource who brought material help and a scientifically informed sympathy. Today's social worker is a malevolent agent of creeping totalitarianism.

These astonishing paradigm shifts are effected without the turn of a hair. It is a sequential, not a dialectical, process and no synthesis of ideas or practices is either attempted or achieved. Ideas and practices are suddenly right or wrong, good or bad, in or out. What this is *not*, although it occasionally attempts to pass itself off as if it were, is a Popperian project of conjecture and refutation. It *is* a process of intellectual entrepreneurism and professional asset-stripping. Ideas and practices are abused in this way because ultimately their integrity and veracity is of less significance than their capacity to act as vehicles for ideologues and practitioners who wish to exert control over the ways in which the issue of juvenile crime is conceptualised and the juvenile criminal is managed. As we have seen, the history of the theory and practice of juvenile justice is, perhaps inevitably, the history of a struggle for power and control rather than a simple progression towards enlightenment and humanitarianism. The most damaging consequence of this is that a heritage of theory and practice is lost from sight in the pursuit of politically acceptable novelty and the promotion of theoretical amnesia.

The retreat from novelty and amnesia: come home, Emile Durkheim, all is forgiven
The consequences of the quest for novelty, the pursuit of political acceptability, the furtherance of sectional interest and pragmatism are all too evident. We have more police officers, magistrates, social workers, probation officers and prison officers doing more and more things to an ever-expanding army of, frequently unemployed, frequently homeless, frequently black, adolescents whose 'crimes' grow less and less serious. Prison sentences grow longer as 'alternative to custody' projects, and the victims of street crime, burglary, and auto-theft grow more numerous.

The ideology that nothing can, or should, be done about the 'social' causes of crime, and that the onus of intervention should be placed instead on the more effective or 'humane' management of deviant populations, has misfired alarmingly. The decision taken by many people professionally involved in the juvenile justice process to treat questions of poverty, race, and law and order as an irrelevance and to concentrate instead on the modification of the behaviour of social workers and adjudicated offenders, may be politically expedient and administratively tidy but it consigns the real-life cops and robbers drama which daily unfolds in the inner city to the category of a mistake occasioned by poor decision making on the part of the police officer and the absence of a necessary skill in the behavioural repertoire of the offender. We need to return to our forgotten theoretical heritage to find ideas with which to conceptualise the contemporary impasse.

For more than a decade, our preoccupation with social reaction has blinded us to the significance of social action and the structuration of social events. Crime may have a meaning and a purpose for its perpetrators who may find in crime an individual solution to their social, economic, or existential predicament. The Brixton Triangle tells us that structurally generated social problems, just like Shakespearian dramas, have an existence which is independent of the particular actors, the criminals, the victims and the agents of the state, who may from time to time and from place to place constitute the dramatis personae who enact them. We need to re-establish the link between social action and social reaction and to locate both within a theory of the ways in which social events are structured. This is what Emile Durkheim tried to do and he called it sociology.

Some things our theory should explain

We need a theory of the ways in which the interactions between a social structure and the cultures and subcultures it generates shape the biographies of individual actors. This theory must explain how these interactions contrive:

1. So to construct the meaning of their predicament, the options for, and the actions of, a group of people seriously disadvantaged by the place they occupy in the social structure, in terms of their class, race, gender, and geography, that they become pre-disposed to the perpetration of criminal acts.
2. So to construct the meaning of their predicament, the options for, and the actions of a similar, but much larger group of people, seriously disadvantaged by the place they occupy in the social structure, in terms of their class, race, gender and geography, who none the less refrain from the perpetration of criminal acts.
3. So to construct the available options for a similar group of people located at a similar place in the social structure, in terms of their class, race, gender and geography that they have a heightened vulnerability to criminal victimisation.
4. So to construct the meaning of events, the available options for, and the actions of a different group of people, with greater social advantage and greater social power in terms of their class, race, gender and the position they occupy in the state apparatus that they are constrained to develop and institutionalise particular modes of anticipation of, and social reaction to, 'crime' and 'civil disorder'.

This theory must then explain how this highly-structured or 'over-determined' confrontation between the perpetrator, the victim, the non-criminal, non-victimised bystander, and the apparatus of state anticipation and social reaction develops through time reaching a climax in the ritual of the court appearance and the castigation or expulsion of the criminal from civil society, and then doubles back on itself to start all over again with a similar cast of players, a similar script and an identical plot. It must explain differentiation, solutions, victimisation, social anticipation and social reaction.

Differentiation
Only if everybody of the same class, race, age, gender, social and economic predicament and neighbourhood committed the same offences with the same frequency could we sustain a theory which located the causes of crime exclusively in the social characteristics of perpetrators rather than in the ideas held in their heads or made manifest in their actions. This was one of the problems with opportunity theory. Opportunity theory specified the invariant social characteristics of the perpetrators of particular types of offences but failed to explain why only a minority of people with these characteristics actually committed offences (Cloward and Ohlin, 1960). As David Matza (1964) observed, the 'hard determinism' of opportunity theory offered us an 'embarrassment of riches' because, on the basis of these social characteristics, it predicted far more crime than was actually perpetrated. This is not to argue, of course, that a specification of the characteristics of perpetrators is unimportant. If it was unimportant then we should expect middle-class white women of 45 with annual incomes in the region of £20,000 to appear as perpetrators of street crime, with the same statistical frequency as young unemployed working-class black men, and they don't. The specification of the social characteristics of the perpetrators of particular offences is of central importance and offers us vitally necessary, albeit insufficient, information with which to construct a theory. A sufficient explanation of the perpetration of offences requires, in addition, an understanding of the meanings developed within the family, the peer group and the subculture, and the structurally available solutions realised by subjects as they attempt to deal with the experience of relative deprivation and the consequent status frustration it induces.

Solutions
As we have seen, the experience of relative deprivation and status frustration throws the subject's relationship with the social order into question. Existence is experienced as problematic, things are not as

they should be, there is a discrepancy or a dissonance which requires a solution.

There are two types of solution. One involves finding an answer, the other involves finding a way out. A solution in the first sense requires a conceptual change, a change in the beliefs of the subject. A solution in the second sense requires an actual change in the relationship between the subject and the social order.

The saintly answer

Pryce's (1979) 'saints' have found a solution in the form of an answer. The question is 'why must we experience tribulation in this life?' The answer is that this life is a test-bed, or entrance examination for the next. One's performance in this life is important to the extent that it will guarantee a rich reward in the next. It is an answer which has sustained some Afro-Caribbean people through slavery, colonialism and migration. Close adherence to the precepts of religion and the elaboration of a detailed and specific set of moral injunctions concerned with how one's day-to-day existence should be conducted enables the saints to monitor the accumulation of righteousness which will ultimately be their passport to transcendence. The reward of religious conformity will be a privileged place in the 'sweet by and by' which will be an exact mirror image of one's present social and economic predicament. On that day the righteous shall wield power and subject the unrighteous, who currently create or compound the saints' tribulation, to their will. Some day, on the other side of the grave, everybody is going to get theirs. There is no escape. All the scores will be settled and the person who today appears to absorb inequality and social rejection passively will be vindicated and elevated to sit upon the right hand of God.

The Rastafarian answer

Rastafarianism offers a different but analogous solution to the problem. Its answer is to transform the Brixton Triangle into 'Babylon', marginalisation and alienation into 'exile' and heaven into Afrika. Dick Hebdige writes:

> Simultaneously the apotheosis of alienation into exile enabled him to maintain his position on the fringes of society without feeling any sense of cultural loss, and distanced him sufficiently so that he could undertake a highly critical analysis of the society to which he owed a nominal allegiance. (Hebdige, 1976: 152)

The saints have been placed in their predicament as part of the divine plan. To complain is to question the intentions of the supreme being who arranged one's predicament and so fatalism, a belief in the inevitability, coherence, and rightness of one's fate, becomes a virtue.

Rastafarians by contrast see themselves, in some ways correctly, as displaced and dispossessed people. The Rastafarians ought to be at home in Afrika but have instead been forced into exile, first in the Caribbean and now in Britain. Their answer to the question 'why must we experience tribulation in this life?'is that Babylon is like that and having inadvertently stumbled into it we must practise the faith, observe the sacraments, and live in peace and love until the time comes for the inevitable 'exodus'. The 'temporary' nature of the stay in Babylon defends Rastas from the third answer.

The annihilation answer

At the extreme end of the 'solution as an answer' trajectory lies madness and death because a possible, available and powerful answer to the question 'why must we experience tribulation in this life?' is that 'I brought it on myself by my own deeds or as a result of my own inadequacies'. Whereas the saints and the Rastafarians are able collectively to locate the cause of their oppression outside of themselves, retreatist opiate abusers (Cloward and Ohlin, 1960), the growing numbers of black young people experiencing 'personality disorders', and the small but growing number of black teenage suicides may be seen as people who locate the causes of their oppression within themselves (Littlewood and Lipsedge, 1982). They are prey to an internalised oppression in which they came to assume personal responsibility for the oppressive political, social and economic circumstances of which they are, in fact, the victims. The solution to the problem is to annihilate the experience, to annihilate the self, or both.

The achievement escape

The achiever's answer to the question 'why must we experience tribulation in this life?' is that we need not if we are prepared to transform the circumstances which bring about that tribulation by our own individual efforts. The achiever's motto could be 'I want my share, I want it here, and I want it now'. The achievers' solution is to find not an answer, but a way out by seizing the few educational and career opportunities which are available and then working and working and working. They may have something of the saints' commitment to behavioural conformity but they want their reward in this life, and unlike the Rastafarians they want it in this country. They are on their way out of the ghetto and up through the class structure. Their objective is higher status and the prosperity which accrues to that higher status. They are here to stay and they intend to carve a new place for themselves in the British social order. As a people who have been oppressed by the rules, achievers know the rules better than anybody else. Achievers combine a knowledge of what it takes to succeed in the white world with a knowledge of what it takes to survive in the black world. Achievers know the price of everything but unlike Oscar Wilde's cynics they also know its value. Black achievers are more likely to be women than men because the roles which offer the possibility of social mobility to black people tend to be those, like the role of social worker or bank clerk, which have traditionally been occupied by women. Middle-class white men are more likely to admit black women to middle-class 'women's' work roles, which, by definition, place them in a subordinate position to middle-class men. To admit black men to 'middle-class' jobs would put black men in direct competition with white middle-class men and this seldom happens.

To be an achiever requires self-denial, self-discipline and a powerful sense of purpose. The bind for black achievers is that they are under constant pressure to do better than their white counterparts, knowing that any success will be claimed by their employer or profession as a vindication of its decision to employ and promote black staff while any failure will be attributed to their race. The black achiever's escape from the ghetto is an ambiguous endeavour. It is an escape from a very obvious oppression which is none the less cushioned by the proximity of those in a similar predicament. It is an escape to a less tangible or restrictive form of oppression which offers material rewards and higher status at the cost of estrangement from the white middle class and the black working class alike. The upwardly mobile black achiever cannot ultimately penetrate the cast-iron facade of the white British class system and is destined to exist alongside that system in an amorphous social space occupied by other successful exiles. The black achiever faces the dilemma of all those who have achieved individual success against the odds. In creating a personal solution to a social problem they opt for social homelessness. Their solution to the problem created by the achievement solution may be to reaffirm their political link with the ghetto and in so doing come to serve as its voice and its representative in a white world.

The delinquent escape

The perspective developed here locates ghetto delinquency among a range of solutions which are adopted by people experiencing the strain induced by their position in the social structure. The selection of subculturally available solutions will be determined by age, gender, reference group and the meanings imposed upon the individual's experience of relative deprivation within the family and the peer group. The impact of this structurally induced strain on those who adopt the delinquent solution, loosens the moral bind, or the controls, which usually hold the subject to the conventional order.

Unlike achievers who struggle out of the ghetto into a bigger world, those who effect a delinquent escape conduct their struggle within the miniaturised world of the ghetto. Their problem is to find a way out of a low-status position in the ghetto in order to achieve a high-status position in the ghetto. The means whereby this solution is effected is the hustle. To be a hustler is to straddle the conventional and the deviant life in a perpetual endeavour to 'keep ahead' and 'stay on top'. Dealing in dope, handling stolen property, and misappropriating the resources of the DHSS are only partly concerned with survival. The hustle is centrally concerned with becoming a 'somebody' rather than the nobody you would be if you let the hostile social, economic, and political forces ranged against you simply 'happen' to you. Being a hustler concerns retaining one's potency, staying smart and being cool. 'You try to keep your balls when all around are losing theirs' (personal communication, 1987).

At the time of the 1981 riots Michael Heseltine observed that the subterranean activities of ghetto youth, if properly channelled, could in fact be their salvation. Heseltine divined that the skills and abilities which enabled some ghetto youth to be effective dope dealers, robbers and pimps, were precisely the skills required for commercial success in Mrs Thatcher's Britain. He advocated the infusion of private capital into the ghetto in order to excavate this rich but latent source of entrepreneurial energy. He realised that the delinquent activity of the ghetto was not a manifestation of a politically subversive counter-culture, but rather a clear reflection of the rampant acquisitive individualism of those at the top of the social and economic heap played out on the miniaturised stage of the unemployed ghetto. This should come as no surprise because if the experience of relative deprivation is about anything it is about shared material goals and differential opportunities for their achievement.

What the delinquent and non-delinquent young black working-class inhabitants of the Brixton Triangle want is similar to what the white middle-class people who live around the corner in Clapham and Wandsworth want. The reality of these shared goals is evidenced by the enthusiasm which both groups share for BMW or Audi motor cars. Young black people tend to own much older models because they have to buy them themselves. The young upwardly mobile middle-class car owners around the corner, by contrast, often receive theirs from employers as part of a package of massively lucrative tax-avoidable perks. 'Vorsprung durch technik' ('nice work if you can get it') as they say in the Railton Road.

The hustle concerns the efficacious and apparently effortless manipulation of the world in the furtherance of one's ends. One must win and look cool at the same time. The hustle alone is not a sufficient means whereby the highest status can be achieved, however. High status is also contingent on demonstrated or perceived machismo and toughness. Like the residents of Cloward and Ohlin's (1960) disorganised slum, the ghetto delinquent is engaged in a relentless struggle to maintain reputation and status in the eyes of a small localised audience. Feuds and vendettas are fiercely parochial while the victims of assaults and robberies tend, as we have seen, to be selected from this immediate audience. This accounts for both the symmetry, in terms of class, race, age and gender, between the offender and the victim and the low levels of reporting of ghetto crime. Those who 'grassed' would be immediately visible, and accessible to those on whom they had 'grassed' or their associates. To report an attack or robbery is to open up the possibility of further violence.

In 1985, in New Cross in south-east London, a 24-year-old black man stabbed a 17-year-old black youth to death in an argument about how fast the 24-year-old's car could go. Two hours later a member of the 17-year-old's family fire-bombed the flat of the 24-year-old's family. In 1982 in the same area, as a result of an argument in a pub, a 19-year-old white youth knocked at the front door of his adversary and when he heard footsteps in the hall fired both barrels of a sawn-off shotgun through the letter-box. Luckily the child who was coming to answer the door did not die. This is 'ghetto mentality', white and black. To perpetrate such horrific and irrevocable deeds for such apparently trivial reasons must be explained in terms of the distortion of perspective which necessarily accompanies social, political and economic entrapment in the ghetto. The perpetrators of these acts were not intrinsically monstrous but their perception of the world was constructed out of an exaggerated form of the 'normal' values of masculinity, dominance, aggression and machismo, and a set of personal, social and economic circumstances which left them with no other place but the ghetto in which to salvage some vestige of self-esteem in the only way available to them (Gregory, 1986). This is not to excuse these acts nor minimise their horror. The point is that violence of this order is a highly-structured, 'over-determined' and hence, inevitable outcome of an avoidable combination of social, political and economic determinants. Criminologists who speak of behaviour like this as if it were a tragic but completely idiosyncratic happening within an otherwise relatively innocuous and exotic working-class youth culture have failed to grasp the point. Ghettoisation kills people.

The delinquent solution is at best a temporary solution. The escape it appears to offer leads eventually to nothing and nowhere. Malcolm X writes:

> hearing the usual stories of so many others. Bullets, knives, prison, dope, diseases, insanity, alcoholism — so many of the survivors whom I knew as tough hyenas and wolves of the streets in the old days now were so pitiful. They had known all the angles but beneath that surface they were poor, ignorant, untrained black men; life had eased up on them and hyped them. I ran across close to twenty-five of these old timers I had known pretty well who in the space of nine years had been reduced to the ghetto's minor scavenger hustles to scratch up room, rent and food money. Some now worked downtown, messengers, janitors, things like that. (Malcolm X, 1966: 315–16)

Victimisation
We have already noted the tendency towards symmetry between the victim and the offender. Intra-class and intra-racial crime is by no means the end of the story, however. The illegal manipulation of their market monopoly by the multinational drug corporations serves to impoverish the poor still further since their excessive profits force up the costs of the NHS and consequently depress the quality of the service. Unpoliced infringements of the laws regulating 'sharp' business practice costs the British public millions of pounds every day and it is the poor who experience these crimes most acutely (Pearce, 1976).

The likelihood of being victimised by the drug companies is about 100 per cent whereas the likelihood of being burgled, robbed or assaulted is substantially lower. Understandably, of course, it is these latter offences which we fear most although our fear of victimisation will not necessarily coincide with the likelihood of victimisation. As we have seen, by and large race, class, gender, age and geography will determine the likelihood of victimisation, but in certain parts of the city geography alone will be sufficient. It may be that what is happening at the southern end of the Northern Line portends the shape of things to come.

London Regional Transport announced in December 1986 that the most dangerous underground stations, those in which passengers or staff were most likely to be robbed or attacked, were Oxford Circus, Clapham Common, Clapham South, Balham and Tooting Common. With the exception of Oxford Circus these stations are all within or close by the Brixton Triangle. The people attacked or robbed in or near these stations were not for the most part young, male, working-class and unemployed. They were commuters and shoppers with goods, money and credit cards. Increasingly the southern end of the Northern Line serves the young upwardly mobile middle classes who live in £100,000 artisan terraces and fall victim to street and tunnel crime. Street crime and burglary are moving beyond the unemployed ghetto into the yuppie heartland. But this is no class war, the attacks are fast, apparently random, hit and run affairs. Proximity and opportunity are the keys to this nastiness at the end of the Northern Line. It may well be that increasingly black and white young people, who have sought a solution to their problem through petty crime will turn away from the lean pickings of the ghetto to the immediately adjacent up-and-coming white middle-class areas in which the accumulation of wealth and consumer goods becomes more and more conspicuous as the burglary clear-up rate drops lower and lower (Kinsey et al., 1985). Poyner observes:

> If burglary prevention was the only criterion for urban planning, the evidence ... such as it is, points to the minimisation of mixed or heterogeneous housing areas and the maximisation of the size of homogeneous housing areas, or put more simply ... Areas of wealthy or middle-class/middle income housing should be separated as far as possible from poorer housing. (Poyner, 1983: 36)

The signs of fortification are everywhere. Alarm systems, security guards, electronic surveillance, and electronically operated access gates are all appearing at the southern end of the Northern Line. There are two nations in Lambeth and this reality is not lost on the inhabitants of either. The evidence of relative deprivation, the key ingredient in the growth of crimes of poverty, is palpable here. As the wealthy, powerful and articulate grow more vociferous in their demands for police protection and the police force expands in response, ghetto unemployment rises and the value of social security payments plummets. This is the political economy of unsafe streets.

Social anticipation and social reaction
As we have seen, we must link 'anticipation' with 'reaction' if we are to explain the consequences of the interaction between the state, its agencies, its agents, and the suspects, perpetrators and victims of juvenile crime.

The policing of the unemployed ghetto is concerned with the apprehension of criminals and the prevention of offending but, more importantly, it is concerned with the maintenance of public order. The levels of petty crime which emanate from the ghetto are regarded by governments and the upper echelons of the police force as a barometer, or early warning system, for future social disorder.

Urban policing is increasingly organised around anticipation of the threat to public order from trade unionists, squatters, IRA terrorists and 'ethnic minorities'. This 'threat' has led, in some urban areas, to the reconstitution of the police force into a quasi-military army of occupation. The deployment of this force in anticipation of social disorder itself becomes a significant factor in the distillation of that social disorder (Hall et al., 1978; Mark, 1978; Lea and Young, 1980). This tendency is compounded by a political hostility to black citizens expressed by successive British governments through their immigration and race relations policies, a 'hands off' policy towards the police and a consequent 'gloves off' policy towards 'militants', 'scroungers' and 'blacks'. In political rhetoric and policing theory it is these categories of people who are the 'enemy within'.

'High profile policing' is a component in, and a potent symbol of, the oppression of the residents of the unemployed ghetto. The message expressed by this policing strategy is that this dangerous volatile people must be contained within the ghetto. Sivanadan (1982) writes: 'Black youths could not walk the streets outside the Ghetto or hang around the streets within it without courting arrest.'

In 1975 the Metropolitan Police Special Patrol Group moved into Lewisham and stopped and interrogated 14,000 people on the streets. At the time a black young man gave this account of the experience:

> To drive a car anytime in Lewisham or New Cross is a big joke, you might as well walk, and when you do that you might as well stay inside, and me no 'fraid of the wicked. I driving through Lewisham to New Cross and get stopped three times, the whole place full with road blocks, transit vans, police cars, the lot — curfew in this town. (Counter Information Service, 1976: 10)

John Lea and Jock Young (1984) have alerted us to the spiral in which higher levels of street crime evoke, in turn, higher levels of quasi-military policing, but they have failed to emphasise or explore the extent to which anticipatory, as opposed to purely reactive, policing gives momentum to this spiral. Anticipatory policing by dramatically and publicly locating all black young people as suspects may well serve to dislodge some of them from their position in the conventional order and propel them into the very behaviour of which they are persistently but usually wrongly accused (Becker, 1963).

The response of the criminal justice apparatus is, as we have seen, similarly conditioned by political ideologies, economic imperatives, vested interest, and party political commitments. Sir Michael Day, OBE, Chief Probation Officer for the West Midlands, writes:

> A government will try to carry its penal philosophy into legislation and resource provision. The 1982 Criminal Justice Act, for instance, is a more judicial and less welfare orientated response to offending than its 1972 predecessor, with greater emphasis on penalties and less on training and

treatment. Policy statements from the Home Office, specifically *The Yellow Book* (The Criminal Justice System) and the National Statement of Objectives and Priorities for the Probation Service, make it clear that cost effectiveness is an important consideration in the continued resourcing of the Probation Service and should be demanded no more than any educational or social welfare provision. So the fear grows that services might be pared down to a narrow range of tasks of proven effectiveness and applied on a principle of offenders' reduced eligibility and from considerations of social control. (Day, 1987: 23)

The repertoire of possible reactions to offenders remains the same but the priority accorded each of them, and hence the amount of money spent on them by governments, effectively determines the form and quality of the state's response to the offender. Cutbacks in expenditure on prison building and police riot equipment constitute a move towards liberalisation. A shift of expenditure in the opposite direction betokens a shift towards authoritarianism. The government through the financial control it exerts over the broad repertoire of responses to crime and criminals will determine in crucial ways the shape and quality of social reaction.

In 1972 Mark Carlisle, a Home Office minister of state, announced that the Probation and Aftercare Service would be the central pillar of the Conservative crime control strategy for the next twenty years. So saying he increased probation officers' salaries by 30 per cent and increased the number of trainee places in the service from 200 in 1972 to 600 in 1975. Between 1972 and 1973 the number of probation officers working in Great Britain increased by 388 from 3939 to 4327. By 1975 the figure had risen to 4735 (Haxby, 1978).

By contrast the projected rise in the number of probation officers for the period September 1986 to March 1987 was 65. In the same period the numbers of additional officers and civilians in the police force rose by more than 3000. Meanwhile the present government remains committed to the provision of an additional 6613 prison places in the period 1984–91 at an estimated cost of £246,200 (*Criminal Justice*, 1984). Whatever position the probation service may occupy in contemporary crime control strategies, it is no longer a 'central pillar'.

Social reaction to crime and offenders at local and national level is shaped by how much money the government is prepared to spend and what it is prepared to spend it on. It is also shaped by governmental postures which encourage or discourage professional groups within the justice system to develop their capacity for 'care' or 'control'. The present government through legislation and public utterance has encouraged police discretion while simultaneously attempting to curb the discretion of probation officers and social workers by enjoining them to enter 'a new partnership with the courts' (sic).

It is only when we have understood the ways in which the reactions of the apparatus of justice and crime control are shaped politically that we can begin to make sense of the behaviour of the individual agents who help to operate the apparatus. To suggest, as powerful protagonists in the juvenile justice debate in the past decade have suggested, that the outcomes of the juvenile criminal justice system are simply a function of idiosyncratic decisions and choices made by the low-level agents, the police officers, social workers and magistrates who operate the machinery is far too simplistic. It is a little like suggesting that a factory which produces televisions does so because the workers on the production line like watching *Dynasty*.

It is within the ebb and flow of changing governmental reactions to crime and deviance that the professionals and academics, who ply their trade in the juvenile criminal justice system, struggle to retain an enduring relevance. It is this ideological ebb and flow which gives the impetus to professional amnesia and theoretical novelty. It is on this terrain, demarcated by governments, that juvenile justice radicals must fight.

If we are searching for the ultimate origins of social reaction then our search must take us far beyond the discussion of the behaviour of low-level system agents which preoccupied the labelling theorists of the 1960s and preoccupies contemporary administrative criminology still. We can begin to throw some light upon the ways in which professional discretion is politically structured by undertaking the kind of analysis attempted in this book. In this analysis we try to understand the percolation of ideology through the filters of politics, policy and bureaucracy into the patterned and consistent practices of system agents. Even when we are able to do this though we are still left with a profound theoretical and practical problem. It is a problem which is in many ways peculiar to Britain and sets Britain apart from most of its European neighbours. The problem is to account for what Giles Playfair (1971) termed our 'punitive obsession'.

The 'punitive obsession'

In 1983 proportionately more people were imprisoned in the UK than in any other Western European country apart from Turkey (Table 8.1).

In the juvenile justice system the numbers of children and young people held in institutions for offenders rose steadily from the mid-1960s and then leapt ahead in the wake of the implementation of the 1982 Criminal Justice Act. A survey conducted by the London

Table 8.1   *Prisoners in western Europe, 1983*

	Number imprisoned in 1983	Number imprisoned per 100,000 population
Western Europe		
Turkey	165,753	371.9
United Kingdom	191,734	340.4
Belgium	22,670	225.8
West Germany	115,326	187.2
Italy	103,196	181.9
Holland	24.500	171.5
France	86,362	158.4
Portugal	13,924	134.6
Spain	50,784	133.7
Greece	7,054	88.7
UK breakdown		
England and Wales	152,414	307.2
Scotland	35,469	688.8
Northern Ireland	3,851	247.6

Source: NACRO, 1986

Boroughs Children's Regional Planning Committee in 1984 noted that there had been:

a huge increase in the use of youth custody (previously borstal) since the Criminal Justice Act came into force on 24 May 1983; though detention centre sentences increased only slightly, and care orders from criminal proceedings declined, the overall effect is very considerable.

	1982/3	1983/4
Detention Centre	27	31
Youth Custody (Borstal)	7	27
7/7 Care Order	7	3
Total	41	61

Overall this is a 49 per cent increase in removal from the community. Specifically, it is a 200 per cent increase in youth custody and, in fact, an even more substantial increase in the total length of youth custody sentences (assuming maximum remission) from 42 months to 135 months, or more than three times as long. Using 1982 Home Office figures for youth custody costs, at £191 per week, this implies a direct increase in cost due to the increase in youth custody sentencing of nearly £80,000, from £34,800 to £112,000. (This figure, of course, includes neither police nor judicial costs; nor the subsequent continuing costs of the extremely high (up to 85 per cent) recidivism likely from youth custody institutions).

Between the 1960s and the present day there has been a substantial reduction in the proportion of Dutch children and young people in trouble of various kinds placed in institutions. 'Placements decreased by 66 per cent in the 0–6 age group, 40 per cent in the 6–13 age group and 15 per cent among older youth' (Junger Tas, 1984: 134). 'Sweden', Pat Carlen (1983: 210) writes, 'has also reduced its prison population; between 1971 and 1973 the number of prisoners fell from 4600 to 3600 which was the lowest figure for 3 years'. Emilia Romagna, the area surrounding Bologna, Italy, has a population of 15,000,000 people. In the summer of 1987 its 'youth custody' population was 2. Ten years ago, before the decarcerating policies of the local authority were instituted, more than 400 boys lived in the 'youth custody centre'.

In Holland, Sweden, and Emilia Romagna, the problem of juvenile crime has been effectively depoliticised. In Britain, it has not. Depoliticisation is a process in which perpetrators of crime cease to be the objects of a political discourse and become instead the objects of a scientific or professional discourse. Depoliticisation usually involves a movement from an emphasis on the free will of the actor to an emphasis upon the ways in which the offender's behaviour is constrained or determined. Often behaviour previously viewed as a sign of wilful badness is redescribed as unwitting or involuntary behaviour symptomatic of a more profound social or psychological disjunction. Theoretically, depoliticisation usually involves a conceptual movement from classical voluntarism to either the 'soft' determinism of Matza or the thoroughgoing hard determinism of criminological positivism. At the level of policy, depoliticisation has meant a shift towards systems which emphasise the concern for the welfare of the offender and de-emphasise a concern for formal justice. This is a shift which British governments since 1969 and their radical-liberal adversaries alike, in the field of juvenile criminal justice, have been unwilling and unable to make.

9 Thinking about change

It is tempting to think that the government, the Home Office and the Department of Health and Social Security do not want an adequate evaluation of their juvenile justice activities.

David P. Farrington

Perfection of means and confusion of goals seems — in my opinion — to characterise our age.

Albert Einstein, *Out of my Later Years*

The situation may be dire but the reformers remain optimistic. They may begin their arguments with a critique of the ideology, functioning, absurdities or cruelties of the British juvenile criminal justice system but they usually finish with positive suggestions for minor modifications which will get the machinery of justice back into efficient working order. Morris et al.'s (1980) assault upon welfare as a manifestation of creeping totalitarianism dwindles into a plea for a child's right to punishment. Thorpe et al.'s (1980) startling exposure of the ways in which collusion between the juvenile bench and social workers jeopardises the liberty of working-class young people, culminates in a blueprint for an Intermediate Treatment curriculum which will appeal to a punitive magistracy. John Holt (1985) urges us to make 'a direct assault upon the rhetoric of law and order' but ends by enjoining social workers to abandon the language of treatment or punishment and to speak instead of reparation and atonement.

Rights

The reformers' critique may start by addressing real social and political problems but the 'solutions' which follow concern modest extensions or limitations of the rights of the child or the rights of the court. Pat Carlen writes:

> Unfortunately, their joint concerns serve mainly to demonstrate that the liberal concept of rights is still as impossible as ever. Thus, whereas Morris et al. claim that punishment is society's and the child's right, Taylor et al. more specifically, want rights for children against adults. Reynolds

however, in criticising them both wants even more and differently located rights — this time for parents and teachers against both children and other adults! (Carlen, 1983: 206)

What begins as an assault on the prison all too often ends as a plea for administrative change or modifications in the day-to-day practices of low-level agents of the juvenile criminal justice system. As the critique develops so its object changes from the structure, functioning and political environment of the system to the behaviour of its subjects and agents.

The critique takes the form of a discourse on rights and the minimisation of intervention and penalties. It highlights anomalies and absurdities in the system as a prelude to the restoration of that system to optimal functioning. There is a concern with the ways in which the utility of penalties can be maximised to produce a system of rational, and hence minimal, punishment sufficient to chasten the offender, and deter those of us who hover on the margins of crime.

This discourse on rights always has the free and equal citizen of civil society effecting a rational choice to do good or evil in the knowledge of the penalties or rewards which will attend his or her actions. This citizen is contrasted in the discourse with the socially, psychologically or biologically determined humanoid who is the object of a social intervention justified in terms of social need or 'welfare'. Needless to say, the freely-willing actor of classicism is presented as a model of the 'real' while the positivistic cabbage against which he is measured is presented as a figment of the social work profession's collective imagination.

This tedious juxtaposition of fictitious caricatures is necessary if the discourse on rights is to be sustained because it hinges on the absolute rationality of the totally free actor. There is, however, a very serious problem involved in attempting to represent juvenile offenders in this way because in reality they simply are not like that. An alternative view of human actors as neither wholly free nor wholly determined but constrained, and sometimes disabled by their social, economic, cultural and existential predicament is more plausible and points to the intellectual bankruptcy of positions which must retain these caricatures as the centrepiece of their arguments. Matza's representation of the subject of the juvenile criminal justice system transcends this false dichotomy:

> I do not propose a free or calculating actor as an alternative to constraint. Freedom is not only the loosening of controls. It is a sense of command over one's destiny, a capacity to formulate programmes or projects, a feeling of being an agent in one's own behalf. Freedom is self-control. If so, the delinquent has clearly not achieved that state. The sense of self-control irrespective of whether it is well-founded exists to varying degrees in modern

man. Those who have been granted the potentiality for freedom through the loosening of social controls but who lack the position, capacity or inclination to be agents in their own behalf I call drifters, and it is in this capacity that I place the juvenile delinquent. (Matza, 1964: 29)

This lack of 'position, capacity, and inclination to be agents in their own behalf', this constraint, is social. It is born out of a lack of means, choices and opportunities or, more specifically, a lack of power. The central problem with the discourse on rights is that it fails to deal with the issue of the differential distribution of power. It not only misunderstands the nature of the deviant actor but it also misunderstands the nature of the social world he inhabits, and it should not. It should not because Emile Durkheim's most compelling criticism of classicism, the discourse on rights, was that in ignoring the enforced division of labour and the consequent maldistribution of social power, classicism elaborated a system of criminal justice on a social fantasy of freedom and equality which gave legitimacy to the activities of the rich and compounded the misery of the poor.

The notion of a deviant actor who is neither absolutely free and equal nor wholly determined presents a serious challenge to reformers who favour a return to the due process of law and the minimisation of social intervention. On the one hand, it erodes the philosophical rationale for a system of 'just deserts' since as Andrew von Hirsch (1978) has argued, it is difficult if not impossible to ensure 'just deserts in an unjust society'. On the other hand, the recognition of social powerlessness as a factor limiting personal culpability would, on the face of it, indicate the need for a social intervention to effect an equitable redistribution of power and wealth as a necessary moral precursor to the introduction of a 'just deserts' model. That we are not clear how this radical redistribution of power and wealth might be achieved simply means that until we find out it will remain a moral necessity to defend the children of the poor against the power of the machinery of justice and the penitentiaries it feeds.

Power

If we wish to act in defence of the children of the poor both as victims of crime and as victims of our notoriously punitive juvenile criminal justice system then we must move beyond the discourse on rights and concern ourselves with changes in the distribution of power and wealth.

Change is most likely to occur when private troubles become 'political problems'. 'Political problems' may be distinguished from 'public issues' in that they pose a direct threat to power and wealth. Public issues like AIDS, acid rain and nuclear waste, require all serious politicians and responsible citizens to hold a considered view. They do not, however, threaten to topple governments or force the 7 per cent of the population which controls (approximately) 84 per cent of the nation's wealth to get their cheque books out. 'Political problems', by contrast, require, for their resolution, a redistribution of power and wealth.

Power and wealth are seldom given away. When power and wealth change hands they do so because the powerful and the wealthy anticipate even greater losses if the particular threat or demand is not met. Reform occurs not when power-holders become aware of the right thing to do about a problem, but when the problematic situation offers them no alternative. In short, power and wealth is relinquished, when and where it is, because the powerful and the wealthy believe that it is in their interest to do so. It should be added that this is seldom done before the alternative response to the threat, the demonstration of the coercive and controlling potential of power and wealth, has been tried and failed.

Back to the Brixton Triangle

The task for those who wish to effect change is to locate the political problem which will trigger a redistribution of power and wealth. It is at least plausible to argue that what has happened, and anxieties about what might yet happen, in the unemployed ghetto of the inner city will give the impetus to social change because what happens in the inner-city ghetto threatens most directly the existing pattern of social relations in Britain.

Unemployment is higher than it has ever been but it is highest among the young people of the unemployed ghetto. Permanent unemployment is a structural feature of all western economies not least because in adopting the new technology these economies are effectively emancipating themselves from labour. Thus the unprecedented prosperity of most of those still in work is paralleled by the unprecedented poverty of most of those who are not. Politicians of all persuasions are alarmed by the explosive contradiction of an irrevocably unemployed and impoverished underclass subjected to bombardment by a governmental rhetoric which links worklessness with fecklessness in an attempt to cajole the 'workshy' into what must inevitably be a frustrating and fruitless search for employment. This transparent attempt to achieve political legitimacy for an economic and political system running out of control rubs political salt into the gaping wound of relative deprivation.

The discrepancy between a rapid expansion in the productive capacity of the system and an equally rapid contraction it its capacity to distribute the benefits of a burgeoning technology in response to the simple survival needs of the poor, adds further fuel for the anticipated conflagration.

Virtually all the social issues confronting British society are located within, or bear disproportionately on, the unemployed ghetto of the inner city. At the epicentre of this coincidence of catastrophes are black children and young people in trouble and in need.

The question of the reform of the juvenile criminal justice system has been politically ghettoised along with the professional workers who have championed the cause of the young offender. The 'political problem' of the black juvenile offender in the ghetto is quite another matter and offers a lever with which to prise apart the 'public issue' of juvenile injustice. It offers this lever because these children and young people are fixed in political rhetoric and popular imagery as 'social dynamite'. They have, by dint of this dubious attribution, become the instruments whereby the marginal public issue of juvenile justice is being transformed into the serious political problem of rioting, and unsafe streets. Nobody can afford to be the first British prime minister to preside over 'no-go' areas on the mainland. It is also becoming a political problem in part because ghetto youth are finding a political voice.

As the crisis in the unemployed ghetto deepens a new generation of black intellectuals begins to assume, for the first time, a professional and political power previously denied them. As we have seen this intelligentsia cannot disappear into the white class system and so its impact cannot be dissipated by absorption. White intellectuals may arise from the working class and come to regard the destiny of white working-class deviants as separate from their own. Black intellectuals cannot escape their origins and allegiances in this way. The confrontation between black children and young people and the apparatus of justice is the actual and symbolic moment at which a usually opaque institutionalised racist oppression which bears on all black people is made transparently clear in the official interventions and judicial disposals to which black young people are subjected. Black politics emerges of necessity as an abolitionist politics of negative reform which on the one hand attempts to resist the violent incursions of the state into the black community while on the other it attempts to link the politically and economically marginal to the mainstream of the political process. Black intellectuals have everything to gain and little to lose. Offered cold comfort elsewhere their prime constituency will remain Britain's black population and their prime concern institutionalised racism.

And the white and the powerful know this. The black intelligentsia will, whether they like it or not, be identified by the white and powerful as the 'enemy generals' empowered to negotiate an end to hostilities on behalf of the army in the ghetto. They will be construed by the white and powerful, who see the urban problem in terms of the threat posed by black young men to the property and person of white families, as the holders of the key to the problems of the inner city. The white and powerful will be wrong but in asking the black intelligentsia to contain social dissent within the ghetto they may have to offer them the means whereby black people can break out of the ghetto. If this happens, then the issue of juvenile injustice will be taken out of the political ghetto with them.

Neo-abolitionism and the radical professional

In Gunter Grass's *The Plebeians Rehearse the Revolution*, Berthold Brecht and the Berliner Ensemble are rehearsing a play about radical social change in a hall in East Berlin. It is 17 June 1953, and the people of Berlin are demonstrating in the streets against the Russian occupation. Brecht's ensemble decides that this uprising is of no real historical significance and so, instead of leaving the hall and joining the people, they stay inside and continue to rehearse a play about a revolution. Like the Berliner Ensemble, radical professionals rehearsing the ritual of justice in the juvenile court have often been confounded by the where? when? how? and who? of a politics which could contest social injustice beyond the juvenile justice system.

The political struggle in the unemployed ghetto combines a resistance to the predatory incursions of the state apparatus and its agents into the lives and liberty of black citizens with a demand for protection from crime and an extension of adequate state services for the poor and the powerless. In doing this it moves beyond the liberal attempt simply to minimise the quantity of state intervention. It moves to a more sophisticated politics in which the quality of state services and the accountability of state agents to the recipients of those services is in question. This stance is epitomised in the demand for the transformation of the police force into a 'police service' through the creation of a system of popular democratic accountability. This model of politics resembles, in many ways, what we might call the 'neo-abolitionism' of the politics developed by NAPO. At its core is an assumption that the state should be accountable to, controlled by, and work in the interests of, the poor and powerless. It is a politics predicated on the contradiction that in as much as state resources may be deployed to suppress or placate the dissent emanating from those trapped at the bottom of the social structure, the struggle for control of those state resources is the only site upon which non-violent class conflict aimed at a redistribution of power and wealth can be enacted in periods of economic recession and widescale unemployment. In the unemployed ghetto of the inner city, state resources are, by and large, the only resources and this gives an added urgency to the struggle. More ominously of course the success or failure of this attempt to extend, and gain control over, state resources may well have a bearing on whether, and to what extent, the conflict becomes violent. The white and the powerful believe this too and this is an important bargaining counter for the black intelligentsia.

The new politics of the unemployed ghetto, this spontaneous neo-abolitionism, has implications for radicals working within the juvenile criminal justice system. As managers of this most politically ambiguous piece of the state apparatus the choices they make about the allegiances they will establish and the alliances they can form will be important ones for the children of the poor. If they decide that their primary allegiance lies with the poor and the powerless they must consider how they should use their power.

Information as power
Professionals in the juvenile criminal justice system have at least five different types of information which would add strength to the political rejoinder from the unemployed ghetto.

1. Information about the structure and the intricacies of the juvenile criminal justice system which would enable non-professionals to understand the workings of the system.
2. Information about the functioning of the system. If some form of system-monitoring has been instituted by the local authority social services department then it should be possible to ascertain the racial origins and antecedents of offenders and the police stations and benches where either diversionary or punitive initiatives are favoured. This type of information would allow non-professionals to identify discrepancies in the system.
3. Information about abuses in the system. As we have seen, only rarely is the routine brutality and lawlessness of the junior penal system subjected to public scrutiny. Professionals within the system are by contrast fully aware of the seamy side of penal and professional practices but they are usually unsure about where to take information which is almost always offered on the condition that the informant will not be identified. By taking all these instances of abuse to a non-professional public the possibility is opened up for the transformation of the sum total of these 'private troubles' into a 'political problem'. This type of information would offer non-professionals an issue around which to organise resistance to the excessive imprisonment of their young people.

4. Information gained from the thousands of interviews and discussions with young people about the impact of the juvenile criminal justice system and its institutions upon the attitudes and identities of children and young people in trouble. This type of information would afford non-professionals the opportunity to appreciate, and therefore achieve a closer identification with, young offenders, by correcting unrealistic stereotypes.

5. Information about alternative strategies for responding to children and young people in trouble and alternative methods of crime control. Increasingly professionals in juvenile justice are developing knowledge and expertise about pro-active crime-control strategies. This type of information allows non-professionals to consider the type of crime control they want in their neighbourhood.

Policy as power

Clearly this 'political' information-sharing can never be an individual initiative. It must emerge from a collective decision on the part of a group of workers in the system to redefine the role, the political constituency, and the political commitment of their agency in a particular way. Unless this redefinition emanates from the policies of the local authority social services department on the issues of race, racism and juvenile justice workers could well find themselves politically beleaguered.

This could of course be a serious political stumbling block except that where and when social services departments have committed themselves to abolitionist policies on juvenile justice they have done so because radical professionals have organised it. This organisation involves a lengthy process of discussion and consultation involving at one end the director of social services who will have to present the policy to the council and at the other, basic-grade social workers who will have to implement it. Enough successful examples exist for us to see that policy change can be effected by the concerted actions of practitioners.

The implementation of abolitionist juvenile justice policies by local authorities has usually had the effect of moving IT from the margins to the centre of local juvenile criminal justice strategies. IT then becomes a base from which attempts to effect political change in other agencies are launched. This redefinition of the role of IT can release workers to engage with and act as facilitators for an effective abolitionist alliance which attempts to influence the functioning of all the agencies and all the agents of the juvenile criminal justice system at a local level.

Horizontal and vertical alliances
Mathiesen (1974) speaks of the need to develop an abolitionist alliance along horizontal and vertical axes in an attempt to reconnect the 'expelled' to the political mainstream. The alliance between juvenile justice practitioners and local authority councillors to produce an abolitionist juvenile justice policy would be located on the vertical axis of the alliance. The move by rank and file members of NAPO to affiliate with the TUC in order to influence the policies of the national executive on crime and offending would be similarly placed.

At the moment a temporary horizontal alliance orchestrated by the National Council for Civil Liberties and articulated by the Prison and Youth Custody Centre Branch of the Civil and Public Servants Association, the POA and NACRO is attempting to achieve a vertical alliance with European jurists. The jurists are expected to rule that the overcrowded conditions in British jails make imprisonment in Britain a cruel and inhuman punishment in which case any prison sentences imposed in the wake of this ruling will be in contravention of European law and hence illegal unless the British government provides twice as much space or locks up half as many people.

Figure 9.1 illustrates the scope for horizontal and vertical alliances which could be constructed around the issue of juvenile injustice in the unemployed ghetto. What becomes evident from a glance at the diagram is the extent to which potential alliances and routes to political power and influence remain unexploited. Local authority IT sections do not, as far as I am aware, maintain a dialogue with black community groups. Workers who have the most frequent contact with young people who are expelled to penal institutions seldom attempt to link them into a political alliance with groupings beyond the prison.

Black community organisations, black prisoners' groups and black social workers and probation officers are beginning to come together on the issue of imprisonment but it remains unclear which vertical connections this horizontal alliance will make. The social welfare trade unions, with the exception of NAPO, are effectively organisations which merely negotiate pay and conditions for welfare professionals, yet it is clearly possible to mobilise them as pressure groups on social issues. This does not happen and so a potentially rich source of political pressure and support remains underused. The European Court has proved itself a remarkably effective source of pressure on the British government and offers a focus for what have until now been disparate but potentially complementary reforming activities. Our ability collectively to formulate social issues as rights which can be translated into legal and social practices will in large part determine how effectively we will be able to get Euro-justice working for us. If we can do this then we may be able to get some help in

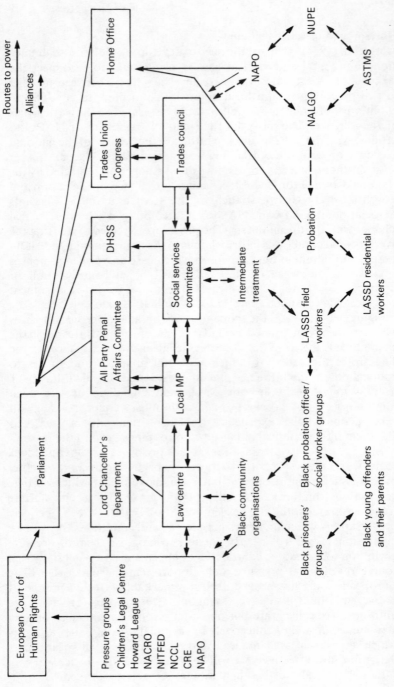

Figure 9.1 Alliances and routes to power

shifting the European social, racial and economic inequality mountains which have appeared in British cities in recent times.

To specify the precise ways in which any abolitionist alliance would, in the event, unfold is not possible since these alliances are of necessity a pragmatic and ever-changing nexus of short, medium and, less often, long-term political interests. As a reactive and opportunistic politics 'neo-abolitionism' must be prepared to change faster and more often than the law and order state it confronts. As Castlereagh once remarked of Britain, it has no long-term allies, just long-term interests.

What are we fighting for?

An alliance which attempts to address the inter-related questions of the victimisation of the poor by the poor, the criminalisation of the poor but innocent by the police, and the excessive punishment of the poor perpetrators of crimes against the poor by agents of the state will mystify the adherents of a 'justice' model. The 'justice' model would have the victim of crime, the falsely accused citizen, and the correctly accused offender as individual moral actors engaged in discreet legal episodes in which social contracts between them (their rights and obligations) are violated. For those who see reform in terms of the manipulation of rights the programme which emerges from the unemployed ghetto will remain inconceivable and unworkable. It is inconceivable because it moves the issue of reform and change from a discourse on rights conducted between the theoreticians and practitioners of the criminal justice system to a struggle to impose some form of democratic control over the system of surveillance, policing and punishment by the actual and potential subjects of the system. They believe, as Durkheim, Marx, Weber and Foucault believed, that 'justice' is not a timeless moral entity against which human endeavour is measured but rather what those with the power to impose their definition on it say it is. The question is not whether 'justice will prevail in the state's response to the unemployed ghetto, but whose justice will prevail'. Nils Christie (1974) argues that radicals should reformulate the concept of justice on the basis of social morality rather than social utility. Such a redefinition of justice would require a substantial redistribution of power. This redistribution of power would have the following components: de- and repoliticisation, civilisation, popularisation and the redistribution of discretion, decentralisation, democratisation and decriminalisation, and prevention.

De- and repoliticisation

We need to depoliticise the young offender, who currently occupies centre stage in the hard-right populist theatre, and repoliticise the aetiology of crime. A Brixton Triangle will predictably generate patterned behavioural responses in the same way that an Eton, an Oxford or a Coldstream Guards will. As we have noted, young people in the Brixton Triangle are not propelled blindly into crime, but crime looms large in the narrow repertoire of 'ways of being' available to them.

We need to restate the obvious. If the rich, white and powerful really believed that conventional social and economic success in our society was simply a consequence of individual worth and effort rather than social environment they would not send their children to exceptionally expensive schools and colleges. Social and economic environment shapes behaviour because it delineates the opportunities we have to do particular kinds of things and hence, to become particular kinds of people. Whatever philosophy we may espouse most of us live our lives as if this were true. This is why parents of all social classes struggle to provide a better environment and the best opportunities they can for their children. Anybody will tell you, 'it's only natural'.

The reintroduction of relative deprivation as a precipitating factor in the perpetration of crime and a mitigating factor in any assessment of culpability is both theoretically and politically necessary. The liberal justice lobby has, by its crude insistence on the absolute rationality of the totally free actor, colluded with a right-wing law and order crusade which has succeeded in dismissing any consideration of structural social disadvantage from the debate. If we are to repoliticise the aetiology of crime we must stress that the social suffering which moves young people to the threshold of serious and persistent juvenile crime, and beyond, is avoidable and has a political remedy.

Civilisation

When I was a youth worker, a 15-year-old boy I knew came to my office after a court appearance. He was not sure what he had been charged with. He said it sounded 'weird' but he could probably write it down. He wrote 'A salt and buttery'. Leroy's brush with the majesty of British justice was marred to a considerable extent because he didn't know why he was in court. When I translated the charge he was flabbergasted since in his view the 'geezer was asking for a smack in the mouth' and he thought he had 'sorted it out' with him anyway. The 'geezer' in question thought so too and was very surprised to hear about Leroy's court appearance. For Leroy this mystifying encounter with the justice system served only to compound his waning confidence in officialdom.

In this story respect for the law is undermined because the whole episode has mystified the defendant. The 'victim' is similarly perplexed and gains no benefit from the process. The state has incurred considerable costs in order to intervene even though the defendant is unrepentant and the victim unconcerned. This type of minor skirmish, neighbourhood disputes, petty theft, and a great deal of 'criminal damage' could be redescribed, not as criminal action which causes affront to the state, but as inconsiderate behaviour which worsens social relationships in the neighbourhood. If we are concerned with the quality of social relationships in a neighbourhood there is an inherent absurdity in whisking wrongdoers out of that neighbourhood and into a juvenile criminal court in which their destiny will be decided by 'experts' who are not party to the dispute. There is a much more powerful argument for an intervention in which the young person who has caused offence is requested to appear at a neighbourhood tribunal at which some agreement about how he or she can make good the damaged social relationships to the satisfaction of the aggrieved parties may be reached. The endeavour is to transform the 'criminal' into the 'civil' in order to achieve a civilisation of juvenile justice.

The tribunal, being an informal civil mechanism, would impose no penalties but it would of course be able to refer the case to a family panel or a public prosecutor if agreement could not be reached. The argument for the lay tribunal is strengthened when we recognise that the juvenile court is in reality a place where working-class children and young people go to admit their responsibility for usually trivial misdemeanours. Often the most serious thing they have done is to create anxiety and disruption within their families and their neighbourhoods, yet the juvenile criminal court has no access to the place where this anxiety and disruption were generated. Civilised lay tribunals could deal effectively with much of the work which is currently dealt with by the juvenile court.

Lay tribunals, by encouraging greater participation by the parties concerned, would be able to explore a wider range of issues than is possible within formal settings. Being less dependent on rules and procedures they would be in a position to challenge existing structures of legality. In accommodating groups as well as individuals they could provide a forum in which disputes affecting the community as a whole, pollution, transport, etc, could be explored. Probably its most important potential difference from formal courts — which are concerned either with retribution, causation and ascertaining responsibility arising from the past; or with therapeutic or rehabilitative concerns which are preoccupied with devising remedies for the future — lies in its ability to make a response which links past, present and future. It could respond to crime as process, rather than simply as an 'event' or 'case'. It would be in a position to monitor local patterns of crime through liaison with local police committees, schools and community organisations. It is widely agreed that informal courts are likely to be more effective in dealing with some forms of intra-class crime than formal processing. Thus an appearance at a community court, facing neighbours and being asked to justify one's actions to them may well be more effective than punishment. Such a process also gives community representatives a chance to confront those who have offended them and express a justifiable anger which probably has more meaning than the incomprehensible rituals of the formal court appearance.

Popularisation and the redistribution of discretion

Pat Carlen suggests how the members of local lay tribunals might be selected:

> Why not, therefore, harness the public concern about law-breaking to a social intervention programme on which, for a specified period, all persons over a certain age would be eligible for either voluntary or compulsory service? (Preparation for such service could be incorporated into social studies lessons in schools.)
>
> I am suggesting that local lay tribunals, operating under the auspices of the expediency principle, 'Why prosecute?' should initially process all juvenile and most other 'crime' where an accused person admits to breaking the law. (Carlen, 1983: 213)

Dr Hans Tulkens, head of the Dutch Prison Administration, cites the reinterpretation of the expediency principle by Dutch public prosecutors as a major factor in the dramatic reduction in the Dutch prison population. He writes:

> As an example of policy development I would mention the remarkable change in interpretation of the law which the right to dismiss a case has undergone. The Act gives the Public Prosecutor the power to drop a charge if he considers that it is in the public interest to do so. Until about five years ago, the interpretation of this provision was: prosecute unless prosecution is not required in the public interest. Now the interpretation is: do not prosecute, unless required in the public interest. This change in the approach to cases illustrates the limited importance the Public Prosecutor attaches to a trial. (Tulkens, 1979: 6)

In July 1983, Commander Newman of the Metropolitan Police issued a directive to his police officers instructing them to avoid prosecution where to do so would be stigmatising for the child or where the prosecution was likely to result in an absolute or conditional discharge (The *Observer*, 31 July 1983). This modest attempt to limit prosecution was unsuccessful but it flowed from a recognition of the fatuity of much formal processing. At the other end of the scale, when the police as prosecutors decide that they will not prosecute but will caution and divert instead, this produces the virtually custody-free zones of the type witnessed in Basingstoke, Southend and Corby. It is at best unlikely, for the reasons outlined in Chapter 7, that these police-initiated diversionary strategies would be attempted as part of the policing of the unemployed ghetto and this reinforces the radical argument for an independent public prosecution service.

A public prosecution service operating the 'why prosecute?' expediency principle could offer the government a means whereby it could limit the flow of cases through the courts and reduce imprisonment. This would have even greater political legitimacy if the prosecution service had the power to initiate non-punitive regulatory interventions. Such interventions might involve agreements that defendants would attend an alcohol abuse programme, a day centre or appear at a lay tribunal instead of being prosecuted. It would be naive to suggest that this might not at times appear coercive to its subjects but they would have the choice and one of those choices would enable them to avoid criminal stigmatisation. Pat Carlen writes:

> Punishment if successful intentionally causes pain and usually has disabling (physical, psychological or financial) consequences for the offender. Regulatory intervention, on the other hand, need have no penal intent; it could be defined as being merely the authoritative rectification of the particular social problems which both occasion and are occasioned by law-breaking. (Carlen, 1983: 213)

The public prosecutor could stem the flow of cases to the court yet, as we have seen, in court the juvenile bench has displayed an alarming tendency to ride roughshod over those legal caveats which enjoin them to use their punitive powers sparingly. This punitive profligacy is defended by governments in the name of the doctrine of the separation of powers which identifies two distinct social spheres, one of which deals in politics and the other in justice. The doctrine maintains that justice must remain independent of politics but this independence is never seen to be violated by the addition of powers and penalties, only by their erosion.

D.A. Thomas (1974) indicates that the bench and the judiciary have effectively ignored 'bold exhortation' to leniency and subverted legal restrictions upon their power to imprison. Box and Hale offer an exhaustive account of measures governments could deploy to limit judges' and magistrates' enthusiasm for imprisonment but conclude that they will not intervene because governments:

> faced with a population they perceive to be increasingly ungovernable, and realising that their economic policies may substantially exacerbate this, particularly amongst certain sections of the community, have not seen any

> pragmatic sense in alienating such a trusted and loyal ally as the judiciary, or abandoning prison as an iron fist of threat, control, and punishment. (Box and Hale, 1986: 93)

Our alliance must reach up to parliament because only parliament can address this thorny constitutional problem.

Decentralisation, democratisation and decriminalisation
The architects of the 1960s juvenile justice legislation realised that in order to create a juvenile justice system which emphasised a concern for the needs and best interests of the child the juvenile bench would have to be effectively excluded from any significant decision-making role in the system.

This was attempted initially, as we have seen, by the decentralisation of control of the apparatus of justice to local authorities with a parallel move to transform the juvenile court into a family panel where the opinions of lay or social/psychological experts would hold sway. The subsequent 1969 CYPA offered a much more modest version of this original initiative and yet had it been implemented it would have ended imprisonment for young people below the age of 18.

The decentralisation of control remains the core issue in the debate about change in the British juvenile criminal justice system. The present government has attempted to exert increasing centralised control over the apparatus of juvenile justice and this endeavour has led inevitably to increases in juvenile imprisonment.

Critics of the 1969 CYPA argue that it failed to offer children the protection of due process of law, thus rendering them vulnerable to excessive intervention or incarceration in the name of 'treatment'. This argument seems to suggest that an initial concern with social need and the best interest of the child must always and everywhere, as a consequence of professional entrepreneurism, degenerate into the violation of a child's rights. We cannot meet this criticism by a bland defence of treatment but we can point out that social deprivation as a precipitating factor in offending must constitute a mitigating circumstance. More generally we can argue that a system of juvenile justice which recognises social need, but, in the interests of the child, places clear limits on the capacity of professionals to intervene on the basis of need is not unimaginable. There is no reason why a young person could not be offered a choice between a fine, a series of meetings with a family counsellor, or some form of reparation. The family panel might well express a view about which option they would see as most useful but the onus would be on the child and the family to choose.

There is no reason why such a family panel should not have a legal adviser who refereed the session rather than chairing it and whose primary concern was to ensure proportionality and the defence of the rights of the child, a kind of in situ public defender and rights watchdog. There is also no reason why the lay element on the panel should not be recruited in the same way as the jury.

Like the neighbourhood tribunal described above, the family panel would serve to divert youngsters out of the justice system to local authority and voluntary facilities and services which can respond to their needs. Such a panel would ultimately be empowered to incarcerate some young people but not to imprison them. Incarceration would be undertaken in accordance with strict and detailed conditions regulating the type and severity of offences for which it was necessary and the duration of the period of incarceration.

Prevention

The lay tribunal and the family panel could serve as the base from which preventive and defensive strategies could be developed. Lloyd Ohlin, whose opportunity theory gave the impetus to the British and US poverty programmes, was subsequently engaged to research the Massachusetts experiment, the most throughgoing decarceration initiative we have so far witnessed. He writes:

> ... our research indicates that the network of relationships which youth maintain in the community have a crucial impact on their ability to stay out of trouble after their release. In fact, it seems clear that the total community experience of the youth before and after his correctional experience may overwhelm even the most constructive elements of the correctional programme. (Ohlin, 1979: 22)

We live and work in a world where every day the predicament of working-class young people in the inner city is worsened. It is a world where the 'network of relationships' is under greater and greater stress. There can be no doubt that the systematic impoverishment of the inner city has strained all relationships and services and in so doing has increased the likelihood of the incarceration of the young. Young people from overcrowded homes, with unemployed or clinically depressed parents are at risk in a multiplicity of ways. Hostels for the young homeless house a high proportion of young people previously in care or who have unsuccessfully attempted to get admitted to voluntary care as a result of a breakdown of family relationships which are in turn a function of social stress. Work is a problem. Housing is a problem. Together they tend to propel young people into deviance and so into the expanding penal institution which is the substitute the law and order state offers for a minimum wage and adequate welfare services. Housing need and welfare rights loom as targets for a sustained intervention. Now is not the time to be saving money. To limit welfare expenditure now is not radical non-intervention, it is not even benign neglect, it is professional negligence. Following the logic of Ohlin's argument any programme of crime control and social defence must address the quality of services available to young people and their families in their worsening predicament. It must press for popular services untainted by association with law and order. It should be noted that in this way it would be possible to claim that one was taking the social nature of crime seriously.

It is interesting that the techniques pioneered by the Wincroft project in the late 1960s (described in Chapter 4) have been resuscitated by projects concerned to combat crime. In their report on their three-year experiment the NACRO Safe Neighbourhoods Unit concludes:

> 12.14. This experience suggests that on estates with a serious crime/vandalism/hooliganism problem that is thought to be caused by indigenous young people, a detached youth worker with a specific job brief should be deployed with responsibilities both for the welfare of the young people, and for reducing crime and deterring the harassment of tenants.
> 12.15. The worker should work closely with relevant agencies and would concentrate on the following:
> —fostering a positive attitude in young people towards their community
> —working alongside other agencies involved with young people, particularly estate-based ones
> —understanding the social structure of the young, getting to know as many as possible, and planning and undertaking activities with them.
> (Bright and Petterson, 1984: 41)

More recently the French government, in response to rioting by young people in Marseilles and Lyons in 1981 and fearing that the situation might assume what they regarded as the crisis proportions it had reached in Britain, introduced a programme called Etés Jeunes. These were programmes of artistic, sporting and cultural activities developed with, and in large part directed by, the poor children and young people of the French inner cities. In 1983, its second year of operation, 100,000 children and young people participated in Etés Jeunes. In the period 1984 to 1986 the police estimated that the reduction in the juvenile crime rate during the period of the programme was 10.4 per cent. In Lille, one of the pilot cities for the programme, the fall was 12 per cent. Because of these summer programmes, Conseils Communales, committees composed of representatives of all the relevant local authority departments and chaired by the mayor, have been established in most large French towns to create a permanent system of social prevention (King, 1987).

These initiatives suggest an intervention in the 'community' and yet 'community', as we are often reminded, may have no negative connotations but it has little reality either in the classical sense, and it would be naive of us to believe that this notional community existed as some kind of curative safety net. This indicates that workers must be imaginative in an attempt to identify the often conflicting and diverse needs and desires of people living in particular neighbourhoods. Perhaps our job is to enable these needs and desires to be articulated in order to establish a, not always polite, dialogue between these interests and to work with young people in order that they might become articulate participants in such a dialogue. Robins and Cohen (1978) have indicated strategies which might be adopted within the youth service to enfranchise young people in neighbourhood debates. Their concept of a Youth Tenants' Association remains an untried but potentially fruitful initiative. To talk out rather than act out the stresses, strains and conflicts existing in deprived inner-city neighbourhoods may not lead to reconciliation but could at least lead to a higher level of tolerance — a rare enough commodity — and it could also be a means whereby previously unarticulated political demands could emerge from marginalised populations. There is no reason why we should not begin to work in these ways, and there is a need for an established body of expertise whereby such work could be undertaken. What interventions of this type do not do is save local authorities money, indeed they make increasing demands on local authority budgets. If we can move beyond a position which only considers the young offender, and ignores the impact of his behaviour, then youth workers and social workers may come to be seen by the victimised neighbourhood as taking crime seriously and therefore worthy of its support and encouragement in the development of non-punitive responses to young people in trouble.

Implicit within all this is the need for participants in an abolitionist alliance to work simultaneously at the political, administrative and face-to-face levels. Too often, creative changes and reforms are neutralised by a failure to identify the appropriate level of intervention.

Since the 1960s official responses to the mistakes made by the children of the poor have become important symbols of political grit and determination. From the mid-1970s black children and young people have borne the brunt of this repoliticisation and in looking at them we see, in exaggerated form, what happens to all working-class children and young people who fall foul of the law. In this period tolerance and compassion were ousted by force and coercion in an attempt to make the dubious political point that what is wrong with this country is exemplified in the bad behaviour of its poor children. In *Two Cheers for Democracy*, E.M. Forster wrote:

> I realise that all society rests upon force. But all the great creative actions, all the decent human relations, occur during the intervals when force has not managed to come to the front. These intervals are what matter. I want them to be as frequent and as lengthy as possible and I call them civilisation. (Forster, 1941: 78)

Whether or not a society responds to the mistakes made by its poorest children with tolerance, compassion, and a willingness to do something about their poverty is perhaps a good measure of how civilised it is.

References

Abel-Smith, B. and Townsend, P. (1965) *The Poor and the Poorest*. London: G. Bell & Sons.

Anderton, J. (1979) Speech to Manchester Lunch Club, 14 June.

Beaumont, B. (1985) 'Probation, Working for Social Change?' in H. Walker and B. Beaumont (eds) *Working with Offenders*. London: Macmillan.

Becker, H. (1963) *Outsiders: Studies in the Sociology of Deviance*. New York: Free Press.

Becker, H. (1967) 'Whose Side are We on?' *Social Problems* 14 (3):239—47.

Bellow, S. (1982) *The Dean's December*. Harmondsworth: Penguin.

Benington, J., Bond, N. and Skelton, P. (1975) *CDP Final Report: Part 1: Coventry and Hillfields: Prosperity and the Persistence of Inequality*. Home Office and City of Coventry.

Berlins, M. and Wansell, P. (1972) *Caught in the Act*. Harmondsworth: Penguin.

Booker, C. (1980) *The Seventies*. Harmondsworth: Penguin.

Bottoms, A.E. (1974) 'On the Decriminalisation of the English Juvenile Court', in R. Hood (ed.) *Crime, Criminology and Public Policy*, pp. 319—45. London: Heinemann.

Box, S. and Hale, C. (1986) 'Unemployment, Crime and the Enduring Problem of Prison Overcrowding', in R. Matthews and J. Young (eds) *Confronting Crime*. London: Sage Publications.

Brewer, C. and Lait, J. (1980) *Can Social Work Survive*? London: Temple Smith.

Bright, J. and Petterson, G. (1984) *The Safe Neighbourhoods Unit*. London: National Association for the Care and Resettlement of Offenders.

Brittan, L. (1985) 'A New Sense of Purpose', *Community Care*, 2 May.

Burney, E. (1985) *Sentencing Young People*. Aldershot: Gower Press.

Carlen, P. (1983) 'On Rights and Powers — Some Notes on Penal Politics', in P. Garland and P. Young (eds) *The Power to Punish*. London: Heinemann.

Cawson, P. and Martell, P. (1979) *Children Referred to Closed Units*. London: Department of Health and Social Security.

Central Statistical Office (annual) *Social Trends*. London: HMSO.

Christie, N. (1974) 'Utility and Social Values in Court Decisions on Punishment', in R. Hood (ed.) *Crime, Criminology and Public Policy*. London: Heinemann.

Cicourel, A.V. (1968) *The Social Organization of Juvenile Justice*. New York: Wiley.

Clarke, J. (1980) 'Social Democratic Delinquents and Fabian Families', in National Deviancy Conference *Permissiveness and Control*, pp. 72—95. London: Macmillan.

Cloward, R. and Ohlin, L. (1960) *Delinquency and Opportunity*. London: Routledge & Kegan Paul.

Cohen, A.K. (1956) *Delinquent Boys*. London: Routledge & Kegan Paul.

Cohen, S. (1979) *How do We Balance Guilt, Justice and Tolerance?* London: Radical Alternatives to Prison.

Cohen, S. (1980) 'It's All Right for You to Talk', in R. Bailey and M. Brake (eds) *Radical Social Work*. London: Edward Arnold.

Cohen, S. (1983) 'Social Control Talk', in D. Garland and P. Young (eds) *The Power to Punish*. London: Heinemann.

Community Development Projects (1977). *Gilding the Ghetto*. London: CDP.

Cook, S. (1982) 'Tension as Black Jail Population Increases', *The Guardian*, 6 July.

Cornish, D.B. and Clarke, R.V.G. (1975) *Residential Treatment and its Effects on Delinquency*. London: Home Office.

Counter Information Service (1976) *Racism, Who Profits?* London.

Dale, R., Esland, G. and MacDonald, M. (eds) (1976) *Schooling and Capitalism*. London: Routledge & Kegan Paul.

Davies, B. (1982) *Restructuring Youth Policies in Britain — The State We're In*. Leicester: National Youth Bureau.

Day, M. (1987) 'The Politics of Probation', in J. Harding (ed.) *Probation and the Community*. London: Tavistock.

Dennington, J. (1981) 'SUS does a Phoenix Job', *Eureka*. (London Intermediate Treatment Association).

Department of Health and Social Security (1972) *Intermediate Treatment*. London.

Department of Health and Social Security (1983) *Further Development of Intermediate Treatment (IT)*, Local Authority Circular LAC (83) 3, 26 January.

Dodd, D. (1978) 'Police and Thieves on the Streets of Brixton', *New Society*, 16 March.

Donnison, D. and Stewart, M. (1958) *The Child and the Social Services*. London: Fabian Society.

Donnison, D., Jay, P. and Stewart, M. (1962) *The Ingleby Report: Three Critical Essays*. London: Fabian Society.

Downes, D. (1980) 'Abolition: Possibilities and Pitfalls', in A.E. Bottoms and R.H. Preston (eds) *The Coming Penal Crisis*. Edinburgh: Scottish Academic Press.

Engels, F. (1874) 'Preface' to *The Peasant War in Germany*. In *Marx–Engels Selected Works*, Vol. 2. Reprinted 1950, London: Lawrence & Wishart.

Evans, R. (1982) *The Theoretical Foundations of Doing IT* (Social Work Monograph) Norwich: University of East Anglia.

Farrington, D. (1984) 'England and Wales', in M. Klein (ed.) *Western Systems of Juvenile Justice*. Beverly Hills: Sage Publications.

Forster, E.M. (1941) 'What I Believe', in *Two Cheers for Democracy*. Reprinted 1972, Harmondsworth: Penguin.

Foucault, M. (1972) *The Archaeology of Knowledge*. London: Tavistock.

Foucault, M. (1977) *Power and Knowledge*. Brighton: Harvester.

Freud, S. (1928) *The Future of an Illusion*. New York: Garden City.

Giller, H. and Carrington, C. (1983) 'Structuring Discretion: Question or Answer?' in H. Giller and A. Morris (eds) *Providing Criminal Justice for Children*. London: Edward Arnold.

Giller, H. and Morris, A. (eds) (1983) *Providing Criminal Justice for Children*. London: Edward Arnold.

Goffman, E. (1961) *Asylums*. New York: Doubleday.

Goldthorpe, J. and Lockwood, D. (1968) *The Affluent Worker*. Cambridge: Cambridge University Press.

Gough, I. (1979) *The Political Economy of the Welfare State*. London: Macmillan.

Gregory, J. (1986) 'Sex, Class and Crime — Towards a Non-sexist Criminology', in R. Matthews and J. Young (eds) *Confronting Crime*. London: Sage Publications.

Guest, C.L. (1984) 'A Comparative Analysis of the Career Patterns of Black and White Young Offenders', unpublished MA thesis, Cranfield Institute of Technology.

HMSO (1960) *Report of the Committee on Children and Young Persons*. Cmnd 1191. London.

HMSO (1964) *Children and Young Persons: Scotland* (the Kilbrandon report). Cmnd 2306. Edinburgh.

HMSO (1965) *The Child, the Family and the Young Offender*. Cmnd 2742. London.
HMSO (1968) *Children in Trouble*. Cmnd 3601. London.
HMSO (1974) *Young Adult Offenders* (the Younger report). London.
HMSO (1976) *Children and Young Persons Act 1969: Observations on the Eleventh Report from the Expenditure Committee*. Cmnd 6494. London.
HMSO (1977) *Intermediate Treatment in London*. London.
HMSO (1980) *Young Offenders*. Cmnd 8045. London.
HMSO (1982) *Criminal Justice Act*. London.
HMSO (1984a) *Tougher Regimes in Detention Centres*. London.
HMSO (1984b) *Criminal Justice*. London.
Hall, S. (1979) 'The Great Moving Right Show', *Marxism Today*, January.
Hall, S. (1982) 'Policing for the Future', speech given to Changing Policing: a conference based on the Scarman report, University of London.
Hall, S., Critcher, C., Clarke, J., Jefferson, T. and Roberts, B. (1978) *Policing the Crisis*. London: Macmillan.
Hargreaves, D. (1967) *Social Relations in a Secondary School*. London: Routledge & Kegan Paul.
Harrison, P. (1983) 'The Victims of Crime', *New Society* 25 (5): 282.
Haxby, D. (1978) *Probation — a Changing Service*. London: Constable.
Hebdige, D. (1976) 'Reggae, Rastas and Rudies', in S. Hall et al. (eds) *Resistance through Rituals*. London: Hutchinson.
Hiro, D. (1971) *Black British, White British*. New York: Monthly Review Press.
Holt, J. (1985) *No Holiday Camps*. Leicester: Association for Juvenile Justice.
Hunt, G. and Mellor, J. (1980) 'Afro-Caribbean Youth: Racism and Unemployment', in M. Cole et al. (eds) *Blind Alley*. Orsmkirk: G.W. and A. Hesketh.
Illich, I. (1973) 'The Hidden Curriculum', in P. Buckman (ed.) *Education without Schools*, pp. 9–19. London: Souvenir Press.
Jackson, G. (1971) *Soledad Brother*. Harmondsworth: Penguin.
Jenkin, P. (1979) 'Opening Address' to Getting on with Intermediate Treatment conference, City Hall, Sheffield, 9 July.
Junger Tas, J. (1984) 'Holland' in M. Klein (ed.) *Western Systems of Juvenile Justice*. Beverly Hills: Sage Publications.
Kettle, M. (1982) 'The Racial Numbers Game in our Prisons', *New Society*, September.
King, M. (1987) 'Social Prevention in France', Paper given at Social Prevention Seminar at NACRO, October.
Kinsey, R., Lea, J. and Young J. (1985) *Losing the Fight against Crime*. Oxford: Basil Blackwell.
Kirwin, K. (1985) 'Probation/Supervision', in H. Walker and B. Beaumont (eds) *Working with Offenders*. London: Macmillan.
Labour Party Study Group (1964) *Crime, a Challenge to Us All* (the Longford report). London: Labour Party.
Laing, R.D. (1968) 'The Obvious', in D. Cooper (ed.) *The Dialectics of Liberation*. Harmondsworth: Penguin
Lambert, J. (1970) *Crime, Police and Race Relations*. Oxford: Oxford University Press.
Landau, S. (1981) 'Juveniles and the Police', *British Journal of Criminology* 21: 143–72.
Lea, J. and Young, J. (1984) *What is to be Done about Law and Order?* Harmondsworth: Penguin.
Little, A. (1962) 'Borstal Success and the Quality of Borstal Inmates', *British Journal of Criminology* 2: 266–72.
Littlewood, R. and Lipsedge, M. (1982) *Aliens and Alienists*. Harmondsworth: Penguin.
London Boroughs Children's Regional Planning Committee (1984) *The Implementation*

of the 1982 Criminal Justice Act. London.

London–Edinburgh Return Group (1977) *In and Against the State.* London.

Lupton, C. and Roberts, G. (1982) *On Record — Young People Appearing before a Juvenile Court.* Portsmouth: Portsmouth Polytechnic, Social Services Research and Intelligence Unit.

Macpherson, C.B. (1962) *The Political Theory of Possessive Individualism.* Oxford: Oxford University Press.

Malcolm X and Haley, A. (1966) *The Autobiography of Malcolm X.* London: Hutchinson.

Mathieson, T. (1974) *The Politics of Abolition.* London: Martin Robertson.

Matza, D. (1964) *Deliquency and Drift.* New York: Wiley.

Matza, D. (1969) *Becoming Deviant.* New York: Prentice-Hall.

Millham, S. (1977) 'Intermediate Treatment: Symbol or Solution?' *Youth in Society* 26: 22–4.

Morgan, P. (1978) *Delinquent Fantasies.* London: Temple Smith.

Morgan, P. (1981) 'The Children's Act — Sacrificing Justice to Social Workers' Needs?' in C. Brewer et al. (eds) *Criminal Welfare on Trial.* London: Social Affairs Unit.

Morris, A., Giller, H., Szued, M. and Geech, H. (1980) *Justice for Children.* London: Macmillan.

Moynihan, D.P. (1969) *Maximum Feasible Misunderstanding.* New York: Free Press.

Muncie, J. (1984) *The Trouble with Kids Today.* London: Hutchinson.

Musgrove, F. (1964) *Youth and the Social Order.* London: Routledge & Kegan Paul.

NACRO (1986) *NACRO Briefing.* London: National Association for the Care and Resettlement of Offenders.

National Association of Probation Officers (1975) *Young Adult Offenders: An Examination of the Younger Report.* London: NAPO.

Ohlin, L. (1979) 'The American Experience', in *Getting on with IT.* London: DHSS.

Parker, H. (1974) *A View from the Boys — a Sociology of Downtown Adolescents.* Newton Abbot: David & Charles.

Parker, H., Casburn, M. and Turnbull, D. (1980) 'The Production of Punitive Juvenile Justice', *British Journal of Criminology* 20(3).

Parker, H., Casburn, M. and Turnbull, D. (1981) *Receiving Juvenile Justice.* Oxford: Basil Blackwell.

Peacock, A. and Wiseman, D. (1966) *The Growth of Public Expenditure in the UK.* 2nd edn. George Allen & Unwin.

Pearce, F. (1976) *The Crimes of the Powerful.* London: Pluto.

Pearson, G. (1977) *The Deviant Imagination.* London: Macmillan.

Pearson, G. (1981) 'Review', *Critical Social Policy* 1: 115–16.

Pease, K., Durkin, P., Earnshaw, I., Payne, D. and Thorpe, J. (1975) *Community Service Orders* (Home Office Research Study 29). London: HMSO.

Personal Social Services Council (1977) *A Future for Intermediate Treatment.* London: PSSC.

Pitts, J. (1979) 'Changes in the Control, Prevention, Anticipation and Surveillance of Youthful Disorder and Delinquency in England and Wales 1965–1977', unpublished MA thesis, Middlesex Polytechnic.

Pitts, J. (1981) 'Abolitionism and Juvenile Justice', *Eureka* (Journal of the London Intermediate Treatment Association) 2: 35–9.

Pitts, J. (1982) 'Policy, Delinquency and the Practice of Youth Control 1964–1981', *Youth and Policy* 1: 9–16.

Pitts, J. (1986) 'Black Young People and Juvenile Crime: Some Unanswered Questions', in R. Matthews and J. Young (eds) *Confronting Crime.* London: Sage Publications.

Pitts, J. and Robinson, T. (1981) *Young Offenders in Lambeth*. London: London Intermediate Treatment Association.

Platt, T. and Takagi, P. (1981) 'Intellectuals for Law and Order — a Critique of the New "Realists" ', in T. Platt and P. Takagi (eds) *Crime and Social Justice*. London: Macmillan.

Playfair, Giles (1971) *The Punitive Obsession*. London: Gollancz.

Power, M.J., Benn, R.T. and Norris, J.N. (1972) 'Neighbourhood, School and Juveniles before the Courts', *British Journal of Criminology* 12: 111–32.

Poyner, B. (1983) *Design against Crime*. London: Butterworths.

Pratt, M. (1980) *Mugging as a Social Problem*. London: Routledge & Kegan Paul.

Preston, R.H. (1980) 'Social Theology and Penal Theory and Practice: the Collapse of the Rehabilitative Ideal and the Search for an Alternative', in A.E. Bottoms and R.H. Preston (eds) *The Coming Penal Crisis*. Edinburgh: Scottish Academic Press.

Priestley, P., Fears, D. and Fuller, R. (1977) *Justice for Juveniles*. London: Routledge & Kegan Paul.

Pryce, K. (1979) *Endless Pressure*. Harmondsworth: Penguin.

Robins, D. and Cohen, P. (1978) *Knuckle Sandwich*. Harmondsworth: Penguin.

Rowbotham, S., Segal, L. and Wainwright, M. (1979) *Beyond the Fragments*. London: Merlin Press.

Rushdie, S. (1982) 'The New Empire within Britain', *New Society*, 9 December.

Rutherford, A. (1986) *Growing Out of Crime*. Harmondsworth: Penguin.

Rutter, M., Maughan, B., Mortimore, P., Ouston, J. and Smith, A. (1978) *Fifteen Thousand Hours*. London: Open Books.

Rutter, M. and Giller, H. (1983) *Juvenile Delinquency Trends and Perspectives*. Harmondsworth: Penguin.

Saville, J. (1957) 'The Welfare State: an Historical Approach', *New Reasoner* 3: 5, 6, 11, 12–17, 20–24.

Schur, E. (1971) *Labeling Deviant Behavior*. New York: Random House.

Senior, P. (1985) 'Groupwork with Offenders', in H. Walker and B. Beaumont (eds) *Working with Offenders*. London: Macmillan.

Sivanadan, S. (1982) *A Different Hunger*. London: Pluto.

Smith, C., Farrant, M. and Marchant, H. (1972) *The Wincroft Youth Project*. London: Tavistock.

Smith, D. (1983) *Police and People in London*. London: Policy Studies Institute.

Spiers, S. (1977) '15- and 16-year-olds in Borstal', unpublished Home Office document.

Spitzer, S. (1975) 'Towards a Marxian Theory of Crime', *Social Problems* 22: 37–42.

Statistical Bulletin (1986) Issue 17/86, June, Home Office.

Taylor, I., Walton, P. and Young, J. (1973) *The New Criminology*. London: Routledge & Kegan Paul.

Taylor, L., Lacey, R. and Bracken, D. (1980) *In Whose Best Interests*? London: Cobden Trust, MIND.

Taylor, W. (1981) *Probation and Aftercare in a Multi-racial Society*. London: CRE and West Midlands Probation and After-care Service.

Taylor, W. (1982) 'Black Youth, White Man's Justice', *Youth and Society*, November: 14–17.

Thomas, D.A. (1974) 'The Control of Discretion in the Administration of Criminal Justice', in R. Hood (ed.) *Crime, Criminology and Public Policy*. London: Heinemann.

Thorpe, D., Smith, D., Green, C. and Paley, J. (1980) *Out of Care*. London: George Allen & Unwin.

Tulkens, H. (1979) *Some Developments in Penal Policy and Practice in Holland*. London: NACRO.

Von Hirsch, A. (1978) *Doing Justice*. New York: Hill & Wang.

WLIHE (1982) 'Black Young People in Trouble and Intermediate Treatment', first year CQSW project, West London Institute of Higher Education.

Walker, H. and Beaumont, B. (1982) *Probation Work: Critical Theory and Socialist Practice*. Oxford: Basil Blackwell.

Walker, H. and Beaumont, B. (1985) *Working with Offenders*. London: Macmillan.

Westergaard, J. (1968) *The Rediscovery of the Cash Nexus*. London: New Left Review.

Willis, P. (1977) *Learning to Labour*. London: Saxon House.

Wilson, J.Q. (1975) *Thinking about Crime*. New York: Basic Books.

Young, J. (1979) 'Left Idealism, Reformism and Beyond', in B. Fine, R. Kinsey, J. Lea, S. Picciotto, and J. Young (eds) *Capitalism and the Rule of Law*. London: Hutchinson.

Young, J. (1986) 'The Failure of Criminology: the Need for a Radical Realism', in R. Matthews and J. Young (eds) *Confronting Crime*. London: Sage Publications.

Index

42, 60, 108, 147−9
public prosecution service 164, 165
punitive obsession 149

Race Relations and Immigration, Select
  Committee Report (1978) 125
Radical Alternatives to Prison (RAP)
  110, 121
radical welfare 63−71, 102; non-
  intervention 83, 84, 135; and
  abolitionism 97
Rastafarianism 139−40
realism, right-wing criminological 44
reform: *versus* revolution 94; positive
  and negative 94; and power 154
repoliticisation 28, 32; and
  remoralisation 43
residential tradition 60−61
revolutionary left 99, 100; *see also*
  'new left'
rights 151
Robins, D. and Cohen, P. 69, 168
Rowbotham, S. 118
rule of law 40, 58
Rushdie, S. 123
Rutter M. and Giller, H. 73

'safe neighbourhood' projects 79, 168
saints 139
Saville, J. 118
Schur, E. 83, 84
secure accommodation 33; care order 46
Senior, P. 74
separation of powers, doctrine of 49
sexual revolution 99
Sims, R. 43
Sivanandan, S. 146
skewed deviant 10, 11
Smith, C., Farrant, M. and
  Marchant, H. 75
Smith, D. 126
social: contract 7, 8, 11; treatment 9;
  disadvantage 68; facilitation and
  normalisation 74; democratic reform
  99; anticipation 145−50; reaction
  145−50
Social Services (Reorganisation) Act
  (1970) 19
Social Work (Scotland) Act (1968) 13
social work/workers 13, 18, 135;
  significance of in juvenile justice

system 19, 20, 21; and totalitarianism
  135
socialism 1, 2, 12
solutions 138−44
Special Patrol Group 146
Spitzer, S. 97
street crime 108, 133
subculture 88
Supervised Activity Order 52, 53
supervision order 19
'sus' (arrest on suspicion) 126, 127
Sweden, declining prison population of
  150

Taylor, I. et al. 8, 10
Taylor, L. et al. 85, 86
Taylor, W. 128
Thatcher, M. 24, 32, 39; and populism
  40; and the family 54; and riots 56;
  and the 'enemy within' 58; and the
  'swamping of our culture' 125
theory: orthodoxy of 135; struggle for
  power and 136; requirements of an
  adequate 137−8
Thomas, D.A. 165
Thorpe, D. et al. 23, 24, 83, 85−9, 151
treatment, and Fabianism 6
truancy: decriminalisation of 33; rise in
  72
Tulkens, H. 164

unemployment, and black young people
  (US) 64; (UK) 125; and relative
  deprivation 154

victimisation 144−5
voluntary sector 32, 39; erosion of 55−6
Von Hirsh, A. 153

Walker, H. and Beaumont, B. 114
'War on Poverty' (US) 66; *see also*
  poverty programme (US)
welfare: and the denial of legal rights 1;
  as a pre-emptive strategy 6, 12; versus
  justice debate 7, 21, 84−6; restructuring of 18, 19, 88; and treatment 79;
  as stigma 105
welfare state 4, 11, 100
West London Institute of Higher
  Education 129
Westergaard, J. 4